Comparative Approach on Development and Socioeconomics of Africa

Baimba Yilla
Marymount University, USA

A volume in the Advances in Finance, Accounting, and Economics (AFAE) Book Series

IGI Global
PUBLISHER of TIMELY KNOWLEDGE

Published in the United States of America by
IGI Global
Information Science Reference (an imprint of IGI Global)
701 E. Chocolate Avenue
Hershey PA, USA 17033
Tel: 717-533-8845
Fax: 717-533-8661
E-mail: cust@igi-global.com
Web site: http://www.igi-global.com

Library of Congress Cataloging-in-Publication Data

CIP DATA IN PROCESS

Comparative Approach on Development and Socioeconomics of Africa
Baimba Yilla
2024 Business Science Reference

ISBN 9798369324035(hc) | ISBN 9798369349038(sc) | eISBN 9798369324042

This book is published in the IGI Global book series Advances in Finance, Accounting, and Economics (AFAE) (ISSN: 2327-5677; eISSN: 2327-5685)

British Cataloguing in Publication Data
A Cataloguing in Publication record for this book is available from the British Library.

For electronic access to this publication, please contact: eresources@igi-global.com.

Advances in Finance, Accounting, and Economics (AFAE) Book Series

Ahmed Driouchi
Al Akhawayn University, Morocco

ISSN:2327-5677
EISSN:2327-5685

MISSION

In our changing economic and business environment, it is important to consider the financial changes occurring internationally as well as within individual organizations and business environments. Understanding these changes as well as the factors that influence them is crucial in preparing for our financial future and ensuring economic sustainability and growth.

The **Advances in Finance, Accounting, and Economics (AFAE)** book series aims to publish comprehensive and informative titles in all areas of economics and economic theory, finance, and accounting to assist in advancing the available knowledge and providing for further research development in these dynamic fields.

COVERAGE

- Wages and Employment
- Corporate Finance
- Theoretical Issues in Economics, Finance, and Accounting
- Economics of Agriculture and Biotechnology
- Microeconomics
- Bankruptcy
- Fiscal Policy
- Comparative Accounting Systems
- Stock Market
- Economic Indices and Quantitative Economic Methods

IGI Global is currently accepting manuscripts for publication within this series. To submit a proposal for a volume in this series, please contact our Acquisition Editors at Acquisitions@igi-global.com or visit: http://www.igi-global.com/publish/.

The Advances in Finance, Accounting, and Economics (AFAE) Book Series (ISSN 2327-5677) is published by IGI Global, 701 E. Chocolate Avenue, Hershey, PA 17033-1240, USA, www.igi-global.com. This series is composed of titles available for purchase individually; each title is edited to be contextually exclusive from any other title within the series. For pricing and ordering information please visit http://www.igi-global.com/book-series/advances-finance-accounting-economics/73685. Postmaster: Send all address changes to above address.

Titles in this Series

For a list of additional titles in this series, please visit:
http://www.igi-global.com/book-series/advances-finance-accounting-economics/73685

Revolutionizing the Global Stock Market Harnessing Blockchain for Enhanced Adaptability
Nuno Geada (ISCTE, University Institute of Lisbon, Portugal) Rohit Sood (Lovely Professional University, India) and Ajay Sidana (Amity International Business School, Amity University, Noida, India)
Business Science Reference • © 2024 • 285pp • H/C (ISBN: 9798369317587) • US $295.00

Six Sigma DMAIC and Markov Chain Monte Carlo Applications to Financial Risk Management
Vojo Bubevski (Vojo Bubevski Consulting, UK)
Business Science Reference • © 2024 • 299pp • H/C (ISBN: 9798369337875) • US $255.00

Artificial Intelligence Approaches to Sustainable Accounting
Maria C. Tavares (ISCA, University of Aveiro, Portugal) Graça Azevedo (University of Aveiro, Portugal) José Vale (ISCAP, Polytechnic Institute of Porto, Portugal) Rui Marques (University of Aveiro, Portugal) and Maria Anunciação Bastos (ISCA, University of Aveiro, Portugal)
Business Science Reference • © 2024 • 312pp • H/C (ISBN: 9798369308479) • US $275.00

Impact of Digitalization on Reporting, Tax Avoidance, Accounting, and Green Finance
Ahmad Alqatan (Arab Open University, Kuwait) Khaled Hussainey (University of Portsmouth, UK) Mounira Hamed (University of Tunis El Manar, Tunisia) and Kameleddine Benameur (American University of Kuwait, Kuwait)
Business Science Reference • © 2024 • 358pp • H/C (ISBN: 9798369316788) • US $270.00

Strengthening Sustainable Digitalization of Asian Economy and Society
Patricia Ordóñez de Pablos (The University of Oviedo, Spain) Mohammad Nabil Almunawar (Universiti Brunei Darussalam, Brunei) and Muhammad Anshari (Universiti Brunei Darussalam, Brunei)
Business Science Reference • © 2024 • 432pp • H/C (ISBN: 9798369319420) • US $290.00

IGI Global
PUBLISHER of TIMELY KNOWLEDGE

701 East Chocolate Avenue, Hershey, PA 17033, USA
Tel: 717-533-8845 x100 • Fax: 717-533-8661
E-Mail: cust@igi-global.com • www.igi-global.com

I dedicate this work to my gorgeous wife, Matoaile, whose unyielding love and support fuels my soul and the man that I am; to my amazing children, Sanaa, Nia, Becca, Brazil, and Bakar, whose boundless spirits infuse my heart with inspiration; and to my loving mother, Hajjah Adama Bintu, whose uncanny wisdom and generosity lifts me (and so many others) to heights that I never imagined possible.

I cannot go wrong with you all by my side, especially in the work of reaching the destined promise of our lives together…bmy

Table of Contents

Section 3

The Conclusion and Recommendation

Detailed Table of Contents

Section 1

The Problem and Research

Chapter 1

Africa, as a land area and birthplace of a people, is as intricate a subject to consider as the present effort to explore the continent's challenges with socio-economic development and the achievement of lasting social transformation. A significant reason why is the enormous diversity found inside of Africa's ecosystem – a variance in people, language, history, and general way of life that often defies mainstream logic and is hardly ever understood in the light of our common humanity. Africa, juxtaposed with the rest of the world in the dominant media, is always viewed as "a backwater" locale because it is wrongly portrayed as a place forever isolated from the best that has been thought, said, and done in the history of our world. So, a crucial task at the onset of this challenging study is to set the scene for a deeper understanding of our subject. What is Africa? How might we define the land and the people given Africa's sheer size and history? What does Africa offer relative to the rest of the world?

Chapter 2

Exploring the relationship between the lives Africans lead and the development challenges that prevail on the continent requires careful deductive reasoning. Such an effort is advanced and made exponentially better with the benefit of context – an understanding of what has been thought and said about development in Africa, the core reasons that experts and scholars have identified for Africa's socio-economic struggles and inability to achieve lasting social transformation. This context from what has been thought and said offers a roadmap to aid the work of careful analysis of our subject. This chapter thus reflects a critical synthesis of the literature on the impediments to socio-economic development in African countries, a synthesis that aligns the study's purpose, research questions, and ideological foundations. The chapter includes a discussion on the theoretical and conceptual foundations of the study and a comprehensive review of the literature.

A careful reading of the literature suggests that what has not been emphasized or prioritized enough about African countries' present predicament is the role of the people and our environment: the choices we make, our cultural context, and our interactions with one another. To be sure, the external and the internal impediments (environmental sources of control and personal control in social learning parlance) promulgated in the literature shed light on how conditions in Africa have been influenced by the reciprocal interaction of choice and culture – the decisions and behaviors of the people in response to our environment, which includes circumstances imposed by outside forces. The depths of these connections are explored in this chapter, specifically what the broader literature conveys separately about choice and culture, how the two constructs influence human development in keeping with the theory of social learning, and why there is a compelling need to explore the relationship between the lives Africans lead and the development challenges that prevail on the continent.

Qualitative research, the methodology of the present study, is a comprehensive and interpretive approach to studying and understanding the experiences of human beings. The research approach allows for a study of an exploratory nature to investigate "human choice and behavior as it occurs naturally in all of its detail" (Johnson and Christensen). In this study, the qualitative research approach provides a pathway, through evidence in the form of a qualitative questionnaire, interviews, research documents, and field notes, to explore, describe, and analyze the relationship between the lived experience of everyday Africans and the challenges of socio-economic development that impede social transformation in African countries. This chapter begins with an exploration of the researcher's positionality and the philosophical assumptions that influence use of the study's methods. The chapter provides an overview of the research design, participants and setting, sources of data, validity, and trustworthiness.

Section 2

The Data and Analysis

This chapter presents the findings from the data collected and analyzed from the qualitative questionnaire and semi-structured interviews, which endeavored to answer three primary questions: (1) How do everyday Africans describe their lived experience in pursuit of socio-economic development; (2) How does choice (decision-making) and culture (environment) influence everyday Africans' ability to develop socio-economically; and (3) How does the lived experience of everyday Africans inform understanding about achieving social transformation? These questions shed light on the intersectionality of choice (personal control), culture (environmental sources of control), and socio-economic development (human achievements) – social constructs that are germane to the endeavors of human development according to this study's theoretical and conceptual frameworks and a close reading of the literature. The chapter details the preparation of the raw data for analysis and descriptive data as well as the research findings.

A narrative inquiry and case study of the experience of the participants' home countries within the context of and in parallel with the participants' narratives is the focus of the next two chapters. The chapters further illuminate answers to the research questions posed in this study and help to fully appreciate the power of choice and culture in our lives. The foundation of the chapters are the research documentation and field notes the researcher authored while working as a foreign service officer during the 2004-2017 period. This period overlapped the time-period of the participants' lived experience narratives. The data provided an on-the-ground, contemporary account of relevant developments in Ghana, Tanzania, South Africa, and Sierra Leone, including economic and socio-political events that unfolded around the same period the participants pursued their own socio-economic development. The case study design, conducted instrumentally, enables the learning of broader lessons about Osie, Zahra, Siya, and Amie's lived experiences in their home countries.

Tanzania and South Africa, the homes of study participants Zahra and Siya, are the focus of this chapter, which offers a narrative inquiry and case study of Tanzania and South Africa within the context of and in parallel with the lived experiences of

Zahra and Siya. As demonstrated in the previous chapter with a deeper dive into the socio-political and economic dynamics of Ghana and Sierra within the space and time as Osie and Amie attempted to piece their lives together, a closer examination of Tanzania and South Africa in the same vein yields a correlation between the nations' political and development trajectory with that of their citizens' socio-economic achievements. Zahra and Siya in particular chart the course of their lives according to the dictates of their environments, which were overwhelmingly influenced by the condition of their nation-states. But Zahra and Siya remained, for the most part, in their home countries, notwithstanding the conditions therein.

Section 3

The Conclusion and Recommendation

This chapter addresses the findings related to the participants' lived experience, the role of choice and culture in shaping the participants' development, and how the participants' lived experience informs understanding about the achievement of social transformation. This chapter also details the important changes, strengths and weaknesses, and limitations of the study. The important changes reflect consideration and planning for achieving representational aims, including the number of participants, their country of origin, and regions of Africa studied. Strengths and weaknesses of the study take a hard look at what methodological elements enhanced or diminished efforts of the study to explore the lived experiences of the participants through narrative inquiry and case study. This deliberate advantages and disadvantages review helps to illuminate the fundamental limitations of study, which relate, positively and negatively, to the research design and sampling approach.

The findings reviewed in the previous chapter offer compelling insights into the lives of the study participants. They shed light on conditions the participants had to navigate in their pursuit of socio-economic development. They also offer a much better vantage point from which to try to make sense of participants' experiences, especially as it relates to implications for the development of the participants, their nation-states, and for the achievement of lasting social transformation. This consideration of the findings' implications is the focus of this chapter, which is written with the aim of elucidating answers about what meaning can be derived from the present study. This chapter deliberates on the important question, what does it all mean? It considers the theoretical and empirical implications of the study findings and offers recommendations for future research and future practice that can

Preface

Imagine being on a flight at a high altitude. Crossing ocean waters and descending lower, the African landscape comes into view. Rainforests, tropical deserts, savanna grasslands, and riveting mountains animate one's eyes. The images are simply spellbinding, nature's way of orienting the mind to its majestic beauty and awesome power. In the picturesque scene below is scattered human activity, people tending to their daily lives – some with hurried purpose, while others move about more carefreely. At this high altitude one can only truly make out the concerns of those at the top. The authorities in government, in commerce, and in other places of significance are busy exacting plans that direct resources to their personal endeavors. Monies are siphoned from national banks. Tenders for public works are given to family and friends. Infrastructure and social services stand neglected, while entire projects for national development are frustrated by willful inaction.

There is a serious disconnect, it appears from this view, between the leaders and those whom they lead, owing to the reality that the government and other authorities do not seem to work in any meaningful way to address the needs of the populace. One thinks out-loud, while surveying this scene below, that surely this must be the source of African countries' challenge with social transformation – the phenomenon that has captured the attention of both Africans and outside observers alike; that perhaps this failure is an outgrowth of the continent's history of colonialism, failed institutions, and globalization. But as all plane rides go, there comes a time when the aircraft must land.

This maneuvering to lower altitude offers yet another view of the African landscape. There is similar human activity at the ground-level, but these activities concern the interactions of individuals, families, and communities. People are busy trying to put their lives together. Their efforts appear to be guided by a blinding force, the mantra "by any means necessary" that can sometimes render people indifferent toward one another. It seems everyone is willing, to some degree or another, to undermine a family member, a friend, or a stranger in order to advance their own self interests.

One can observe from this ground level view that the worrisome kind of individualism persists among the people – a me first mentality that betrays the collectivist mindset of not-too-long ago generations of Africans. Could this be the source of the continent's discontent, one thinks to herself – perhaps an outgrowth of problems stemming from the continent's geography, systems, and body politics? This question, the cause of African countries' perennial low-income status and failure to advance socio-economically, despite the countries' abundance in human capital, mineral and marine resources – has proven to be a consistently vexing phenomenon.

THE PROBLEM

Experts tell us that African countries endure enormous strain to advance socio-economically for a variety of reasons. These external and internal impediments, as the late American University Professor George Ayittey (1998) categorized them in one of his seminal works, offer insights on the factors contributing to the chaos on the continent. Yet the impediments, as presented in the literature, do not tell the whole story, much like the imaginary flight over the African landscape offered in the foregoing paragraphs. To be sure, Africa has immense wealth and yet it is home to over half of the nations in the world whose people live below the poverty-line. The continent also contains two-thirds of the poorest nations in the world (World Bank, 2023).

While the data is clear about which countries and regions of the world struggle with socio-economic development, there has been far less agreement on the causes, especially concerning related developments in Africa. Many have offered insights on the continent's impediments, which range from theories on development, leadership and institutions, to politics, the legacy of colonialism, and the impact of globalization (Acemoglu and Robinson, 2013; Achebe, 1998; Ake, 1996; Ayittey, 1998; Ekeh, 1986; Haugen and Musser, 2012; Juma and Oluoch, 2013; Lin, 2014; Mawere and Mwanaka, 2015; Sachs, 2006; Settles, 1996).

These research contributions are significant but they do not tell the whole story. They do not, for example, invest fully in examining the lives of the people to answer a fundamental question: what role do everyday Africans play in the struggle for our personal development and the advancement of our nation-states? To answer this question and perhaps understand the true nature of Africa's enduring socio-economic struggle, we need to examine the issue with a different lens, one that provokes us to think seriously about how the choices we make and the cultural environment in which we make them informs understanding about our struggles.

The recommendation to employ this kind of an investigative lens, a qualitative narrative inquiry and case study of the lived experience of everyday Africans, is rooted in established ideas about how change is affected in society, namely (a) social learning theory on the determinants of human behavior and accomplishment; (b) choice and culture as vital antecedents for the sustenance and elevation of the human condition; and (c) leadership as a social process – not a "great man" theory – of reciprocal engagement between people for a common good (Arendt, 1958; Arnold, 1869; Bandura, 1974; Barker, 1997; Gemmill and Oakley, 1992; Soyinka, 2000). The lessons offered by these established ideas are monumental and they serve as the ideological foundation for the work that we embark on in this volume.

IDEOLOGICAL FOUNDATIONS

Lasting social transformation is an endeavor that cannot be accomplished without the mutual efforts of a society's population and governing bodies. The catalysts for such transformation, such as education according to Singh (2019), is made possible through the inputs and tireless support of the population and the deliberate actions of the peoples' governments – what is or becomes the culmination of a shared national purpose. This shared purpose is produced through recognition and practice of leadership by members of society as a social process, which leads to collective engagement for achievement of the common good. But how does all of this come about? It begins with the determinants of human behavior and accomplishment, as theorized by social learning.

Social Learning Theory

Social learning is the psychological theory that explains how people learn and, by extension, how we behave. Albert Bandura (1977), who introduced the theory in 1977, explained that observation, modeling, and imitation of others are the primary ingredients for our learning. Specifically, Bandura posited, learning and human behavior is determined by "the bidirectional influence process" of personal control and environmental sources of control, constructs that can be better understood in layman's terms as choice or agency and culture or environment. All of us observe the behaviors of others either directly or indirectly (think social media). We are likely, social learning tells us, to imitate the said behaviors if they are rewarded, but we instinctively and intuitively avoid them if the said behaviors are punished. This corresponding experience compelled Bandura to observe that if human behavior is determined by a "bidirectional influence process" of personal control and environmental sources of control (choice and culture), then "Human accomplishments [including socio-economic development] result from the reciprocal interaction of external circumstances [culture or environment] with a host of personal determinants including endowed potentialities, acquired competencies, reflective thought, and a high level of self-initiative" [choice or agency] (p. 867).

Applied to the leadership of human development, social learning denotes that people engaged in the said process have an interactive and negotiable relationship with one another, and that we are always cognizant of the ways in which we influence other people. Social learning thus gives life to the conceptual framework that underpins the present qualitative narrative inquiry and case study, which is a representation of the relationship or intersectionality between the variables of choice (personal control), culture (environmental sources of control), and socio-economic development (human accomplishments). The present study's focus on choice and culture emanates from the profound relevance of these constructs to human and social development, as revealed in the literature.

Choice, Culture, and Leadership

Choice and culture, the literature informs us, interdependently enable social change (Arendt, 1958; Arnold, 1869; Bandura, 1977; Barker, 1997; Gemmill and Oakley, 1992; Soyinka, 2000). Combined, they make change possible through the development of the social process of leadership, the idea from Gary Gemmill and Judith Oakley (1992) and Richard A. Barker (1997) that leadership encompasses the components of process and ethics (what Barker defined as a spiritual definition of life), which enables individuals to create a vision of a future good and, through this vision, come together to establish community mores that regulate our interactions.

The social process of leadership emerges when people are taught skills and when people are grounded in specific social realities that raise greater awareness and responsibility. This learning or growth process thus obliges focus on choice (decision-making) and the consolidation of an enabling culture (environment) that aligns thinking and behavior toward service of a common good (Arnold, 1869; Soyinka, 2000). Figure 1 below attempts to incorporate

Bandura's (1977) emphasis on personal control and environmental sources of control to explain human behavior and accomplishments; Gemmill and Oakley (1992) and Barker's (1997) theory on leadership as a social process; and Matthew Arnold (1869) and Wole Soyinka's (2000) theory on culture as the catalyst for leading change in society.

Figure 1. Relationship between choice and culture and the social process that yields development

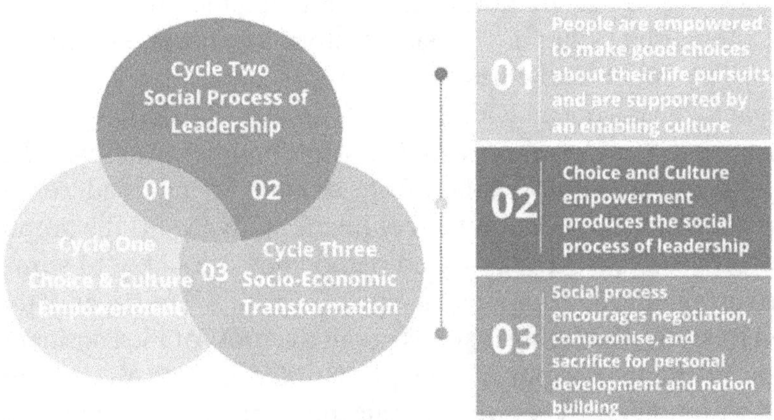

The figure showcases how Africans' lived experiences, with a focus on choice and culture, can illuminate the trajectory of our personal and national development efforts. It displays the importance of the intersectionality between choice (personal control), culture (environmental sources of control), and socio-economic development (human accomplishments) – the study's conceptual framework, which makes the assumption that if people are empowered to make good choices about our life pursuits, and we are supported, rather than hindered, by our cultural environment, we might be better equipped to navigate the conditions that influence our socio-economic development. Examining this assumption and determining whether there is evidence supporting the chain of relationship between choice, culture, and human accomplishments extends the existing research.

THE RESEARCH

With regard to evidence supporting the relationship between choice and culture and the influence of these constructs on socio-economic development, the existing research is limited. The research concerning the continent's struggling development efforts seems primarily focused on governance, failed development theories and factors related to political systems, history, globalization, neo-colonialism, or bad national leaders, in keeping with Bruce Gilley's (2010) pronouncements in *The end of the African renaissance*. The Canadian-American scholar argued, rather emphatically from an internalist point of view, that "blaming outside factors has never explained Africa's maladies. The direct blame lies with corrupt leaders" (p. 93).

Munyaradzi Mawere and Tendai R. Mwanaka's (2015) *Democracy, good governance and development in Africa* offers another example. The volume of essays, constructed by scholars from around Africa to address the issue of sustainable development on the continent "[advanced] the argument that good governance and African-based democracy are likely to stimulate and promote sustainable development in Africa'' (p. viii). The pages of the volume provided thought-provoking insights about the roots of the continent's socio-economic challenges, from the people being besieged by a "coloniality" mindset, to the need to revive African indigenous institutions, education, and values. The volume's pages also declared as problematic the continued use of the "imperial" methodologies that are "empowered by certain political and economic systems championed by the global north" and through which Africa and development in Africa is researched, studied, and understood – notwithstanding the difference in conditions and contexts whenever Africa is juxtaposed with the global north (p. 195).

Such arguments have merit and they do reflect a genuine attempt by scholars to make sense of the prevailing conditions on the continent. Yet they do not go deep enough. They do not adequately address the role of the people – the choices we make and the culture that shapes those very choices, not unless the arguments offered turn to the exploitation of the continent by the ruling elite, also known as our national leaders. Thus, more evidence is needed to support the intersectionality of the choices that the people make, the culture in which we make those choices, and how the two constructs work to power (or not) the social process we need to overcome our struggles. The purpose and significance of this kind of a research endeavor is difficult to overstate.

PURPOSE AND SIGNIFICANCE

The present qualitative narrative inquiry and case study explores the relationship between the lives Africans lead and the development challenges that prevail on the continent. The rationale supporting this exploration is that the choices ordinary people make and the culture in which we make them have proven to make change possible in human affairs (Arendt, 1958; Arnold, 1869; Bandura, 1977; Barker, 1997; Gemmill and Oakley, 1992; Soyinka, 2000). The combined framework of social learning, choice and culture as the catalyst for change, and leadership as a social process support the inquiry, analysis, and interpretation of the examined data, which emanate from three questions: (1) how do everyday Africans describe their lived experience in pursuit of socio-economic development; (2) how does choice (decision-making) and culture (environment) influence everyday Africans' ability to develop socio-economically; and (3) how does the lived experience of everyday Africans inform understanding about achieving social transformation?

In answering these questions, the study fills an existing gap in the literature concerning understanding about African countries' struggles with socio-economic development. It puts into better perspective what has thus far been explored and characterized within the literature as the causes of the continent's material and social underdevelopment and helps us to understand the reason such arguments, as presently constructed, are insufficient explanations (Ayittey, 1998; Acemoglu and Robinson, 2013; Ake, 1996; Sachs, 2006; Lin, 2014). The clarity gained from the present study on the roots of Africa's troubles ultimately positions us to consider workable solutions, to develop a roadmap for change that is focused on the people, the vast majority whose living conditions reflect precisely the reason Africa's standing in the world is so low.

To be sure, African countries rank dead last in practically every human development index category, according to the World Population Review, giving credence to the derisive label of Africa as "the third world of the third world." The label, while unfortunate, speaks to the hard and undeniable realities on the ground. African countries and African people are threatened by political instability and social upheaval, to say nothing of struggles with the survival matters of "access to healthcare…low income and low life expectancies, coupled with high birth rates'' (World Population Review, 2022). These dire conditions are further exacerbated by a void, at an alarming scale on the continent, of leadership – the social process variety that compels citizens to engage each other in the advancement of our communities and nation-states.

African countries' present-day conditions of widespread poverty perpetuated by an absence of the social process of leadership are critical matters of human rights and social justice. African people, not unlike other peoples of the world, have a right to life, which can only be made possible through socio-economic security and lasting social transformation. There is no greater purpose, with regard to these considerations, than determining how the said security and transformation can be harnessed and applied for improving the living conditions and the quality of life of the people. We all therefore stand to benefit from the application of the present study findings in our own lives and, in so doing, learn how to better navigate our lives in ways that set the stage for us to advance the common interests of our communities.

ORGANIZATION OF THE STUDY

The study is organized in three parts. Part One begins with a scene setter in Chapter 1. This chapter offers a basic contour of the continent with regard to our people, our history, our potential, our successes and our challenges in the socio-economic development space. A comprehensive review of the literature follows in Chapter 2. The review examines what has been said about the impediments to development in Africa and how Africa's related struggles have been investigated. This effort includes a look at the ideological foundations of the present study, as well as a synthesis of key findings in scholarly articles, dissertations, books, and online publications. Chapter 3 identifies and goes deeper into the nexus of impediments to development, specifically the constructs of leadership, choice and culture. Chapter 4 introduces the study's design for action, including details of the methods used to collect the qualitative data required to answer the research questions.

Part Two of the study opens with Chapter 5, which provides the analysis of the data collected from the qualitative survey questionnaire and semi-structured interviews of the study participants. Part Two continues with a narrative inquiry and case study of the experience of the participants' home countries within the context of and in parallel with the participants' narratives. This participant and country juxtaposition further illuminates answers to the research questions posed in the study. Ghana and Sierra Leone comprise Chapter 6. Tanzania and South Africa round-out Chapter 7.

Part Three of the study offers, in Chapter 8, a thorough explanation of the fundamental discoveries of the study, as well as the important changes made during and the limitations of the study. In Chapter 9, we deliberate on the important question, what does it all mean? Here we consider the theoretical and empirical implications of the study and offer recommendations for future research and future practice that can be applied to improving outcomes in African countries. Chapter 10 offers concluding perspectives through the researcher's engagement in the obligatory practice of narrative inquirers, wherein "researchers also engage in narrative inquiry into their own lived and told stories as part of the process of coming alongside research participants" (Johnson and Christensen, 2020 p. 406). The aim of this effort is to expound upon and contextualize the lessons of this study through a personal example.

The definition of terms used in the study follow, along with a closer look at the landscape of our study's focus in Chapter 1.

Baimba Yilla
Marymount University, USA

REFERENCES

Acemoglu, D., & Robinson, J. A. (2013). *Why nations fail: The origins of power, prosperity, and poverty (Pbk* (C. Business, Ed.).

Achebe, C. (1998). *The trouble with Nigeria*. Fourth Dimension Publishing.

Ake, C. (1996). *Democracy and development in Africa*. Brookings Institution.

Arendt, H. (1958). *The human condition*. The University of Chicago Press.

Arnold, M. (1869). *Culture and anarchy: An essay in political and social criticism*. Macmillan.

Ayittey, G. (1998). *Africa in chaos*. St. Martin's Press.

Bandura, A. (1974). Behavior theory and the models of man. *The American Psychologist*, *29*(12), 859–869. doi:10.1037/h0037514

Bandura, A. (1977). *Social learning theory*. Prentice Hall.

Barker, R. A. (1997). How can we train leaders if we do not know what leadership is? *Human Relations*, *50*(4), 343–362. doi:10.1177/001872679705000402

Barrett, M. S., & Stauffer, S. L. (2009). *Narrative inquiry in music education: Troubling certainty*. Springer. doi:10.1007/978-1-4020-9862-8

Clandinin, D. J., & Rosiek, J. (2007). Mapping a landscape of narrative inquiry: Borderland spaces and tensions. In D. J. Clandinin (Ed.), *Handbook of narrative inquiry: mapping a methodology* (pp. 35–75). Sage. doi:10.4135/9781452226552.n2

Ekeh, P. (1986). Development theory and theAfrican predicament. *Africa Development. Afrique et Developpement, 11*(4), 1–40. https://www.jstor.org/stable/24486618

French, H. (2021). *Born in blackness: Africa, Africans, and the making of the modern world, 1471 to the second world war.* Liveright Publishing Corporation.

Gemmill, G., & Oakley, J. (1992). Leadership: An alienating social myth? *Human Relations, 45*(2), 113–129. doi:10.1177/001872679204500201

Gilley, B. (2010). The end of the African renaissance. *The Washington Quarterly, 33*(4), 87–101. doi:10.1080/0163660X.2010.516612

Haugen, D. M., & Musser, S. (2012). *Africa.* Greenhaven Press.

Juma, T. O., & Oluoch, K. K. (2013). System failure causes of conflict in Africa as a social transformation. *International Affairs and Global Strategy, 17*, 2013.

Lin, J. Y. (2014). *The Quest for prosperity: How developing economies can take off.* Princeton University Press.

Mawere, M., & Mwanaka, T. R. (2015). Democracy, good governance and development in Africa. Langaa Research & Publishing CIG.

Oakes, J.M., and Rossi, P. H. (2003). The measurement of SES in health research: current practice and steps toward a new approach. *Social Science & Medicine (1982), 56*(4), 769–784. . doi:10.1016/S0277-9536(02)00073-4

Sachs, J. B. (2006). *The end of poverty: Economic possibilities for our time.* Penguin.

Settles, J. D. (1996). *The impact of colonialism on African economic development.* Chancellor's Honors Program Projects. https://trace.tennessee.edu/utk_chanhonoproj/182

Singh, R. (2019). *Education: An effective engine and catalyst of social transformation.* Eurasiareview.com.

Soyinka, W. (2000). Culture, democracy and renewal. *Trends in Organized Crime*, *5*(3), 110–117. doi:10.1007/s12117-000-1039-2

Storr, W. (2020). *The science of storytelling: Why stories make us human and how to tell them better*. Abrams Press.

World Bank. (n.d.) *World Poverty Overview 2023*. World Bank. https://www.worldbank.org/en/topic/poverty/overview

Worldatlas. (n.d.). *Least Developed Countries 2022*. World Population Review. https://worldpopulationreview.com/country-rankings/least-developed-countries

DEFINITION OF TERMS

Case Study: A detailed study of subjects or topics, including people, groups, places, events organizations, or phenomena, commonly used in educational and other research studies.

Choice: The act of making a decision for one's life pursuits when one is faced with multiple options or possibilities. Choice is synonymous with decision-making and agency in this study.

Culture: An approach to or a way of life that centers the thinking and behavior of a people. Culture, which includes artifacts or material objects and symbols (ideas, values, and beliefs of a people) is synonymous with environment in this study.

Everyday Africans: The men and women of Africa's rural communities and urban centers who are parents or caregivers; citizens who toil the land, devote themselves to vocational occupations, or work in other professional capacities to earn a living wage.

Leadership: The components of process and ethics (what Barker (1997) defines as a spiritual definition of life), which enables individuals to create a vision of a future good and, from this collective vision, create community mores which define behavioral standards, role expectations, and contractual commitments (Barker, 1997; Gemmill and Oakley, 1992).

Narrative Inquiry: A way of thinking about and studying experience as a story. Its focus, according to Clandinin and Rosiek (2007), "is on an individual's experience as well as on the social, cultural, and institutional narratives within which individuals' experiences are constituted, shaped, expressed, and enacted" (p. 35).

Socio-Economic Development: Socio-economic development (status), as Oaks et al., (2003) defined the construct, is a measure of access to resources and a function of one's material, human, and social capital in relation to others. The combined total of this economic and sociological measurement, the authors contend, "uniquely locates the status of individuals in the social structure" (p. 776).

Social Transformation: Social transformation requires a shift in the collective consciousness of a society. It is the process of change in institutionalized relationships, norms, values, and hierarchies over time. It is the manner in which society changes due to economic growth, science, technological innovations, and war or political upheavals. (https://www.worldatlas.com/articles/what-is-social-transformation.html).

Section 1

The Problem and Research

Chapter 1
The Landscape

ABSTRACT

Africa, as a land area and birthplace of a people, is as intricate a subject to consider as the present effort to explore the continent's challenges with socio-economic development and the achievement of lasting social transformation. A significant reason why is the enormous diversity found inside of Africa's ecosystem – a variance in people, language, history, and general way of life that often defies mainstream logic and is hardly ever understood in the light of our common humanity. Africa, juxtaposed with the rest of the world in the dominant media, is always viewed as "a backwater" locale because it is wrongly portrayed as a place forever isolated from the best that has been thought, said, and done in the history of our world. So, a crucial task at the onset of this challenging study is to set the scene for a deeper understanding of our subject. What is Africa? How might we define the land and the people given Africa's sheer size and history? What does Africa offer relative to the rest of the world?

INTRODUCTION

Africa is the second-largest and second most-populous continent in the world covering 11.2 million square miles and roughly 20 percent of the world's land area. The continent is bordered by the Mediterranean Sea to the north, the Red Sea to the northeast, the Indian Ocean to the southeast, and the Atlantic Ocean to the west. Africa is watered by great rivers, including the Congo, the Niger, the Zambezi, and the Nile, the latter of which has become, because of climate change and water supply concerns, a considerable source of friction

DOI: 10.4018/979-8-3693-2403-5.ch001

among the river's neighboring countries over questions about access and control. Some of the most impressive natural wonders in the world call Africa home. The Serengeti Plains, Victoria Falls, Mount Kilimanjaro, and Table Mountain are just some of the immensely beautiful nature scenes that have captured the imagination of world travelers, to say nothing of the continent's beaches, unparalleled wildlife, and abundant mineral deposits.

In the history of man, Africa's foremost significance remains its confirmed status as the birthplace of humankind and of modern-day humans. Africa is where Homo sapiens emerged some sixty thousand years ago to populate and render the world as it exists today. Historian Martin Meredith (2011) explained in *Born in Africa: The quest for the origins of human life* that Homo sapiens from Africa proved to be the source of early technology, language ability, and artistry that enabled our species to evolve from living in forests and on savannah grasslands, to adopting a beachcombing lifestyle and, eventually, to settling communities. From their original homeland in northeast Africa, many Homo sapiens spread across other parts of the continent largely in response to climate change and the unrelenting will to survive. An even smaller group of emigrants, according to archaeological records and genetic evidence, likely crossed the western shore of the Red Sea along the straits of Bab al-Mandab to enter the Arabian peninsula from the Abdur reef in what is present-day Eritrea. Over the course of thousands of years, these early African emigrants spread farther across the southern Arabian coastlines, gradually migrating east to India, the southern end of Asia, Australia, New Guinea and Tasmania, while others headed westward to establish settlements in the Levant, East and Central Asia, Europe, Siberia, Alaska, and the Americas. Meredith (2011) expounded further that,

As they spread out across the world, far-flung branches of the modern human family began to diversify, adapting variously to the different climates and ecologies they encountered. Local populations developed distinctive local features. In northern latitudes, they acquired a lighter skin color in response to different levels of ultraviolet radiation. The diverse trajectories they followed led to a vast array of languages, cultures and religions. New technologies allowed agriculture and settled communities to flourish (Meredith, 2011, p. 193).

Archaeological records found in East and Southern Africa demonstrate an array of innovation which came into existence inside of Africa, including toolmaking, language, and the capture and control of fire that led to the production of cooked food to aid in the development of the human body and brain. Smelting iron is but one example of Africans' technological innovation, which advanced the human species in such a profound way that it bears brief mention here in the same manner W.E.B. Dubois (1915) captured it in his telling of Africans' contributions to the modern world through the words of Franz Boas, the German-American anthropologist and pioneer of modern anthropology. Dubois wrote in *The negro* that according to Boas,

It seems likely that at a time when the European was still satisfied with rude stone tools, the African had invented or adopted the art of smelting iron. Consider for a moment what this invention has meant for the advance of the human race. As long as hammer, knife, saw, drill, the spade, and the hoe had to be chipped out of stone, or had to be made of shell or hard wood, effective industrial work was not impossible, but difficult. A great progress was made when copper found in large nuggets was hammered out into tools and later on shaped by melting, and when bronze was introduced; but the true advancement of industrial life did not begin until the hard iron was discovered. . . Neither ancient Europe, nor ancient western Asia, nor ancient China knew the iron and everything points to its introduction from Africa (Dubois, 1915, p. 57).

According to Dubois and others who followed suit with their own research, Africans proved to be vastly innovative in other areas of human development contrary to what many of us were taught in our history classes in American schools. To be sure, as Homo sapiens marched toward the establishment of settler communities around the world, organizing themselves along sophisticated socio-political bodies, those left behind in Africa were equally up to the task. Later empires of Ghana, Mali, Kongo and Songhai were exemplary. These African societies leveraged their social and political organization, agricultural and industrial skills to create kingdoms of states that boasted an array of specialists who delivered services to the masses. Among them were farmers, blacksmiths, carpenters, miners, ceramists and textile manufacturers, and they all combined through the administration of their societies to establish a buoyant and prosperous system of domestic and foreign trade. It was this commercial acuity, coupled with Africans' immense wealth in gold and the trading of the latter to outsiders, that further amplified Africa's burgeoning contribution to the development of the modern world (French, 2021).

But alas, the wicked irony of our modern existence is that thousands of years after the early African emigrants left their home in Africa to settle the rest of the world, some of their descendants returned to the motherland and mingled together with Africans under the auspices of conducting trade (initially for gold) without the immediate knowledge (one must assume) of their genetic lineage with the Africans. The differences in physical appearance, language, cultures, and innovations – the very byproducts of their evolution outside of Africa – convinced the returning descended emigrants to castigate Africans as different and, somehow, sub-human. American scholar Howard French (2021) affirmed this historical reality in *Born in blackness: Africa, Africans, and the making of the modern world, 1471 to the second world war* when he described what some considered the "index case, or first victim, in the formation of the transatlantic slave trade centered on dark-skinned Africans" (p. 67).

French (2021) observed that the Portuguese, who engineered the capture of a "black Mooress" and several others along the coast of present-day Mauritania during a 1441 expedition, placed great significance on the skin color of their captives and their "pagan" religious orientation. Yields of more captives from subsequent raids reinforced and "mobilized" during the 1440s "the notion that the Black peoples who inhabited this part of Africa, which was coming under exploration by Europeans for the first time, were uniquely wretched and lacking in the redeeming attributes of civilization by virtue of their color" (p. 69). Skin color and religion were, of course, only useful justifications for the Europeans, who held a much deeper motivation to render possible what Meredith (2011) highlights as the hallmark of early human achievement: agriculture and the flourishing of settled communities. The returning descended emigrants out of Europe thus gradually instigated (lest we forget that Africans were also complicit) bondage of their African kin in order to secure the labor required for the agricultural revolution that would generate unconscionable wealth for themselves in their adopted lands outside of Africa and from the very places they would go on to conquer and colonize.

The slow development of abolitionist thought in the world, in parallel with Africans' defiance of their bondage through revolts, eventually prevailed to force an end to the slave trade (both transatlantic and above the Sahara), albeit some four hundred years later, compelling Africans to persevere through the trauma while concurrently enduring the lingering practices of discrimination that permeates their present-day existence. This history of Africans in bondage to labor for the commercial benefit of their fellow humans and what ensued in its aftermath, namely the partitioning and colonization of both the African land and people for further subjugation and exploitation, takes us to conditions of the present-day.

At a structural level, the continent is now 54 different countries or nation states with drastically varying levels of income to account for the economic security of over a billion people. Out of the 54 countries, development experts, including those of the World Bank, deem 22 countries to be plagued by conflict and therefore unstable, while another 13 are landlocked with very small populations and limited human and material resources (World Bank, 2024). Africans' history of being enslaved and colonized cannot be ignored in light of these conditions, especially not when we are moved to examine the troubling socio-economic struggles that prevail on the continent.

To be sure, the harm inflicted on African people through the trauma of slavery and colonialism has permeated through the years, bringing to mind what J.H. Harris (1912) observed even a century or so ago in his dissection of the atrocities in the Congo under the direction of Leopold and his Belgium state. "The real catastrophe in the Congo," Harris penned as a member of a community of witnesses of the ordeal in that period, "was the desolation and murder in the larger sense. The invasion of family life, the ruthless destruction of every social barrier, the shattering of every tribal law, the introduction of criminal practices which struck the chiefs of the people dumb with horror–in a word, a veritable avalanche of filth and immorality overwhelmed the Congo tribes" (p. 38).

The "avalanche" inflicted by the descendants of Homo sapien emigrants who settled in today's Europe and Mediterranean lands was not limited to the Congo. Not by a long stretch. No, the avalanche overwhelmed all of Africa's people and land, resulting in what Harris so aptly described as "the desolation and murder in the larger sense" of the African person, family, and society. It is difficult to embrace a counter-argument or anything remotely contrarian under the weight of such evidence. As Dubios (1915) observed in making the point that slavery rendered impossible further advances toward civilization in Africa, "It would be conservative…to say that the slave trade cost Negro Africa 100,000,000 souls. And yet people ask to-day the cause of the stagnation of culture in that land since 1600" (p. 78)!

Invoking the catastrophic history of slavery to explain why conditions in Africa are the way they are is very appropriate, but so too is the need to look for answers not limited to or confined by historical events from which current generations are so far removed. Half a century since slavery and the life-span now separating us from the colonial period, the question can be asked: what aspect of Africans' enslavement still endures to adversely impact socio-economic development on the continent and, given Africans' political independence beginning with Ghana in 1957, what specific role do Africans play in the modern phenomenon of African countries failing to achieve enduring socio-economic development and lasting social transformation? The answer to the first question, the enduring negative influence of slavery and colonialism, is less obscure – as a review of the literature in chapter 2 reveals – and because of what the world today in general would have us think or believe about Africa.

AFRICA IN THE WORLD

Africa's intrinsic value to its people and the world, some have claimed, is greatly diminished because nature and man (both European and African) have combined to render Africa "a hell on earth" (Sowell, 2005). Slavery and colonialism notwithstanding, the argument goes, Africa's "social degeneration" derives from Africa's geography (no navigable waterways for commercial transport), isolation from the wider cultural universe, the existence of small tribal societies vulnerable to invasion or manipulation, and misguided African leaders educated in western countries who implement unworkable policies in attempt to spur economic growth. We will cover impediments to Africa's development in the next chapter, but the consequence of this dubious narrative and its continued airing in the public domain is much of the world defining Africa as a place that can offer little to advance modern human civilization in a way other continents have and continue to do with their technologies, human capital, and natural resources.

The people of Africa are also erroneously characterized by some in the world today as being homogeneous. This is largely so because we mostly share a skin color (south of the Sahara) and are mistakenly considered by more than a few as belonging to one nation. Africa is not a country but a continent made up of regions, sub-regions and nation-states, whose similarities can be dwarfed by the differences present in each area by way of language, cultural heritage, religion, and colonial influence. The latter alone can transform the nature of discourse about the continent with regard to the diametrically opposing socio-cultural views of Indigenous African tongues, Francophone, Anglophone, Arabic, Spanish, and Portuguese speaking peoples of the continent, whose divergent political outlooks are shaped by the very languages we speak and the history we have lived.

The world today has a similar tendency to separate North Africa from the rest of Africa – the bigoted idea that the Sahara desert, until sustained European contact beginning in the 1400s, had disconnected Africans living below the desert from civilization, despite historical evidence to the contrary that informs us about the Empires of Ghana, Mali, Kongo, and Songhai and their established trade with the peoples of the Maghreb, Asia and the Europeans in the territories of present-day Portugal and Spain in the 1300s

(French, 2021). While differences of language, culture, and socio-politics exist, including North Africans' Arabic and Mediterranean orientations, history and contemporary experience demonstrates that the people of the African continent are very much alike in how we live and fashion ourselves and our communities for social mobility.

The peoples of Algeria and Tunisia, despite their own socio-cultural, linguistic and political dispositions, are as African as the peoples of the nation-states of Kenya and the Democratic Republic of the Congo. This is so because Algerians, Tunisians, Kenyans and Congolese, much like their brothers and sisters on the continent share the spirit of humanity, one bonded, on the African soil, by a shared experience of struggle and triumph through togetherness. Being African is, therefore, not determined by artificial borders, skin complexion, or even religion or politics but rather by a historic willingness of a people to persevere through community.

The fact of humanity's common ancestry – all of us originating from the same species in Africa – pretty much slams the door shut on any attempts to separate or make distinctions between the peoples of Africa, if not the peoples of the entire world all together. Our differences, which are embedded in our separate cultural evolutions over the course of time, informs our value and potential to the rest of the world. Africa's score on the latter scale is profoundly underrated.

AFRICA'S POTENTIAL

The continent's potential lies with our people. The specter of poverty or having to do far more with far less over the years has created a resilient population that pushes the envelope on innovation to attain that which is necessary to survive. Very few in the world today are unaware of the financial services revolution that has gripped Africa by way of mobile banking, wherein citizens in both urban and rural areas are able to leverage their cellphones, in the absence of access to brick and mortar banks, as a platform to receive and transfer money with the click of a button. Many are also aware of the burgeoning film industries and crowdsourcing technologies that have risen to prominence because of the ingenuity of African entrepreneurs to meet the needs of the people where our national governments have failed us, as detailed in Dayo Olopade's (2014) *The bright continent: Breaking rules and making change in modern Africa.*

There are countless more examples still, including the innovators United Nations Development Program (UNDP) Resident Representative in Ghana,

Angela Lusigi (2022), highlighted in *Harnessing Africa's creativity and innovation to drive human development.* Notably, Lusigi informed us about a Ghanaian social entrepreneur who launched Craft Education, a behavioral therapy and special needs platform that provides equitable access to education for children with learning disabilities. Lusigi also introduced an Ivorian woman and her team, who developed an artificial intelligence enabled facial recognition software to remotely identify Africans – a much needed technology for proper identification that can be the gateway to a host of human services. These innovations were made possible by driven and creative Africans who did not wait for the enactment of government policies to address what they observed as societal needs.

Africans are well positioned to extrapolate this same innovative spirit to the world for the very reason that demographers are bullish about what the future holds for the continent's burgeoning population. While major power centers like Japan and China face the dire prospects of low fertility rates and population aging – jeopardizing their outlook on economic growth and political influence, Africa is in the catbird seat of a demographic revolution. The continent's population is projected to reach 2.5 billion by 2050, according to the United Nations, which would translate to Africa having more than 25 percent of the world's population. This staggering figure presents a potential boon for socio-economic development on the continent, including an increase in demands for goods and services. Currently a market of 1.4 billion people, Africa's projected population increase (again 2.5 billion people) would firmly cement the continent as the largest free trade area in the world.

Beyond her people, Africa is blessed with natural resources, including oil, gas, minerals, and fertile land. Oil and gas production remains the dominant source of revenue for many African countries. As Brickstone, an industrial and infrastructure developer on the continent observes, these revenues can be redirected "into trade, manufacturing and industry – leveraging digitalization, technological advancements and enhanced financing to develop diversified industries continent-wide" (Brickson, 2024). But we know that this revenue stream will eventually run its course given clear signs that investments in oil and gas projects across the continent will be adversely impacted by growing environmental and socio-political concerns. Africa can, nevertheless, favorably leverage this change in the world toward usage of low-carbon materials by exploiting existing resources such as oil and minerals (nickel, lithium, cobalt, graphite, manganese, and copper) that are required for the manufacturing of products needed for green economies worldwide, to include solar panels, batteries and other components for electric vehicles.

But if Africa's potential rests with her people, then her salvation lies in the fertile land with which she is endowed. The continent "has 60 percent of the world's uncultivated arable land," a share of the proverbial global pie that points to the untapped potential of the continent's agricultural sector and implications for the world (Hodder, Migwalla et al., 2023). Africa does not only have the land to grow food for self-feeding of Africans and to create millions of jobs within auxiliary industries while doing so, the continent can also generate surplus food for trade to feed the rest of the world. Not unlike the times when Zimbabwe was known, rightly or wrongly, as the bread-basket of Africa due to that country's prolific commercial farm yields in the 1980s, Africa has the potential to leverage key drivers for growth of its agricultural sector that concurrently promotes profitable, sustainable development and helps to meet the globe's food supply demands.

Delivering on these key drivers for an agricultural revolution – paying attention to our institutional framework (governing mechanisms and politics), producing a quality strategy, and strengthening the factors that enable delivery mechanisms for the creation of rural economic growth – is wholly dependent on prioritizing our goals and taking deliberate action. And this very consideration, executing the steps required for Africa to maximize her potential not just in agriculture but in all sectors and areas of human life, brings us closer to exploring the second half of the question posed earlier: what specific role do Africans play in the modern phenomenon of African countries failing to achieve enduring socio-economic development and lasting social transformation? The question compels consideration of what is working and not working in Africa and how this reality influences sustainable development projects on the continent.

THE POSITIVES

There is an effort, however big or small, across all of Africa to achieve sustainable development. These efforts are informed and cheered on by the international community, which takes a carrot and stick approach to encourage cooperation from African nations. The United Nations (UN) and its Sustainable Development Goals (SDGs) is but one example. The specific SDGs for Africa include a targeted focus on growing infrastructure, energy, and clean water and sanitation among several social service needs, which also align with and advance the development agenda that Africa's national leaders have separately promulgated through the auspices of the African Union (AU). This concerted effort by the AU to bring attention to matters of mutual concern to Africans at the continental level is another positive step being taken in Africa to address development needs.

The same can be said about a handful of African countries at the national level, those whose governments have taken steps well beyond the UN-mandated SDGs to deliver to their citizens better living conditions, better healthcare and more access to education. As outlined in the Legatum Prosperity Index 2023, an annual ranking of world nations based on factors such as wealth, economic growth, and human services, several African countries are succeeding in key areas. Their prosperity, as in the example of Mauritius which is the only country on the continent that is ranked in the top 50 globally (47th to be exact), stems from the successful implementation of policy reforms in services such as education and healthcare. Botswana, South Africa, Morocco, Tunisia, Namibia, Ghana, Algeria, Egypt Senegal, Rwanda, Kenya, Seychelles and Côte d'Ivoire stand-out for praise even if, as the institute makes clear about the least prosperous countries that have seen signs of improvement, these countries "have greater potential than is being realized" (Legatum Institute, 2023).

The continents' general disposition toward the consolidation of an internal trade market is another positive trend. This effort has been readily apparent for some time with the formation of the continent's five main regional economic blocs, including the Economic Community of Central African States and the Arab Maghreb Union (AMU). Notwithstanding the military and political oversight responsibility of some of these blocs, they are by-and-large devoted to promulgating inter-regional trade. This means they work together to eliminate barriers (tariffs), to adopt common barriers for non-members and to allow a free movement of resources, including people, within their territories. The net-result of these coordinated efforts is the establishment of free trade, the generation of market access, and the creation and protection of jobs.

This drive toward integration for socio-economic gain is also felt at the continental level. The days of pan-Africanism with Ghana's Kwame Nkrumah and the Congo's Patrice Lumumba pulling the strings to unite Africa as a nation – a United States of Africa – might well be in the past, but today's leaders on the continent have committed to marshaling their combined powers for economic development through integration, namely the signing in March 2018 of the African Continental Free Trade Area Agreement (AfCFTA). This agreement creates a single common market across Africa for economic growth and also promotes social development. Many experts contend that with its full implementation, i.e. the embrace by member states of significant policy reforms and measures to facilitate trade, AfCFTA stands to dramatically increase productivity in the economic sectors that reign supreme in Africa:

natural resources, manufacturing, and services. The World Bank, for example, estimates potential income gains of $450 billion dollars from the agreement, which would allow "African countries to bring 30 million people out of extreme poverty and to raise the incomes of 68 million others who live on less than $5.50 per day" (World Bank, 2020). This would reflect the start of real economic growth for the nations of Africa should it all pan-out as predicted.

Another positive trend in Africa that bears mention is the general disposition of most Africans toward achievement. The vast majority have a motivation – better yet a deep seated hunger – to improve their socio-economic standing and those of their relatives. This motivation might seem driven by the simple desire to keep up with one's peers. While there is some truth to the latter, many Africans are motivated by the struggles they have had to overcome. The crucible experience of material poverty (going without life's basic needs); the recurring exposure to political violence; and the psychological effect of constantly being reminded of one's own mortality all combine to fashion an innate drive to succeed, to improve upon the circumstances that influence our livelihoods and our stations in life. It is this drive (and life conditions) that spurs the creative juices that have led to incredible innovations.

Take, for example, the work of Côte D'Ivoire national and waste management specialist Noel N'guessan. The young Ivorian developed in 2021 Kubeko, a technology that addresses the real problem of post-harvest waste in his home country. Post-harvest waste in Côte D'Ivoire combines with similar occurrences across the continent to yield low agricultural production and, by extension, a significant loss in income for farmers in Africa relative to the rest of the world. N'guessan's set of low-cost bio waste processing systems, as Ventures Africa shared in a profile of the engineer in 2021, produces fertilizers from the waste generated by the processing of harvest yields such as banana and cassava. The engineer's composter and biogas system allows farmers to turn a profit from what creates a deficit for them. Notably, farmers are able to produce organic fertilizers from the processed waste to use for farming and, in so doing, increase their earning potential.

When asked what influenced or motivated him to develop his technology, N'guessan pointed to what he witnessed around him. "Fundamentally," he said, "it is poverty. Farmers cannot be perpetually impoverished. It leads to a slew of issues, particularly with the young population migrating to cities and the negative image that farming has" (Ventures Africa, 2021). N'guessan's very honest response about the enduring impact of poverty puts into perspective the positive trends in Africa that have thus far been outlined. He places a bulls-eye on the reason Africa, even with the successes that the continent lately enjoys, is still hamstrung by serious challenges. Just what are these challenges?

THE CHALLENGES

Perhaps the best place to start with Africa's challenges is where we began regarding positive trends. Africa's effort to address sustainable development at the continental and national levels is, at best, spotty, as many stakeholders know all too well. For starters, there are still an estimated 462 million Africans who live in extreme poverty in 2023. This is one-third of the population that survives on less than $2.15 per day (World Bank, 2023). The statistic offers a vivid portrait of where things are from the standpoint of, among other basic human needs, food insecurity. But there is more to consider. According to the UN's 2023 Africa Sustainable Development Report, progress on the continent concerning achievement of the established goals "has been uneven, with significant differences among sub regions, countries, and rural and urban areas" (United Nations, 2023). With clean water and sanitation, for example, disparities between rural and urban communities resolve to complicate what is otherwise viewed as a 'marked improvement' from years past. Notably, two countries from the 48 participating are meeting established benchmarks while "Three in five Africans, or 411 million people, still lack safely managed drinking water" (United Nations, 2023).

On a national level, this translates into a country like Nigeria having somewhere around 70 percent of its population living without access to clean water and sanitation. The latter, which does not get nearly enough attention, is an even more debilitating problem. Dirty water, poor toilets, and a lack of hygiene facilities are a concern all over Africa. If in doubt, consider once more the example of Africa's most populous country. Over half of Nigeria's population (116 million people) live without access to proper toilet facilities (WaterAid, 2024). This is a remarkable number of people going without life necessities that are as basic as they get. The struggle to meet such basic needs thus contextualizes the inadequate results for the other established sustainable development goals, namely affordable and clean energy, innovation, industry and infrastructure, sustainable cities and communities, and partnerships. The UN's progress report observes:

A reality check of the progress made on the SDGs at the midpoint towards 2030 reveals significant challenges. The latest global-level data and assessments from custodian agencies paint a concerning picture: of the approximately

140 targets that can be evaluated, half of them show moderate or severe deviations from the desired trajectory. Furthermore, more than 30 percent of these targets have experienced no progress or, even worse, regression below the 2015 baseline. This assessment underscores the urgent need for intensified efforts to ensure the SDGs stay on course and progress towards a sustainable future for all (United Nations, 2023).

Challenges with achieving the SDGs in Africa resolve to challenges present in the body politic of the nations, namely the struggle for political power. These perennial fights are as palpable in Africa, if not more so, than in any other place in the world. Evidence can be found in the number of attempts made on the continent (hundreds since the post-independence era) to force a change in government through unconstitutional, some would say, illegal means (Powell and Thyne, 2011). Why these political fights take place offers instructive lessons. For reasons both historic and endemic, the need to control a nation's largesses has long been the foundation of political authority on the continent. What this means is that political authority or influence in a vast number of countries lies not with the people, who elect their representatives, but rather in access to the national resources that convey the means of control necessary to garner both power and wealth.

Such inverse political orientation or governing outlook by elected or appointed officials leads to domestic hostilities, as those locked out of the power that controls the nation's resources see no other means to prosper than wrestling the said power from the hands of those in which it resides. The instability that thus ensues from a war, a running conflict or even a fragile peace in which opposing sides agree to disagree and revert to malice toward each other severely detracts from the business of the people. Delivering on easy deliverables such as food security, clean water and sanitation becomes problematic, to say nothing of the more dynamic elements of social development. Durable infrastructure in the form of adequate housing, healthcare, energy, transportation, banking, education and employment, and the rule of law from which supportive policies and regulations emanate are among the laundry list of the peoples' business that goes unmet or is never addressed at standards comparable to what prevails in the rest of the world.

It is tempting here, by providing concrete examples, to compare African countries with others in the world that have delivered on development agendas to meet the needs of their citizens. After all, doing so has been the traditional yardstick employed for audiences to appreciate just how far African nations have lagged behind or how far they have come in terms of development, especially relative to peer countries. But social comparisons of this variety, much like those individuals make in our personal lives when it comes to socio-economic considerations, can be harmful. Unfavorable comparisons in particular decrease psychological well-being and, over time, erode the self-esteem and confidence required of a people to manage their affairs. Pouring over the conditions in Qatar, South Korea, or even an enormous country like China, for example, will do nothing to change Africa's predicament, not unless the conditions being studied can somehow manifest into trade and investment between these countries and those in Africa.

What we can and should give some thought to is what these countries have in common that propels them in the development space. The commonality that they have is the presence of a general consensus among their people for national advancement – even if at times this consensus is strained or it waivers under the weight of unavoidable politics. Notwithstanding Qatar's hereditary semi-constitutional monarchy and China's one-political party monopoly, all three countries mentioned advance the lives of their people through the development and execution of supportive policies and regulations that serve the public interest. While the politics some employ in the process of this nation building project might be self-serving and while there is the existence of some level of corruption and resistance to partisan criticism from those in power (partisan politics is even banned in communist China), the emphasis on achieving broad economic growth and social development to improve the lot of the country and all of the people within it is never questioned or lost on anyone. Those in power by-and-large work with their people to build consensus about what needs to be done to move the country forward. And the major outlines of this consensus, once established through legislation, are not summarily disposed of just because an election happens to force a change in who controls the levers of national power every four, five or six years.

As maddening as the development conditions in Africa might be, it is the lack of this kind of sustained national consensus in many African countries that ultimately works to rob the people of their promise. Sierra Leone, one of the countries we look at in some depth in this study, is but one example. A fundamental challenge in Sierra Leone is the lack of national cohesion, which is reflected in the representation of the people within their national government. There exists a real north/south divide in the country, wherein the people in these regions side with one of the nation's primary political parties over the other. This reality dramatically shapes how the country is governed based on who is in power. As an example, over a majority of the current senior members of the Administration are of one group. Cabinet and other senior posts, including strategic positions within the military, police and civil service corps, are given to ethnic and tribal loyalists without due consideration for qualification, merit or national representation.

And worse still, meaningful dialogue on the needs of the people, to whom the government is supposed to be responsible, is vastly absent. The government either consults the limited number it favors or simply goes it alone in developing programs such as the highly touted yet failing Free Quality School Education (FQSE) initiative. For background, FQSE was introduced by the current Administration in 2018 to reduce financial barriers to accessing education in government-approved schools for the country's children. Its shortcomings become readily apparent when the views of the parents and children the initiative is intended to support are taken into consideration. From the latter's perspective, free school is well and good but it needs to be accompanied by ancillary policies that support the family holistically, especially those who rely on their children in the home to make ends meet so that the said children do not go to school on an empty stomach and, as a consequence, show up to the classroom ill-prepared to learn.

Beyond overcoming the issues of poverty and rural community realities, FQSE is heavily focused on access to education not learning and therefore does not adequately address the country's current educational achievement gaps, namely:

(a) establishing a system of clear, rigorous goals for learning, as well as regular measuring and reporting on progress, including the introduction of a quality curriculum;
(b) making funding schools a priority, to include building new facilities and improving existing ones, investing in resources, textbooks, and technology, and improving teacher pay; and
(c) raising standards for teachers – with the understanding that underqualified teachers are tied to poor outcomes for students.

The government tried to address these concerns in its later formulation of the Sierra Leone Education Sector Plan 2022-2026 and, to its credit, sought the input of a host of stakeholders to ensure a far more collaborative outcome and policy document. Notwithstanding these efforts, what the Sierra Leone experience demonstrates is that national dialogue regarding the steps necessary to advance a nation and her people is not an idle consideration. Along with inclusive policies and a balanced representation of the people in their government, national dialogue is the foundation for nation-building and, perhaps even more significantly in the case of many African countries given their recent histories, for establishing the kind of participatory political culture that can serve as a check against potential ethnic-based conflict while also enabling the construction of a national identity, culture, and shared purpose.

Adler et al., (2011) remind us in *Building a collaborative enterprise* that having a shared purpose helps to promote cohesion. "Collaborative communities seek a basis of trust and organizational cohesion that is more robust than self-interest, more flexible than tradition, and less ephemeral than the emotional, charismatic appeal of [popular charismatic leaders]." In this way of living, the focus of nations in Africa becomes less about the wants of a particular person or faction and more about the common goal of the collective. African citizens are thus enabled under such conditions to outline how we position ourselves in our own countries in relation to competitors and partners, as well as to determine what key contributions to individuals and society will define our success.

A question that leaps to mind, in light of the social benefits just outlined, is why this way of thinking and behaving – prioritizing the establishment of a shared national purpose – is not a common practice within African nations? Dialogue does take place to be sure, as exemplified by the development efforts mentioned earlier that are being pursued at the continental (AU) and regional (economic bloc) levels. There is an openness to such multilateral and bilateral engagements in Africa by government authorities. But discussions at the national level, wherein governments openly seek the input of their own citizens on matters of national development, occurs with far less frequency, if it does at all. Some would respond to the question with conviction that the vast majority of African people are just not empowered in their respective nations; more to the point, they have far more pressing bread and butter issues to worry about than to entangle themselves with the machinations of governments that appear to be indifferent to their needs.

Perhaps there is some merit to this argument. One has time for little else in life when the said life is a constant balancing act on the edge of a sharp blade. The argument does, however, bring into focus the question raised earlier – the same one that animates this study and informs its ideological underpinnings. Given Africans' political independence beginning with Ghana in 1957, what specific role do Africans play in the modern phenomenon of African countries failing to achieve enduring socio-economic development and lasting social transformation? This overarching query bleeds into the specific research questions that will be explored in depth in this study, specifically how do everyday Africans describe their lived experience in pursuit of socio-economic development; how does choice (decision-making) and culture (environment) influence everyday Africans' ability to develop socio-economically; and how does the lived experience of everyday Africans inform understanding about achieving social transformation?

These questions all seek to understand the relationship between the lives Africans lead and the development challenges that prevail on the continent. They help to crystallize the role that we the people play in the struggle for personal and national development – the experiences of our lives that, upon closer examination, bring into sharper focus the arguments that have been offered thus far to explain what ails our communities. But before we can begin the work of exploring these questions in any meaningful way, we first need to understand the factors or elements that have been said to impede socio-economic development in Africa. We embark on this work in Chapter 2.

REFERENCES

Brickstone. (n.d). *Oil and gas in developing positive growth in economies in Africa*. Brickstone. https://brickstone.africa/oil-and-gas-in-africa-positive-growth-economies

Du Bois, W. E. B. (William E. B. (2007). The Negro. Oxford University Press.

Harris, J. H. (1912). *Dawn in darkest Africa*. E.P. Dutton.

Hodder, M. (2023). *Africa's agricultural revolution: From self-sufficiency to global food powerhouse*. White & Case. https://www.whitecase.com/insight-our-thinking/africa-focus-summer-2023-africas-agricultural-revolution#:~:text=Africa%20has%2060%20percent%20of,Africans%20than%20any%20other%20sector

Legatum Institute. (n.d.). *The Legatum Prosperity Index 2023*. Legatum Institute. https://prosperity.com/about-prosperity/prosperity-index

Lusigi, A. (2022). *Harnessing Africa's creativity and innovation to drive human development*. United Nations Development Program. https://www.undp.org/ghana/blog/harnessing-africas-creativity-and-innovation-drive-human-development

Meredith, M. (2011). *Born in Africa the quest for the origins of human life* (1st ed.). PublicAffairs.

Nakatani, H. (2023). Aging and shrinking population: The looming demographic challenges of super-aged and super-low fertility society starting from Asia. *Global Health & Medicine*, *5*(5), 257–263. doi:10.35772/ghm.2023.01057 PMID:37908514

Olopade, D. (2014). *The bright continent: Breaking rules and making change in modern Africa.* Houghton Mifflin Harcourt.

Powell, J., & Thyne, C. (2011). Global Instances of Coups from 1950-Present. *Journal of Peace Research*, *48*(2), 249–259. doi:10.1177/0022343310397436

Prasad, D. (2021, November 24). *Regional integration and the African Continental Free Trade Agreement: from parallelism to harmonisation.* International Bar Association. https://www.ibanet.org/regional-integration-afcfta#:~:text=The%20African%20Continental%20Free%20Trade%20Area%20agreement%20%28AfCFTA%29,across%2054%20members%20of%20the%20African%20Union.%20

Sowell, T. (2005, July 14). Geography and man have all but killed Africa. *Deseret News*. https://www.deseret.com/2005/7/14/19902079/thomas-sowell-geography-and-man-have-all-but-killed-africa

UN. (2019). Selected Results of the 2019 UN World Population Projections. *Population and Development Review, 45*(3), 689–694. . doi:10.1111/padr.12288

UNICEF. (n.d.). *Sierra Leone - education.* UNICEF. https://www.unicef.org/sierraleone/education

United Nations. (n.d.). *The sustainable development goals report 2023.* UN. https://sdgs.un.org/sites/default/files/2023-07/The-Sustainable-Development-Goals-Report-2023_0.pdf

Ventures Africa. (2021, December 28). Seven notable innovations in Africa in 2021. *Ventures Africa.* https://venturesafrica.com/five-notable-innovations-in-africa-2021/

Ventures Africa. (2021, July 29). Meet Noel N'Guessan. The innovator helping farmers monetize biowaste in Cote d'Ivoire. *Ventures Africa.* https://venturesafrica.com/meet-noel-nguessan-the-ivorian-innovator-helping-farmers-generate-an-income-from-waste/

Wang, F. (2023, January 18). Why China's shrinking population is a big deal – counting the social, economic and political costs of an aging, smaller society. *The Conversation*. https://theconversation.com/why-chinas-shrinking-population-is-a-big-deal-counting-the-social-economic-and-political-costs-of-an-aging-smaller-society-198056

WaterAid. (n.d.). *Nigeria*. https://www.wateraid.org/uk/where-we-work/nigeria

Williams, A. S. (2021). *White malice: The CIA and the covert recolonization of Africa* (1st ed.). PublicAffairs.

World Bank. (2020, Jul 27). *The African continental free trade area*. World Bank. https://www.worldbank.org/en/topic/trade/publication/the-african-continental-free-trade-area

World Bank. (n.d.). *World Poverty Overview 2023*. World Bank. https://www.worldbank.org/en/topic/poverty/overview

Chapter 2
Impediments to Development

ABSTRACT

Exploring the relationship between the lives Africans lead and the development challenges that prevail on the continent requires careful deductive reasoning. Such an effort is advanced and made exponentially better with the benefit of context – an understanding of what has been thought and said about development in Africa, the core reasons that experts and scholars have identified for Africa's socio-economic struggles and inability to achieve lasting social transformation. This context from what has been thought and said offers a roadmap to aid the work of careful analysis of our subject. This chapter thus reflects a critical synthesis of the literature on the impediments to socio-economic development in African countries, a synthesis that aligns the study's purpose, research questions, and ideological foundations. The chapter includes a discussion on the theoretical and conceptual foundations of the study and a comprehensive review of the literature.

INTRODUCTION

What has been thought and said about African countries' perennial low-income status and failure to advance socio-economically is an extraordinary effort by a community of writers to make sense of a vexing social phenomenon. The research findings and opinions vary in the voluminous catalog, yet there is a general alignment of what writers think are the factors contributing to Africa's socio-economic challenges and inability to achieve lasting social transformation. This alignment is reflected in the categorization of the impediments hindering Africa and Africans' development as either external or internal in origin.

DOI: 10.4018/979-8-3693-2403-5.ch002

The late Ghanaian scholar George Ayittey (1998) summed it up well in *Africa in Chaos*. Writers with an externalists view, he explained, identify the root impediments as "colonial legacies, Western Imperialism, the slave trade, an unjust international economic system, and [exploitative] multinational corporations, among others." Those with an internalist view place the blame on "incompetent leadership and the establishment of defective political and economic systems in postcolonial Africa" (p. 26). Geography and the environment are similarly included in the internalist perspective.

A thematic analysis and synthesis of the identified impediments exposes, as Albert Bandura (1963) might have observed "the bidirectional influence process" of environmental sources of control and personal control; the "reciprocal interaction" of outside forces coupled with personal or internal forces which determine human behavior and accomplishment. The analysis and synthesis uncovers the extent or outcome of this reciprocal interaction between the external and internal impediments, specifically the confluence of choice (decision-making/agency) and culture – what can be called the nexus of the impediments to socio-economic development in Africa. This nexus, the need to study it further, represents the gap in the literature – a gap that makes it difficult to understand the relationship between the lives Africans lead and the development challenges that prevail on the continent. The inspiration for this perspective is not only what the literature does not tell us about development efforts in Africa but also what established ideas compel us to consider about our humanity.

THEORETICAL AND CONCEPTUAL FOUNDATIONS

Social Learning Theory

Social learning theory was developed by Canadian-American psychologist Albert Bandura (1963) to help increase our understanding of the determinants of human learning and behavior. It promotes the idea that human learning and behavior is determined by "the bidirectional influence process" of environmental sources of control and personal control, which yields or leads to human achievements. The theory is based on the traditional behaviorist approach to human development, which offers a basic law of association model to explain human behavior. As explained by Professor Malcolm Watson (2002) in his audiobook *Theories of human behavior*, individuals, according to the traditionalist model, learn from and respond to a stimulus from the environment, i.e. stimulus/response or SR association.

Watson (2002) clarified that Bandura (1974) added two important elements to this traditionalist approach to introduce his theory of social learning. First, Bandura emphasized that people learn expected contingency from observations. We act or behave, in response to a stimulus, based on what we believe from having experienced a stimulus. Second, Bandura emphasized that humans learn primarily through observation and imitation of others. This "vicarious reinforcement" suggests that "we might expect a contingency [from a stimulus] but we don't have to experience it firsthand. We can observe contingency from others; therefore, this [process] is social" (Watson, 2002).

If human behavior is determined by "the bidirectional influence process" of environmental sources of control and personal control, Bandura (1977) observed, then "Human accomplishments result from reciprocal interaction of external circumstances with a host of personal determinants including endowed potentialities, acquired competencies, reflective thought, and a high level of self-initiative" (p. 867). It is this formulation of the determinants of human behavior, social learning, that gives life to the conceptual framework of this study, which is a representation of the relationship or intersectionality between choice (personal control), culture (environmental sources of control), and socio-economic development (human accomplishments).

The conceptual framework makes the assumption that if people are empowered to make good choices about our life pursuits, and we are supported, rather than hindered, by our cultural environment, we might be better equipped to navigate the conditions that influence our socio-economic development. This assumption is important based on Bandura's emphasis on vicarious reinforcement. As Watson (2002) observed, vicarious reinforcement is evidence for (or it "explains") many situations in which humans learn new behaviors or change old ones, even as they are not penalized or rewarded for these behaviors. It also demonstrates that humans are complex thinkers. Specifically, "[humans] have to see a similarity of [themselves] to the other person [they] are observing to believe that the contingency occurs not only for that person but is also valid for [them]" (Watson, 2002).

Choice and Culture and Leadership

The conceptual framework assumption is also important because of lessons from established ideas about choice and culture. The constructs, as the literature informs us, interdependently enable social transformation (Arendt, 1958; Arnold, 1869; Bandura, 1977; Barker, 1997; Gemmill and Oakley, 1992; Soyinka, 2000). Combined, they make change possible through the social process of leadership, the idea from Gary Gemmill and Judith Oakley (1992) and Richard A. Barker (1997) that leadership encompasses the components of process and ethics (what Barker defined as a spiritual definition of life), which enables individuals to create a vision of a future good and, through this vision, come together to create community mores which define behavioral standards, role expectations, and contractual commitments.

Change thus requires the social process of leadership, and here again is where Bandura's (1977) social learning theory proves relevant. Applied to leadership, the theory denotes that people engaged in leadership have an interactive and negotiable relationship with one another, and that we are always cognizant of the ways in which we influence others with whom we are engaged in leadership.

The social process that is leadership emerges when individuals are provided training in skills such as communication, building coalitions and compromising. It emerges through development of individual emotional and intellectual capabilities, as well as through education in the "social patterns and moral orders that produces an integration of conceptual knowledge, ideals, insights, experiences, and sources of behavior" – all of which contribute to the "process of integrating individual ethics into community mores" (Barker, 1997, p. 360). The acquisition of this training, development and education Barker outlined raises greater awareness and responsibility in the individual through a focus on choice (decision-making/agency) and the consolidation of an enabling culture that, according to Mathew Arnold (1869) and Wole Soyinka (2000), aligns thinking and behavior toward personal growth, service, and participation for individual betterment and community advancement.

If choice and culture make change possible for individuals and society through the establishment of the social process of leadership within and among people, then our focus in determining Africa's challenges needs to be trained on Africans' roles in the development equation. How do everyday Africans describe their lived experience in pursuit of socio-economic development; how does choice (decision-making) and culture (environment) influence everyday Africans' ability to develop socio-economically; and how does the lived experience of everyday Africans inform understanding about achieving social transformation? These are the questions that need further exploration when it comes to understanding the plight of Africa in the development space. This is because the literature, to which we now turn, fails to adequately demonstrate the nexus of choice and culture within the debate over impediments to development in Africa and, as a result, the relevance of social learning to the same.

PAST RESEARCH AND THEME ANALYSIS

Empirical Research

Choice and culture (or variations of the terms) and their association with development in Africa find space and receive empirical analysis in isolation in the works of both Africans and non-Africans vested in understanding the continent's present-day socio-economic conditions. Among the works are the journal articles *Infrastructure and inclusive growth in sub-Saharan Africa: An empirical analysis* by Mutiira et al. (2020) and *Health expenditure and economic growth in sub-Saharan Africa: An empirical investigation* by Nicholas M. Odiambo (2022). Both articles make the case for development in Africa from an internalist view that centers on the consideration of choice and culture or personal control and environmental sources of control without, in some instances, explicit use of or reference to these constructs.

Using an inclusive index to test the infrastructure and inclusive growth relationship with data from 31 sub-Saharan African countries, for example, Mutiira et al. (2020) concluded that inclusive growth is predicated on infrastructure, as well as the other determinants of inflation and human development. While inflation is a negative determinant, the latter, which includes education, literacy rates, health and life expectancy, is a particularly instrumental determinant of economic growth in sub-Saharan Africa, the authors observed.

Odiambo (2021) arrived at a similar conclusion in his examination of the relationship between health expenditure (a form of human development) and economic growth in sub-Saharan African countries. Using panel data from 2008 to 2017, the author shared there is a "distinct" cause and effect relationship between public health expenditure and economic growth in lower income countries but no causality was found in middle income countries. He went on to note that the reverse is true regarding private health expenditure: "A short-term causality from economic growth to health expenditure is found to prevail in middle income countries but no causality is found to exist in low-income countries" (p. 79). So, notwithstanding variations in income, a nation's choice or decision to invest in the health of its people – human development – is a significant consideration for the economic prospects of the said nation.

Another empirical study examined is *Values and development in Southern Africa*, a book edited by Müller, Mekgwe, & Mhloyi (2013), which looked closely at the dynamics of culture and social influence, especially the role of values, in shaping development in Southern Africa. Of particular interest in the book is Chapter 5, "Linking values and development: An empirical analysis," by Hennie Kotze and Stefanie Schulein (2013). The authors examined the relationship between African value orientations and development through use of the Afrobarometer Network survey data from six countries in the Southern African region, including South Africa and Tanzania, countries of focus in this study. The Afrobarometer survey items were identified under four dimensions: (1) Human qualities (subdivided into "paternalism/ dependency," "consensus-seeking and pursuit of justice vs. pursuit of law"); (2) Human relationships ("community vs. individual interest," "social capital" and "identity"); (3) Power ("gender equality"): and (4) Cosmology (but no items in the survey adequately gauge cosmology).

While the authors admitted that the four dimensions "may in themselves not fully tap the full range and immense diversity of African values," they contended that the four dimensions provide a useful place to start for their study and for expansion of future studies (p. 139). The limitations of the study precluded the finding of significant results. However, trends emerged that the authors believed warranted further study. Specifically, links with development were apparent in the value orientations of gender, consensus-seeking, and individualism. For purposes of the present study, gender and consensus-seeking is included in the culture construct and individualism is included in both the culture and choice constructs.

Regarding gender and development, the authors concluded that "there seems to be a clear linear relationship between level of development and level of support for gender equality in these countries." The countries studied practice patriarchal politics, which renders women inferior and unequal to their male counterparts and places limitations on their agency in the development arena (p. 149). Regarding consensus-seeking and development, the authors concluded that an inverse or negative relationship existed. "An excessive emphasis on reaching agreement/consensus on certain issues may lead towards an intolerance of dissent, thereby preventing diverse voices from being heard... In fact, the desire to agree, which is supposed to safeguard the rights and opinions of individuals and minorities, is often exploited to enforce group solidarity and oppressive group conformity" (p. 142). Southern Africans' gender and consensus-seeking orientations (what social learning theorists would consider external or environmental sources of control) negatively influence development efforts in the region, according to the study, because the latter negates diversity of thought and the former marginalizes and renders unequal half of the population.

Regarding individualism and development, the authors wrote, "a strong Pearson's correlation (r=.884) was found, coming close to significance at p=0.74. South Africa and Botswana are particularly striking in that they both show high levels of development coupled with an emphasis on individualism. This strong relationship seems to highlight the need for individual entrepreneurial spirit in terms of bringing about development within the respective countries" (p. 145). In other words, agency or choice (an individual's ability to determine the course of his or her life and what social learning theorists would consider a personal control) is a necessary precondition for the passion, energy, and creativity required for development. The Southern African nations examined, according to the study, were better positioned in the development arena where agency or choice was an accepted orientation, but they struggled where the same orientation was subordinate to a collectivist orientation.

Strength beyond structure social and historical trajectories of agency in Africa, edited by Bruijn, Dijk, & Gewald (2007), is another book that offered empirical examination of conditions in Africa through the prism of agency (choice). The anthology of empirical research "develops an alternative interpretation of Africa's predicament by emphasizing the strengths of people, organizations and institutions in overcoming the constraining structures that are present in the everyday lives of many Africans today" (p. 2). An exploration of the relationship between agency and specific circumstances in the African experience, including the challenges of social change, was the primary concern of the contributing authors.

Chapters such as "Dreams and agency during Angola's war of independence" by Inge Brinkman, "Les enveloppes pour Papa Daniel: La transformation des relations domestiques dans les ménages des Congolais de la diaspora" by Julie Ndaya, and "Agency in and from the margins: Street children and youth in N'djaména, Chad" by Mirjam de Bruijn, looked deeply at agency through a layered study of its association with reflexivity. The chapters also examined where to locate agency, its interplay with structure (environment) and how it can be both enabling and constraining, how agency becomes the product of a certain group identity, and how it can serve as an emic theory of causations – so much so that "It becomes clear in the cases presented in this volume that these ideas about agency are strongly related to the confrontations that people have in their lives" (p. 13).

The book's culminating argument is that agency, acknowledged as the foundation of human creativity and resilience, has a great importance to and influence on the weak condition of African existence and, by extension, on the predicament of the individual lives that inhabit the continent. This perspective is identical to social learning theorist application of the construct (as personal control) in explaining what determines human behavior and accomplishments. Humans learn through observation and imitation, and we act (make decisions) in response to what we observe to influence our environment just as our environment works to influence our behavior. Our accomplishments (existence or predicament) therefore result from the "reciprocal interaction" of outside forces (our environment) coupled with our personal control or agency, as Bandura (1974) observed in his formulation of the social learning theory.

Mawere and Mwanaka's (2015) *Democracy, good governance and development in Africa* similarly leveraged empirical analysis to investigate Africa's current predicament, including the struggle with socio-economic development. The book's exploration of the root cause of Africa's problems greatly emphasized the external factors that have negatively influenced growth and social transformation. Yet, in a few of the works authored by Africans themselves, there is also recognition of the role internal factors play in the development trajectory of the continent, including Africa's institutions, educational systems, and values. Regarding the external factors, authors contributing to the book focus attention on the negative influence of Western culture and economic practices on African people, leading to Africans' acceptance of a "coloniality mindset" and a disregard for indigenous knowledge, institutions, and values. Chapters such as "Mandela and coloniality in South Africa," "Envisioning African democracy in the twenty-first century" and "Reviving African Indigenous Institutions for Democracy, Good Governance and Development: Lessons from Zimbabwe'' are exemplary.

Regarding the internal factors, contributing authors explore themes central to Africans' personal control, themes such as culture, ethics or values orientation, politics, unity, and level of education, all of which converge to negate or hamper progress toward development. Chapters such as "Towards a United States of Africa: Concepts, issues, and methodologies," "Culture, ethics and politics for a better and sustainable Africa: The Mozambican experience," and "Education for sustainable development in Africa: An appraisal with focus on Nigerian experience" are exemplary. The book's exploration of Africa's problems through the prism of external and internal impediments not only mirrors the thematic analysis of the established literature of the African predicament, it also illuminates the strength of the social learning theory on the determinants of human behavior and accomplishment.

The hard to dismiss conclusion from reviewing these empirical studies is that choice (agency) and culture (environment) – both internal and external – are sources of control that converge to influence the conditions Africans experience in the struggle for personal and national advancement. The literature on the impediments to Africa's development seems to overlook or fails to make this connection more explicitly, however. This failure leads audiences to make the false connection between Africa's developmental challenges with either external impediments or internal ones and, as a consequence, encourage solutions that are inadequate or inappropriate, just as the literature's historical delineation of the problem perpetuates.

EXTERNAL IMPEDIMENTS TO DEVELOPMENT

Legacy of Slavery and Colonialism

Slavery is where Africa's problems begin with a legion of writers and observers who make the continent's development challenges a cornerstone of their scholarship and life's work. As observed in our review of Africa's landscape in Chapter 1, there is hardly an argument that can be made to counter or refute the overwhelming influence of Africans' centuries-long forced enslavement on the psychological and material condition of African people. Slavery eviscerated the African man, family and society. Yet, just as it is legitimate to cite this history as a source for what hinders Africa's development, it is also appropriate to look for answers not confined by a history from which we are so far removed. A less historically inhibiting place to start then, in contemplating the externalists' concern with Africans' contact with outsiders, is the much more recent attempts by the said outsiders to fashion empires out of territories in Africa.

More than a few authors make the argument that African countries' inability to develop has its roots in the legacy of colonialism — the 75 years, from the late 1800s into the early 1900s, during which the vast majority of the continent and its people were subjugated to European rule. Britain, France, Belgium, Spain, Portugal, among them, were singularly focused on exploiting Africans for the extraction of natural resources to both feed and develop the citizens of Europe. In doing so, Europeans systematically destroyed Africa's political, economic, social, religious, and cultural identity and replaced them with European systems, which continue to negatively influence developmental efforts on the continent. For the writers who focus their attention on the impact of colonialism, Achebe (1994), Fanon (1963), Kincaid (1988), Njoh (2006), Settles (1996), and Soyinka (1975), to name but a few, Africans' intense contact with Europeans and later subjugation is the foremost consideration for what is broken and why Africans are unable to make any effective and lasting change.

Ambe J. Njoh (2006) studied the problem in depth in *Tradition, culture and development in Africa.* Njoh employed a qualitative (deductive) analysis to assess how African traditions and customs, coupled with Western civilization's efforts to destroy them, can have an impact on development in Africa. Njoh contended that "the Eurocentric values, customs and traditions that have been adopted in Africa since the colonial era have hurt, rather than helped the development process" in Africa (p. 3). She argued that Europeans were gravely concerned that the Africans' way of life, our culture or system of meaning, was an obstacle to the European colonial development objectives. The Europeans therefore embarked on a campaign of forcefully changing Africans. Their aim "was to transform Africans into 'Black Europeans.' Part of these elaborate efforts entailed a heavy dose of ethnocentricity on the part of Europeans and propaganda campaigns designed to deride African traditional practices while exalting European values" (p. 3). The end result of this process was a complete transformation of how Africans' lived, how they viewed themselves and each other, and how they interacted to create meanings that informed their political, economic, religious, and social lives.

In what concrete ways did this transformation hinder development? Frantz Fanon (1963), Wole Soyinka (1975), and Chinua Achebe (1994), all notable social critics of their respective times, contended it taught Africans to devalue their own traditions and systems and to embrace ones that are foreign to the African identity, including the adoption of European names and languages. This adoption supplanted the existing culture, while also changing the formation of politics, the exercise of law, religious practice, and the administration of commerce. Politically, Africans were forced into manufactured nation states that did not reflect the existing ways in which Africans grouped themselves. Tribes were separated, while many more were lumped together with those of a different ilk, resulting in countries like Nigeria having over 250 ethnic groups and years of divisions and dissension.

According to Njoh (2006), in focalizing the extraction of natural resources and production of crops only for European consumption, Africans were forced to end economically productive activities such as industry and trade in which they were engaged among themselves and with others farther afield. The same economic focalization for the benefit of Europeans produced the construction of physical infrastructure — railroads, roads, hospitals, and schools — along coastal cities, where Europeans and their ships awaited extractive goods for transport to Europe, at the expense of Africa's interior landscape. Moreover, Christian religious practice became a burden on Africans' time; it burdened them with payment for related activities, and it created what Njoh (2006) labeled "cleavages and hostilities amongst previously unified groups" (p. 43-46).

Fannon (1963) deconstructed colonialism using a similar deductive analytical lens. The West Indian psychoanalyst and social philosopher analyzed the psychology of the colonized people and their path to liberation, concluding that the traditional societies of the colonized have been "ruptured" and "disrupted" by Europeans. Their salvation thus lay in remaking themselves by abandoning the imported political, economic, and social systems of Europeans, and in embracing the traditions and systems known to the colonized prior to contact with Europeans. Fanon fascinated this researcher with his criticism. None prove more poignant than his elaboration on the merits and impact of a national culture, following his dissection of the role the bourgeoisie elites played in African nations in manipulating the established political and economic systems in order to serve their narrow, material interests. In his observations about the so-called elites, Fanon concurrently aligned himself with arguments that placed emphasis on the need for Africans to improve their politics (institutions) and to reclaim their culture — the legacies of colonialism — as effective means to jump-start development.

Kincaid (1988) demonstrated the same level of concern as Fanon did about the impact of colonialism on the colonized in her book-length essay concerning her experiences in Antigua, home to people transplanted from West Africa. Her words in *A small place* on the importance of identity, culture, and independence within the context of her country's experience evoke a degree of anger usually associated with revolutionary activists. She wrote in plain and resentful language that,

Antigua is a small place, a small island...It was settled by Christopher Columbus in 1493. Not too long after, it was settled by human rubbish from Europe, who used enslaved but noble and exalted human beings from Africa . . . to satisfy their desire for wealth and power, to feel better about their own miserable existence, so that they could be less lonely and empty — a European disease. (Kincaid, 1988, pp. 80-81).

Apparent in the discourse on colonialism is its push-pull effect on the people. As an external imposition, Europeans' subjugation of Africans compelled Africans, as the authors' referenced detailed in their works, to respond in ways that pushed Africans farther from their identity and way of life. The influence of this external source of control and how Africans' reacted to it (their personal control, even as it was under great duress) reflects the basic principle of the social learning theory. Colonialism's end in the 1950s and 1960s did not, however, mean an end to interference in the affairs of African nations.

Foreign Influence

A prevailing complaint regarding Africa's struggles with development was the undue influence foreigners exercised in the economic and political affairs of the continent's nation states after a majority gained their political independence. Martin Meredith (2006) investigated the origins of this reality with a penetrating look at how Africa's modern nation states came into being in *The state of Africa: A history of fifty years of independence*; how, for example, the French were able to carve out spheres of influence on the continent during the Independence movement by compelling most of its former colonies into membership in the French Community. This resulted in a sort of conjoining or linkage of every facet of the life of the young "francophone" nations, which France then leveraged for its economic advantage (Meredith, 2006).

In addition to establishing a shared currency for francophone Africa linked to France's own currency, authorities of the French nation also placed their own nationals in strategic areas of interest within the government agencies of the new African nations, particularly within the economic, security, and military sectors. Meredith (2006) observed that the British, Belgiums, Spanish, and Portuguese operated in similar fashion, setting the stage for their influence of events that would prove catastrophic for African nation states, including rampant abuse of state resources, violent government take-overs, armed conflicts, and genocides in places like Rwanda and Darfur.

The colonial powers were not the only ones meddling in Africa. Following the two world wars in the 1940s, the United States and the Soviet Union were locked in a battle over ideology for 45 years. Their capitalism versus communism struggle consumed the world, rendering Africa (among other developing regions) a battleground for political influence (Dower et al., 2021). African nations chose sides, drawing the ire of the super-power they rebuffed. Those that remained neutral watched their counterparts who took sides get rewarded with financial and security assistance. The end result was the complete mismanagement of relationships and resources gained from the quid-pro-quo arrangements, as well as the initiation of proxy wars that would cause scores of Africans to die and forever change the course of their nations' histories (Proxy Wars During the Cold War: Africa, 2018).

Yet foreign influence on the continent did not end with the cessation of hostilities between world superpowers. While the United States and the Soviet Union (Russia) cooled engagement and the former colonial powers in Europe nursed their interests, a new power emerged to flex its own muscle in the name of securing natural resources to accommodate its rapid growth. Journalist and Columbia University Professor Howard French (2015) documented Africa's dramatic evolution in becoming China's second continent in a matter of two decades. French leveraged his years of work and travel on the continent to catalog China's exportation of its innovations and importation to China of Africa's natural resources. He observed that the Chinese were

Engineering a kind of modern-day barter system in which developing countries pay for new railroads, highways, and airports through the guaranteed, long-term supply of hydrocarbons or minerals, thus helping Chinese companies win massive contracts. In hundreds of other deals, China's Export-Import Bank and other big, state-controlled "policy bank" counterparts have teamed up to offer attractive project financing that is usually tied to the use of Chinese companies, Chinese materials, and Chinese works. (French, 2015, p. 4).

But what goes unnoticed, French continued, is "China's export, in effect, of large numbers of its own people who are settling in as migrants and long-term residents in far-flung and hitherto unfamiliar parts of the [African] continent" (p. 5). The intensity of China's contact with Africa and what it has yielded in many quarters has Africans once again deeply concerned. The Chinese are contributing to large-scale corruption and the mismanagement of local economies, deepening existing political cleavages, which in turn intensify the struggle for power.

But equally worrisome, Craig E. Johnson (2017) observed in *Meeting the ethical challenges of leadership: Casting light or shadow*, is the impact the Chinese are having on the social fabric and cultural character of African communities, in which many Chinese have demonstrated a level of racism toward and intolerance of their hosts that is akin to the way European colonizers behaved years earlier. This is not an idle or unwarranted concern. Johnson (2017) confirmed in a case study designed to assess the ethical impact of China's penetration of and involvement in Africa:

A manager at a Chinese motorcycle company was deported after calling Kenyans, including President Uhuru Kenyatta, "monkeys." "I don't like here, like monkey people," he said on a video posted on Twitter. "I don't like talk with them, it smells bad, and poor and foolish, and black. (Johnson, 2017, p. 391).

The Chinese, like the European and other western nationals before them, were prioritizing their own economic interests and values in engagements with Africans — a self-centered practice that permeated yet another external impediment to Africa's development efforts: the international market and banking system.

Market and Banking System

Many other experts, including Lin (2014) focused attention on the economic policies, derived from the West, that adversely impacted or stunted Africa's growth. In *The quest for prosperity: How developing economies can take off*, the former lecturer in Beijing and senior vice president and chief economist of the World Bank Group analyzed the challenges to development. He explained the reasons why some countries succeed while others fail, and he offered a new structural economic framework to promote development, namely that countries focus their economic activity in the sectors and industries with which they are well endowed. In doing so, Lin offered a reminder about the bone-headed economic policy decisions Africa's leaders made on the heels of Independence, based on the advice of experts from the West. In the case of Ghana under President Kwame Nkrumah, Lin wrote, the country favored capital-intensive infrastructure projects, when the young nation did not have the capital to do so, instead of relying on labor-intensive projects within the sectors that the nation was naturally endowed. Africa's leaders, Lin observed, wanted to achieve development at the pace and rate of developed countries in the West. So they mimicked what they saw working in the West without due consideration of the implications for their own financially strapped nations.

Ake (1996), Riddell (1992), and Nyerere (1985) placed greater emphasis on the role of the international market and banking system. Their concern extended to unfair policies, including constant changes in relative prices paid in international trade and the debts and debt service charges of so-called 'Third World countries.' Nyerere (1985), the late former President of Tanzania in his March 1985 address, *Africa and the debt crisis*, to a combined meeting of the Royal African Society with other British voluntary bodies at the Royal Commonwealth Society in London, succinctly outlined the damage done to economies like his own in Tanzania. Nyerere noted the vicious cycle of debts, debt services and never-ending high interest rates for the same. But he also cautioned against the very process of African nations seeking debt from international institutions like the International Monetary Fund (IMF), which forced situations that made the African nations' "economic conditions worse and imperil [their] social and political stability" (p. 493-494).

Nyerere's observation was one Ake (1996) and Riddell (1992) and countless others picked-up on in the wake of the Bretton Woods institutions' (IMF and World Bank) imposition of structural adjustment programs across Africa during the 1980s through the 1990s. To extend loans to address acute budget shortfalls, these international bodies compelled African nations to radically change their economies through currency devaluation, a reduction of

Government spending via austere measures such as wage freezes, interest rate hikes, removal of subsidies, lifting of price controls, an increase in exports, and the liberalization of imports. The measures were socially and politically destabilizing. The countries that rejected them were not only denied credit but also compelled to pay their high interest debt to the IMF and World Bank.

Synthesis

The impact on Africa of the legacy of colonialism, direct foreign influence after Independence, and an unfair international market and banking system cannot be overlooked. Combined they present formidable impediments to growth, in addition to creating a level of instability that negates any kind of dialogue for consensus building on a path forward. Yet, the very fact that they are external influences means Africans have a degree of control on their reach and impact. As an example, in much the same way Fanon did, Kincaid (1988) kept a steady focus on colonialism but also drew attention to the role of her people. She accused Antiguans in *A small place* for mimicking the British in the conduct of their affairs to such an extent that the Antiguans' behavior was indistinguishable from that of their former colonial masters. This adoption of the British way of doing things infuriated Kincaid because, from her perspective, the behavior, in response to European subjugation, was at the root of the Island's exploitation and socio-economic ruin.

Achebe (1983) and Njoh (2006) also came around to Fanon and Kincaid's full-circle analysis of their own countries. In *The trouble with Nigeria*, Achebe took his fellow citizens to task for mirroring the behaviors of their leaders, for succumbing to the kind of indiscipline, for example, that motivated average men to relieve themselves in public spaces as and when nature called. Achebe, in effect, challenged his countrymen to lead from where they were, to employ their best selves in the stewardship of their nation. In *Tradition, culture and development in Africa*, Njoh did the same by employing Africans "to emulate the examples of Asian countries, which have made tremendous socio-economic progress without sacrificing their belief systems, culture and tradition" (p. 48).

Thus the recognition by Fanon, Kincaid, Achebe, and Njoh of the roles that Africans play and can play in the development of ourselves and the advancement of our nations — despite the serious consequences and effects of colonialism the authors outlined — is an instructive lesson to consider. Their literary works collectively highlighted the very real harm contact with Europeans has done to Africans materially, psychologically, and otherwise. But they also acknowledge a fundamental truth about the human spirit and condition: humans can influence, even control our own fates, if we so choose. Engagement with foreigners need not come at the expense of Africans' sense of self-worth, as Njoh reminded us. And the pain in doing so, as Nyerere instructed, could well necessitate that Africans turn inward for reflection and engagement with each other.

The authors were admitting that external or environmental sources of control had stunted Africa's growth, but internal factors or personal control, owing to the behavior of the people, were similarly degrading the continent's ability to flourish. While the admission is apparent in the authors' works, it is not made explicit or connected in a way that allows readers to consider the "bidirectional influence" of the environment and human agency, in the way social learning theory asks of us, to help bridge understanding about Africans' role in the evolution of our present-day condition. We are left to think, rather unfortunately, that an external factor or factors are the sole reasons for our lot, instead of leaning into lessons concerning the determinants of human behavior and accomplishment and, as a result, exploring the relationship between the lives Africans lead and the development challenges that prevail on the continent for a deeper understanding. The internist perspective, to which we now turn, leaves us in a similar quandary.

INTERNAL IMPEDIMENTS TO DEVELOPMENT

The Environment (Geography)

The environment or geography, to be more precise, is identified by internalists as one of the primary impediments to development in poor countries, especially in Africa, which comprises the majority of the poorest countries in the world. The geography as impediment argument has its origins, according to Acemoglu & Robinson (2013), in the writings of Montesquieu, a French political philosopher, who argued that the divide between rich and poor countries was rooted in their respective geographic dispositions. Montesquieu maintained that cool or moderate climates produced rich nations, while warmer, tropical climates yielded poor countries. The philosopher during Europe's period of enlightenment went on to observe that people in tropical climates were lazy and prone to be ruled by despots (Montesquieu & Nugent, 1949).

Montesquieu's observations were to later form the cornerstone of discussions about the climate and soil of poor countries as key impediments to their development. William D. Nordhaus (2005), Jeffery Sachs (2006), and Jared Diamond (1997) each advanced theories about the adverse impact of both climate and soil on development. Nordhaus, in *Geography and macroeconomics: New data and new findings*, used spatial data on economic activities of nations to describe the link between economic activity and geography. He concluded that "Tropical geography has a substantial negative impact on output density and output per capita compared to temperate regions" (p. 3515). Jeffery Sachs (2006), the American economist and a Sterling Professor of Economics at Yale University, used storytelling and analysis in *The end of poverty: Economic possibilities for our time* to describe the world economy and what nations can do to mobilize resources toward the achievement of sustainable economic development. In his research, Sachs pointed to what he described as "the frequently overlooked problems of physical geography" to explain why countries fail in their efforts to grow economically. He outlined the heavy financial burden undeveloped countries experience with transport costs, for example, "because they are landlocked, situated in high mountain ranges, or lack navigable rivers, along coastlines, or good natural harbors" (p. 57).

Sachs also outlined the impact of diseases like malaria, which lead to poor health and productivity of the labor force, as well as the poor quality of topical soils because they cannot maintain nutrients and are easily eroded by heavy rains. Similarly, American geographer and historian Jared Diamond (1997) emphasized the inability of some countries to domesticate plants and animals. Diamond asserted such a development would have spurred greater farming and innovation in those countries. But instead the countries, including those in Africa, were consigned to remain hunter-gatherer communities, as Acemoglu & Robinson (2013) confirmed in their own analysis of the argument in *Why nations fail: The origins of power, prosperity, and poverty.*

Politics, Institutions, and Economic Policy

Politics, institutions and economic policies is another major impediment for Africa's development from the internalist perspective. The proponents of this position focus on the national systems designed to regulate political engagement in society, uphold the rule of law, and expand opportunities for economic growth. They argue that the countries still struggling to advance experienced a "divergence" in the way their politics and institutions operate, to a point it creates disincentives for the people to willingly engage in economic activities that would contribute to the overall development of the nation.

Acemoglu & Robinson (2013) do a masterful job in *Why nations fail: The origins of power, prosperity, and poverty* by explaining "that while economic institutions are critical for determining whether a country is poor or prosperous, it is politics and political institutions that determine what economic institutions a country has'' (p. 43). The authors examine the historical political formations of the Americas, Asia, Europe and Africa to make their case. They conclude that it is the result of the composition of the politics, how power is distributed, that determines a nation's economic success. The decisive role for the development of countries, they insist, is played by institutions.

Ayittey (1998), Ake (1996), Ekeh (1986), Juma and Oluoch (2013) echo similar arguments regarding the impact of failed politics and institutions on development. Juma and Oluoch in particular focus on the idea of social transformation in *System failure causes of conflict in Africa as a social transformation,* an analytical effort to assess the causes of conflict and how "addressing system failure causes can cause social transformation" (p. 11). The authors provide the example of Sudan and Somalia, where governments reneged on prior promises for equitable distribution of power and resources among the various groups of people (clans and tribes). These, they argue, are "Systems failure(s), suggesting lack of properly functioning institutions, poor leadership that are characteristics of undemocratic governments" (p. 16).

Lin (2014), in *The quest for prosperity*, extended the argument of institutional failures to the national bodies or representatives responsible for devising and implementing economic policies. He explored the reasons developing nations have failed to develop, and offered a prescription for economic growth, which is centered on nations leveraging what Lin termed "comparative advantage." Instead of leveraging the industries or commodities with which their nations were endowed, African leaders and others of the world made bad development choices leading to the vicious circle of unsustainable pursuit. They invested in industrialization programs (heavy industries like steel) to modernize their countries when they did not have the capital to make such investments.

Synthesis

African leaders' economic policy choices, as Lin posited, reflected a lack of understanding of the relationship between the economic structure and the development levels of their countries. Said another way, Africa's policymakers were ignorant. Lin did not make this argument. He went out of his way, in fact, to articulate the extraneous reasons or pressures African leaders felt, on the heels of their nations' independence, in electing to implement the economic policies that eventually ruined their countries. Both the decision of Africa's leaders and the rationale behind the decision (protecting the economic interest of the elites and patronage of constituents for political support) nevertheless carried the same implication. Africa's leaders were clueless or proved to be willfully so purely out of self-interest. The desire to remain in power was an overriding consideration. It subjected socio-economic policy and the institutions and politics governing the said policy to manipulation by those in control of the state.

There is disagreement on the impact of geography on development in the literature. Some experts were dismissive of the argument, taking aim at the unstated, racial intentions of men like Montesquieu, while others characterized the argument as not satisfactory or dynamic enough to fully explain the challenges, including some of the historical contradictions we have witnessed with the development of tropical climate countries across the world in past and more recent history. Acemoglu & Robinson (2013) were particularly expressive in this area. They contended, based on their reading of history, "There is no simple or enduring connection between climate or geography and economic success" (p. 50).

Both sides of the argument have some merit. Geography can be an impediment to development, as the present author has had the opportunity to experience firsthand. Scores of Africans die each year from curable diseases resulting from the climate and the poor state of healthcare systems, which devastates the continent's labor force. Crops from commercial and subsistence farming fail because of bad soil, inclement weather, or debilitating droughts. The continent is also vastly populated with people still engaged in hunter-gathering practice, as opposed to people who more broadly leverage technological innovations to expand farming and other industries like fishing for domestic consumption and trade.

These internal circumstances – how Africans organize or manipulate our land, sea, politics, institutions, and policies – are considerations of personal control. While significant, they do not on their own explain the roots of the challenges for African people to develop ourselves and our communities because of what we know about the origins of human accomplishment. There is more at play, which illuminates some of the reasons many turned to another internal consideration for an explanation: the failure of leadership argument.

Failure of Leadership

Failure of leadership is the internalist impediment to development in Africa that receives the most attention, including from noteworthy scholars of the continent. Readers heard echoes of the argument from the works of Bonsu (2002), Ayittey (1998), Ake (1996), and Fannon (1963), even as these scholars placed the majority of their focus on other serious impediments such as political and institutional breakdowns and the legacy of colonialism. Perhaps the best known and often quoted proponent of the failure of leadership argument was Nigerian author Chinua Achebe (1983). Achebe trained his focus on the country of his birth in *The Trouble with Nigeria*, yet his characterization of Nigeria, the most populous country on the continent and now one with the largest economy, reverberated in nearly all of the other nations. He blamed Nigeria's leaders for the country's impoverished conditions, economic mismanagement, recurrent coups, armed conflict, and aimless direction. His reasons for doing so are instructive, as they pull back the curtain on the disposition of many of those who point fingers at the men at the top for answers to Africa's problems.

A novelist in the late 1950s, Achebe found his voice as an activist and social critic about a decade later just as his Igbo people developed nationalist aspirations in response to political and economic oppression at the hands of Nigeria's federal government. At the time, the Igbo people believed they were marginalized within the federal system and benefited little from the country's wealth, much of which was being derived from the lucrative oil production right under their noses in the Niger Delta.

According to Forsyth (1969), the Igbos believed they were left with no choice but to secede and create the independent state of Biafra after successive military coups triggered pogroms against their people. This decision, in May 1967, predictably drew the ire of the federal government, which sent in troops to prevent the secessionist movement. In a twisted irony, Achebe authored *A man of the people* just before the onset of these tumultuous events. It was a novel about a fictitious West African country that became engulfed in a military coup, in much the same way the real Nigeria had experienced in 1966 at the hands of predominantly Igbo men in the military. Suspicion about Achebe's foreknowledge of the first real coup, or even direct involvement in it, grew. As a result, Achebe and his family were targeted and eventually forced to flee their bombed-out home in Lagos and take up residence in the newly minted capital of the Biafra Republic in the southeastern part of the country.

Achebe sided with his people out of loyalty and a sense of duty once Biafra was created. He took on a visible role as a foreign ambassador, despite multiple threats to himself, in order to help garner support for the war effort and to communicate the plight of the Igbo people to the rest of the world. But as the secessionist efforts waned and the dust of the armed conflict settled on a fragile peace that did nothing to address the grievances of the Igbo or end the corruption, Achebe turned to what he knew best to dissect his country's lingering problems. He penned *The trouble with Nigeria*, which he defined as "simply and squarely a failure of leadership . . . The Nigerian problem is the unwillingness or inability of its leaders to rise to the responsibility, to the challenge of personal example, which are the hallmarks of true leadership" (p. 1).

Achebe's challenge to Nigeria's leadership was inspired by the political instability that gripped the country in the 1970s and 1980s, particularly as the military forced itself on the body politic of the nation. But the country's monumental failures in managing the Nigerian economy in that period also played a role. Achebe was as much aghast about the military power-grabs and political ineptitude as he was about the country's civilian and military leaders squandering through corruption the 280-billion dollars in oil revenues Nigeria earned during the 1970s as the world's sixth largest oil producer.

Achebe's clarion call for better or changed leadership is reflected in the works of scholars who come after him, those seized with the same anger and frustration, often based on personal experiences, at "the leaders" for their corruption and arrested development of Africa's march toward prosperity. Bonsu (2002) offers a useful example. He made the case for leadership as the panacea in *Leadership: The missing variable in the economic development of sub-Saharan Africa*. Specifically, Bonsu used a qualitative, deductive case study approach to explore the links between leadership, culture, and economic development in Africa, and to assess and articulate the immoral cultural behavior of African leaders and why it has impeded economic development on the continent. Echoing Achebe, Bonsu asserted that Africa's leaders have failed to establish a culture (a moral and scientific variety) conducive to development.

But he also went on to make the following observation: "leaders legitimize and interpret behaviors that lead to cultural norms…that the kind of culture and how a culture of a society changes to suit a mutual quest depends on a leader's beliefs" (p. 88). Given Bonsu's own deliberate focus on culture, his argument then begs the question: what of the role of the people? Can leaders truly establish culture or do they simply amplify it? Is not a leader a product of his or her community or environment? If so, is establishing culture therefore a communal consideration or, at the very least, a mutual one between leader and followers? What then of the role of the people and their culture in the development of their nation states?

These questions reflect the same external and internal control considerations that social learning theorists employed to inform understanding about determinants of human behavior and accomplishment. Our condition, the theory argues, is derived from the confluence of our environment and agency, our choices and our culture. Both operate interdependently to make our achievements possible. The observation then that a leader or his beliefs establishes culture would seem inconsistent or even contradictory. We therefore need a deeper understanding of leadership to gain some clarity.

LEADERSHIP

The literature reveals a serious debate on leadership — what it means, its application, and how it is socially constructed in the ever-changing world in which we live. The latter query proves particularly relevant for the discussion on development in Africa given the emphasis by some on the failure of Africa's leaders to develop our people and advance our nations. Specifically, the question about the social construct of leadership seeks to clarify whether leadership is a construct of "a man at the top" or a person in authority. The question labors to understand whether we should think of leadership, according to Mitchell and Tucker (1992), as the ability to exercise control and accomplish things or, as Nwadike (2011) observed, whether we should "stop thinking of leadership as an aggressive action and acquisition of power, and [view it] more as a way of thinking about our lives, education, jobs, and credibility" (p. 2).

Richard A. Barker (1997) offered a compelling critique of the constructional framework that has been used to develop prevailing leadership theories, including transformational leadership, which has been universally embraced as one of the most effective leadership orientations because it inspires positive change in those who follow. Barker (1997) argued in *How can we train leaders if we do not know what leadership is?* that leadership is what people have turned to for resolution of individual and societal problems. Yet, the issue is that the problems to be solved have been ill-defined; "they have been defined according to old and inappropriate paradigms. So, the proposed solutions just do not work when applied to the modern world" (p. 345). Barker (1997) identified the structure of a feudal kingdom as the paradigm upon which modern problems have been based, a paradigm that promotes "an image of a powerful male leader who sits atop a hierarchical structure directing and controlling the activities of subjects toward the achievement of the leader's goals" – goals that amount to the military defense and acquisition of territory (p. 346).

Barker (1997) contended that defining leadership by pointing to someone who sits in a high position or as having abilities and traits that allow one to transform a lackluster organization does not work if the goal is "freedom, education, or social development" (p. 350). We need a new paradigm for these modern societal considerations because they are human endeavors that require the navigation of complex social and political processes. Barker (1997) thus argued for viewing leadership as a social (community development) endeavor that encompasses the components of process and ethics – what he defined as a spiritual definition of life, the source of behavior derived from the real conditions of society that forcefully pilots the development of conscious moral systems. Barker elaborated that,

When mores or their cultural context become incongruent with individual ethics and are perceived to be in need of change, the ethics of a group of individuals, driven by personal insight and experience, align to motivate the group to produce desired change. That is the process defined here as leadership (Barker, 1997, p. 354).

Barker (1997) conceded that people naturally have conflicting values or ethics because of their varying social experiences. These differences amplify whenever people interact with one another. What aligns these differences of individual ethics, for the attainment of a common goal or the highest good, is the social process of leadership. So, within this framework and, in answering the previous question raised from a reading of Bonsu's (2002) *Leadership: The missing variable in the economic development of sub-Saharan Africa*, "it is not the leader who creates leadership [or cultural norms], it is leadership that creates the leader" and cultural norms (Barker, 1997, p. 354).

The reciprocal interaction between individual and society informs the ethics of the individual, which the individual then leverages during engagement with others to yield leadership for the achievement of a greater or common good. It is a process not unlike how social learning theorists explain the determinants of human behavior, the bidirectional influence process of external sources of control and personal control, which then yields human accomplishments. Leadership, a social process, is the byproduct of human engagement and Barker (1997) was not alone in making this observation. In fact, Gemmill and Oakley (1992), who first defined leadership as a social process, took the debate a step further.

In *Leadership: An alienating social myth*, the authors characterized leadership as a myth that functions to reinforce existing social beliefs and structure about the necessity of hierarchy and leaders in organizations. This myth about leadership pushes people toward devaluing their own intellectual and emotional skills, in pursuit of protection from the fears and challenges of the real world. We need to recognize leadership for what it is, the authors concluded, not for what we have been conditioned to believe. Otherwise, we undermine our best selves. They wrote,

> *When members of a group are faced with uncertainty and ambiguity regarding direction, they often report experiencing feelings of anxiety, helplessness, discomfort, disappointment, hostility, and fear of failure. Frightened by these emerging emotions and impulses, which are ordinarily held in check by absorption into the prevailing social system, they collude, largely unconsciously, to dispel them by projecting them onto "leadership" or the "leader" role. The projection allows organizational members to avoid directly confronting the emerging emotions and regress to a form of social order with which they are familiar (Gemmill and Oakley, 1992, p. 2).*

This is a powerful observation that conjures up images of people the world over abdicating our responsibility to affect change from where we are because we can say, disingenuously, that someone else is in charge. Looked at from this perspective then, the position that African countries' failure to develop rests with the failure of our leaders is not altogether accurate or even fair. It is not the leaders who have failed but rather the social process between the people which produces leadership that has failed. This awareness, in addition to compelling responsibility for our own actions, trains focus on the limitations of the internalist argument concerning development in Africa. The argument generally points fingers at the cadre of people in positions of authority or power to explain the wrongs of a society in the development space. It is an insufficient argument because the people of society bear equal, if not more, responsibility in the work of nation building. This recognition of the role of the people in connection with the outside forces that combine to influence our lives illuminates what the literature has thus far failed to make explicit – the nexus of the impediments to development in African countries that reflects the push-pull effect of our environment and our agency on our living condition. We explore the depths of these connections in Chapter 3.

REFERENCES

Acemoglu, D., & Robinson, J. A. (2013). *Why nations fail: The origins of power, prosperity, and poverty (Pbk* (C. Business, Ed.).

Achebe, C. (1994). *Things fall apart.* Anchor Books.

Achebe, C. (1998). *The trouble with Nigeria.* Fourth Dimension Publishing.

Ake, C. (1996). *Democracy and development in Africa.* Brookings Institution.

Arendt, H. (1958). *The human condition.* The University of Chicago Press.

Arnold, M. (1869). *Culture and anarchy: An essay in political and social criticism*. Macmillan.

Ayittey, G. (1998). *Africa in chaos*. St. Martin's Press.

Bandura, A. (1974). Behavior theory and the models of man. *The American Psychologist*, *29*(12), 859–869. doi:10.1037/h0037514

Bandura, A. (1977). *Social learning theory*. Prentice Hall.

Barker, R. A. (1997). How can we train leaders if we do not know what leadership is? *Human Relations*, *50*(4), 343–362. doi:10.1177/001872679705000402

Bolden, R., & Kirk, P. (2006). Transforming communities through leadership development: A Pan-African example. *British Academy of Management Conference.*

Bonsu, O. K. (2002). *Leadership: The missing variable in the economic development of sub-Saharan Africa*. ProQuest Dissertations Publishing.

Bruijn, D. R. & Gewald, J.B. (2007). Strength beyond structure social and historical trajectories of agency in Africa. Brill.

Castaneda Dower, P., Gokmen, G., Le Breton, M., & Weber, S. (2021). Did the Cold War Produce Development Clusters in Africa? *IDEAS Working Paper Series from RePEc*.

Ekeh, P. (1986). Development theory and theAfrican predicament. *Africa Development. Afrique et Developpement*, *11*(4), 1–40. https://www.jstor.org/stable/24486618

Fanon, F. (1963). *The wretched of the earth*. Grove Press.

Forsyth, F. (1969). *The Biafra story: The making of anAfrican legend.* Penguin Books.

French, H. (2015). *China's second continent: How a million migrants are building a new empire in Africa*. Vintage Books.

Gemmill, G., & Oakley, J. (1992). Leadership: An alienating social myth? *Human Relations*, *45*(2), 113–129. doi:10.1177/001872679204500201

Goldin, I. (2018). *Development: A very short introduction*. Oxford University Press. doi:10.1093/actrade/9780198736257.001.0001

Hammarlund, C., & Andersson, A. (2019). What's in it for Africa? European Union fishing access agreements and fishery exports from developing countries. *World Development, 113*, 172–185. doi:10.1016/j.worlddev.2018.09.010

Haugen, D. M., & Musser, S. (2012). *Africa*. Greenhaven Press.

Juma, T. O., & Oluoch, K. K. (2013). System failure causes of conflict in Africa as a social transformation. *International Affairs and Global Strategy, 17*, 2013.

Kincaid, J. (1988). *A small place*. Penguin.

Lin, J. Y. (2014). *The Quest for prosperity: How developing economies can take off*. Princeton University Press.

Mawere, M., & Mwanaka, T. R. (2015). Democracy, good governance and development in Africa (Mawere & T. R. Mwanaka, Eds.). Langaa Research & Publishing CIG.

Meredith, M. (2006). *The state of Africa: A history of fifty years of independence*. Free Press.

Müller, H., Mekgwe, P., & Mhloyi, M. (2013). *Values and development in Southern Africa*. Council for the Development of Social Science Research in Africa. doi:10.2307/j.ctvk8vz4z

Mutiiria, O. M., Ju, Q., & Dumor, K. (2020). Infrastructure and inclusive growth in Africa: An empirical analysis. *Progress in Development Studies, 20*(3), 187–207. doi:10.1177/1464993420927507

Njoh, A. J. (2006). *Tradition, culture and development in Africa: Historical lessons for modern development planning*. Ashgate Publishing.

Nugent, T. (1949). *The spirit of the laws (trans.)*. MacMillan.

Nyerere, J. (1985). Africa and the debt crisis. *African Affairs (London), 84*, 493–4. Google Scholar.

Odhiambo, N. M. (2021). Health expenditure and economic growth in Africa: An empirical investigation. *Development Studies Research, 8*(1), 73–81. doi:10.1080/21665095.2021.1892500

Olopade, D. (2014). *The bright continent: breaking rules and making change in modern Africa*. Houghton Mifflin Harcourt.

Overview. (n.d.) World Bank. https://www.worldbank.org/en/topic/poverty/overview

Proxy Wars During the Cold War. (2018). Atomic Heritage Foundation. https://www.atomicheritage.org/history/proxy-wars-during-cold-war-africa

Riddell, J. (1992). Things fall apart again: Structural adjustment programs in Africa. *The Journal of Modern African Studies*, *30*(1), 53–68. doi:10.1017/S0022278X00007722

Sachs, J. B. (2006). *The end of poverty: Economic possibilities for our time.* Penguin.

Singh, R. (2019). *Education: An effective engine and catalyst of social transformation.* Eurasiareview.com.

Soyinka, W. (2000). Culture, democracy and renewal. *Trends in Organized Crime*, *5*(3), 110–117. doi:10.1007/s12117-000-1039-2

Worldatlas. (n.d.). *Least Developed Countries 2022.* World Population Review. https://worldpopulationreview.com/country-rankings/least-developed-countries

Chapter 3
Nexus of Impediments to Development

ABSTRACT

A careful reading of the literature suggests that what has not been emphasized or prioritized enough about African countries' present predicament is the role of the people and our environment: the choices we make, our cultural context, and our interactions with one another. To be sure, the external and the internal impediments (environmental sources of control and personal control in social learning parlance) promulgated in the literature shed light on how conditions in Africa have been influenced by the reciprocal interaction of choice and culture – the decisions and behaviors of the people in response to our environment, which includes circumstances imposed by outside forces. The depths of these connections are explored in this chapter, specifically what the broader literature conveys separately about choice and culture, how the two constructs influence human development in keeping with the theory of social learning, and why there is a compelling need to explore the relationship between the lives Africans lead and the development challenges that prevail on the continent.

INTRODUCTION

Slavery, colonialism, and foreign influence were just some of the external impediments that were extensively cited in the literature. While the transatlantic slave trade of Africans is not a particular focus of the literature review conducted for this study because it is so far back in our history, there is ample evidence to confidently state that the trade flourished with the acquiescence of Africans. This includes Africans' willing and organized sale of Africans to Europeans for European goods, to say nothing of Africans welcoming

DOI: 10.4018/979-8-3693-2403-5.ch003

Europeans with open arms during the latters' early pursuit of the continent's gold deposits (French, 2021). Put plainly, the choice Africans possessed to determine the course of our early contact with Europeans is the same choice that existed for us when, after colonialism and independence, we allowed foreign influence to prevail in our political and economic lives.

Thus, while external or environmental sources of control have stunted Africa's growth, it is internal factors or personal control – the decisions that we have made to respond to or counteract those external or environmental sources – that have similarly degraded the continent's ability to flourish. The choices (and behavior) of our national leaders readily come to mind when such an observation is made about African countries' continuing struggles. It is a convenient explanation, but as the literature informs us about the scope of leadership and the associated ideological paradigm that should be our focus in these modern times, our national leaders, as awful as many have been, are scapegoats. The absence of the social process between the people which produces leadership is the culprit. And this reality is rooted in how the convergence of choice and culture in our lives has disproportionately influenced conditions for the worse in African countries.

The literature on impediments to development in Africa fails to make this connection – the combined influence of the reciprocal process of choice and culture in our lives on conditions in Africa. But we will see, through further examination of what the broader literature conveys separately about choice and culture, how the two constructs influence human development – in keeping with the ideas of the social learning theory, and why there is a compelling need to explore the relationship between the lives Africans lead and the development challenges that prevail on the continent.

CHOICE

The literature is expressive about human choice, which is often referenced in the language of freedom, agency, or action. Each of these words carry their own connotation, depending on the context in which they are applied. Each also combines to underpin what is arguably one of the most hotly debated social constructs in human history: free will versus determinism. The debate is a riveting exploration of the significance of choice in human affairs. It need not stall us here, however, for our concern for this study rests not in the origin and formation of choice but in the undisputed fact that humans have the capacity to make choices. This focus is embodied in the common sentiment expressed about the essential nature of humanity, as author and anthropologist Gary Chapman (1992) articulated in *The 5 love languages*. "We are creatures of choice," Chapman observed. "That means that we have the capacity to make poor choices, which all of us have done" (p. 131).

More on poor choices in a moment. We must first explore the meaning of choice. The classic definition is the act of making a decision for one's life pursuits when one is faced with multiple options or possibilities. T. M. Scanlon, Jr. (1986) told us in *The Significance of choice* that the "term applies not only to something that an agent does...but also to what an agent is presented with…[choice] encompasses both an action and a situation within which such an action determines what will happen" (p. 177). For Scanlon, choice is significant and it has value beyond the instrumental variety. "The reasons people have for wanting outcomes to be (or sometimes not to be) dependent on their choices has to do with the significance that choice itself has for them" (p. 180-181). While choice promotes outcomes, which is significant in and of itself, its concurrent value is its profound significance to our humanity — a point illustrated elsewhere in the literature.

Leotti et al. (2010) addressed the significance of choice for humans through a deductive analysis of the literature and provision of empirical evidence in *Born to choose: The origins and value of the need for control*. The authors combed through findings on the "neural substrates of the need for control" from animal studies, clinical populations, and neuroimaging research to determine that choice (its presence or absence) has a massive effect on how our emotions, cognition, and physiology are regulated (p. 457). Our perception of and need for control is born out of a physiological and biological need. It is how we have managed to ensure the evolutionary survival of our species. The significance of choice is thus appropriately germain, even existential to our humanity. Leotti et al. (2010) observed, to support the latter argument, that "individuals exercise control over the environment by making choices…Thus, to choose is to express a preference and to assert the self. Each choice – no matter how small – reinforces the perception of control and self-efficacy… and removal of choice probably undermines this adaptive belief" (p. 457).

This idea of control (choice and decision-making) being instrumental to our humanity is similarly reflected in the writings of Hannah Arendt (1958), one of the more notable scholars whose perspective on choice is couched in the language of action — the capacity to speak and act; our faculty for words and deeds. In her phenomenological analysis of the forms of activity that are fundamental to the human condition (labor, work, and action), Arendt instructed us that action corresponds to our plurality as distinct individuals. She wrote,

Men can very well live without laboring, they can force others to labor for them, and they can very well decide merely to use and enjoy the world of things without themselves adding a single useful object to it; the life of an exploiter or slave-holder and the life of a parasite may be unjust, but they certainly are human. A life without speech and without action, on the other hand...is literally dead to the world; it has ceased to be a human life, because it is no longer lived among men" (Arendt, 1958, p. 176).

Our capacity to make choices, to take action in pursuit of our life goals and to give voice to this endeavor signifies our very existence, while concurrently setting in motion the course of developments that will determine the kind and quality of life we live. The existence of this agency is as true for the people of Africa as it is for any other people in the world, particularly so in the 60-plus years since Africans gained political independence and the choice to determine the course of our lives. What has transpired in African countries with regard to the latter consideration is what brings us back to Gary Chapman's (1992) focus on poor choices.

Chapman's deliberation on poor choices forces us to consider the internal impediment to development of failed leadership in African countries. We have discovered through a reading of the literature that failure of our leaders does not adequately explain the continent's woes, but it is important to revisit this impediment to illuminate the role of choice. The challenge in Africa is not just that the rulers are making poor choices. It is also that the poor choices are enabled by the people through selection of the same rulers. This selection is further compounded by the fact that the rulers, upon entering office, are left to their own devices where matters of the state are concerned. They are seldom, if at all, held accountable for the poor choices they make because of society's abandonment of the social process of leadership – the leveraging of our ethics to engage others, negotiate, compromise, and sacrifice for the greater good.

Cappelan et al. (2020) drew our attention to the adverse effects of choices in *Choice and personal responsibility*. This work is an analysis on "what is a morally relevant choice" and it places into context the severity of the choices made in African countries in the domains of governance and nation building. The authors acknowledged that choice is an exercise of agency, but they also conceded that choice leads to the "acceptance of inequality" in society. This finding is relevant, the authors wrote, because it helps to understand how "fairness preferences" influence perspectives on "redistributive policies." The authors made clear that "where institutions allow for more freedom of choice, there will be less demand for redistribution" (p. 4-5). More freedom in society results in people demanding less from society.

In African countries, the choices people have made, notably the selection of rulers and society's abandonment of the social process of leadership have produced governments ill-equipped to govern. Due to efforts by the same governments to entrench their hold on power through patronage of supporters (thus provoking a limitation on freedom of choice), African societies have experienced an increase in demands for redistribution of the nation's wealth and yet those same demands go unfulfilled election after election. Thus, strategies for reducing inequality and promoting sustainable economic, environmental, and social development are rendered unreachable by the very nature in which Africans' have thus far elected to exercise our agency. Our poor choices restrict freedoms in society. This restriction raises calls for redistribution of the national wealth. When the calls go unheeded, social tensions caused by inequality escalate and the people either disengage from participating in the national life of the nation or they end up placing an at-all-cost premium on securing political power which, in turn, becomes an enduring function of our national culture.

CULTURE

The literature reflects considerable debate on culture, what it is, how it is measured, and what is its impact on social transformation efforts. On the first question, a classic definition is "behavior peculiar to Homo sapiens, together with material objects used as an integral part of this behavior. Thus, culture includes language, ideas, beliefs, customs, codes, institutions, tools, techniques, works of art, rituals, and ceremonies, among other elements" (Britannica, 2023). This study's focus on socio-economic development compels a similar yet narrower definition, one that succinctly defines culture as an approach or way of life that centers the thinking and behavior of a people. The artifacts or material objects of a culture are undeniably significant. Yet it is the symbolic culture, the nonmaterial objects that include ideas, values, beliefs and symbols of a people that must necessarily be the focus in any discussion about human development.

Does culture, as thus defined, have any value, relevance or place in the discussion about socio-economic development? Acemoglu and Robinson (2013) were not convinced. They concluded, on their way to trumpeting politics and institutions as the real impediments to development, that the culture theory does not work because what are emphasized (religion, ethics, values) are "just not important for understanding how we got here and why the inequalities in the world persist. Other aspects, such as the extent to which people trust each other or are able to cooperate, are important but they are mostly an outcome of institutions, not an independent cause" (p. 57). Other experts, Goldin (2018), Lin (2014), Bonsu (2002), Ayittey (1998), Ake (1996), Juma and Oluoch (2013), either overlooked culture or mentioned it in the context of Africans needing to come together since our leaders have failed us.

Kuada (2010), in *Culture and leadership in Africa: a conceptual model and research agenda*, employed a theoretical framework analysis to argue that previous studies have seen African culture as either defining the uniqueness of leadership on the continent or constraining leadership development. He suggested the presence of both degrees of influence on leadership. Kuada identified culture's impact on leadership, which in turn, he wrote, influences economic development paradigms. This view reinforced the outsized role leaders have in development efforts. Kuada seemed to make the argument that leaders, whom culture greatly influences, are the determining factor in countries being able to turn their economies around. He placed the burden for national development on a select group of people at the top, which, as previously discussed, is an inappropriate paradigm for the kinds of development that are our focus and goal in these modern times.

In *Cultural determinants of economic growth: Theory and evidence*, Dieckmann (1996) employed a theoretical approach to identify connections between culture and economic growth both within indigenous growth models and by using cross-country growth regressions. He concluded that "economic performance is also a product of national culture: Individuals are raised in families, and trained in schools and universities, and they absorb the values prevailing in one particular society. As a consequence, economic growth experiences are culturally bounded" (p. 316). Dieckmann's take on the issue was a progressive one, even if he was silent on the opposing view.

Anthony C. Ajah (2014) was more expressive in *On truthful narrative-identity and a development model for Nigeria*. Ajah used theoretical analysis and case study to make the case for a "culture-agency" model of development in Africa. He concluded that other models (modernization, economic development, dependency, human development) encourage 'irresponsibility.' Ajah supported his position by pointing to the logic that development results from human actions."Human actions are results of human choices. Human choices are results of human valuation systems. Valuation systems are aspects of a people's culture. Thus, the best development model is one that puts the members of every society at the center of their development process and developmental activities" (p. 531).

Underlying Ajah's position is his analysis of an Igbo expression that means "truth is life" and Paul Ricoeur's (1986) idea of narrative-identity to establish a link between social development and a people's ability to be truthful about who they are. Ajah came around to this consideration about the need for truth telling for his home country, Nigeria, in asking "whether it is reasonable for the major ethnic groups in Nigeria to continue to live together as a single country" given that the country has experienced nothing but ethnic strife, coups, corruption and mismanagement since independence from Britain in 1960 (p. 539).

Ajah highlighted a concern many Africans have about their existing nation-states given their nation-states' composition of divergent ethnicities that, as power shifts allow, have taken turns to plunder the national resources at the expense of those locked out of power. Notwithstanding the many challenges Africans have endured, including development models which have not worked, we cannot deny that it is Africans who have been making the choices in practically all spheres of our lives. These choices are embedded in established values, which manifest through the way of life (the culture) Africans have created.

Intriguing or tempting as it may seem to start afresh with new national boundaries in Africa, as Ajah ponders for Nigeria, history demonstrates that people of different ethnicities can and do share national borders in a peaceful, prosperous manner. So a more effective solution for Africa, in addition to contemplating the role of choice (decision-making), might be to explore further this very idea of truth-telling and culture.

Daniel T. Osabu-Kle (2000) leaned into the idea of culture as a source for socio-economic advancement in Africa. In *Compatible Cultural Democracy*, Osabu-Kle used historical analysis of pre-colonial Africa and case study of multiple contemporary African countries to demonstrate the merit of Africans infusing their traditional culture in the politics they practice for the achievement of conditions suitable for development. Osabu-Kle blamed the adaptation of foreign political practices in Africa, such as Western-style democracy (partisan politics), by Africa's elites or leaders for Africa's inability to transform. Simply, he wrote, "The cultural preconditions for the institutions of Western democracy (including bureaucracy, incorruptible civil service, a well-grounded private sector, and individualism) are non-existent" (p. 73). He proposed an embrace of Africa's indigenous political culture, characterized as having a "consensual" nature, "with a balance between centralization and decentralization to check abuses of power" (p. 95).

While Osabu-Kle leaned into culture to make the case for development, his efforts seemed entirely focused on what he presented as the need for a revival of pre-colonial Africa's indigenous political system. The culture Osabu-Kle referred to or preferred for Africans to embrace thus applied to the way Africans organized the institutions through which we make decisions. Osabu-Kle essentially made the case, much like we heard from Acemoglu & Robinson (2013), Ayittey (1998), Ake (1996), Ekeh (1986), Juma and Oluoch (2013), and Lin 2014), that institutions are the primary determinants of successful development.

Looking farther back in history, Matthew Arnold (1869) viewed culture as a transformative change agent for his country, England, in the mid-to-late 1800s. The English poet and social critic lived in England during the Victorian Age (1837–1901), a period of great social change and upheaval because of an explosion in population and the Industrial Revolution. England experienced inequities that manifested in deplorable work and living conditions for the average man on the street. Citizens seemed to stop caring about the welfare of their fellow man and about their own communities. They became increasingly focused on their own self-interest, showing more reverence for external, material considerations than the development of their own intellectual and spiritual life.

Arnold posited, in his collection of essays titled *Culture and Anarchy,* that faith in culture was the answer to England's social ills. Arnold defined culture as the pursuit of perfection, an inward condition of the mind and spirit that promotes both the scientific passion to see things as they are, for knowing, and the moral and social passion for doing good. Culture's ultimate aim, Arnold contended, is "to render an intelligent being yet more intelligent" but also "to make reason and the will of God prevail" (34). Arnold believed culture had an important role to play for his society, and ultimately mankind because his own society had become 'mechanical' and 'external.' Culture, Arnold argued, is able to redress this imbalance because its characteristics, if embraced with purpose, are strong enough to overcome the English peoples' faith in machinery — what Arnold described as freedom, population, wealth, religious organizations, bodily health and vigor.

As an elite member of the society he criticized, Arnold was rightly put to task by some who questioned the motives behind his criticisms. How could he possibly be a voice of reason for the ordinary man given that he lived a far more privileged life than the average Englishman (Arnold was an inspector of Nonconformist schools who traveled across central England during the time railway travel was *en vogue*)? It might also seem odd or even counterintuitive to raise the criticisms of a citizen of a former colonial power in Africa in a discussion about what ails the same Africa that the said colonial power had a hand in subjugating and exploiting.

To know the best that has been thought and said in the world, as Arnold would have observed, is always the aim in affecting social transformation. Arnold's nationality is far less important than his message. But let us concede, for the sake of argument, that Arnold is a flawed messenger; that he, in fact, wrote about a people and a time – the Industrial Revolution and England of the Victorian Age – that is dissimilar to the people and time of concern in this study – the globally connected post-Independence African continent of the Information and Digital Age. Might there be other, more contemporary, perhaps even African voices who view culture as Arnold did?

Playwright, Poet and Professor Wole Soyinka (2000) is a contemporary voice from Africa that the literature unveils. Soyinka's name is synonymous with the struggle for social justice in Africa in general and in his beloved homeland, Nigeria, in particular. His plays and writings – The Swamp Dwellers (1958), The Lion and the Jewel (1959), Season of Anomy (1973), and Death and the King's Horseman (1975), to name but a few – are iconic representations of the indelible mark he has made on society's collective conscious. The significance of his voice is further cemented by the Nobel Prize in Literature that he received in 1986 for producing literature that "fashioned the drama of existence," according to the committee that granted him the award.

Soyinka used various literary genres to dramatize the living conditions of his people while resisting dictators and oppressive governments on the African continent. Yet it was through simple prose, a speech Soyinka delivered to the International Monetary Fund's Board of Governor's annual meeting in 1999, that his profound belief in culture as the catalyst for change was made unambiguously clear. Soyinka reflected on his first-hand experience of what he termed "cultural renewal" with (visits to) Palermo, the capital city of Sicily to make his case. Palermo and her people were in 'distress' during Soyinka's first visit years earlier. There was a certain decadence about the place. The people were withdrawn and alienated, owing in part to the pervasive influence of the Mafia and organized crime, which operated like a "State within a State" and used corruption and violence to reign over Sicily with impunity (p. 113).

On his second visit years later, Soyinka told his audience, he discovered a new Palermo. The streets and environs were vibrant. The people were not estranged or indifferent toward one another but rather connected. They were openly agreeable and invested in their respective endeavors while participating in the social mobilization of the city. It was a complete reversal of his first experience. "How was the miracle of Palermo achieved," Soyinka asked (p. 113)? It was no miracle, Soyinka affirmed. The city's "liberation" was a "Renewal," and renewal most especially in the cultural domain" (p. 113). Soyinka walked his audience through what he meant by culture.

[I]t helps to differentiate between culture as understood or as projected, on the one hand, as a kind of glamorized occasion that merely seeks to deodorize a reality of civic alienation, lend spurious prestige to the violent overloads of a captive domain, and, on the other, the culture of participation, of social mobilization that was initiated – for example – during the struggle against the Mafia and accompanies the current process of consolidation of the victories over the Mafia, the complete transformation of the mentality of defeatism in the older generation, side by side with the nurturing of a new generation in the principles of the very human ordinariness and entitlement of creativity and democracy (Soyinka, 1999, p. 113-114).

Soyinka believed, based on what he witnessed from the Italians in Palermo that the people in the city had fully embraced personal and civic responsibility; that they were engaged in the struggle of life and "producing – not for some alienated, coercive masters – but for their own self-realization" (p. 114). They were directing their energies not on having something but in becoming something – the very same observation Matthew Arnold (1869) made over a hundred years earlier about what the English needed to prioritize in their lives to overcome the decadence and alienation that had permeated their existence.

The salient message Soyinka conveyed to the Board of Governors of the IMF in his speech was the significance of culture to a society's advancement, and he offered this message in the obvious language he knew the gathered Economists would surely recognize and understand. National development ought not to be understood through a calculated focus on Gross National Product but rather through an examination of the capacity of the human being – the social and technical skills we develop; our ability to think critically, to creatively express our manifest desires, to pursue our individual goals while accepting our responsibility to others, to fight alienation, indifference, and a defeatist mentality that operate to stifle human progress.

Soyinka seemed to be quietly advising his IMF audience that Palermo's transformation could be replicated in Africa, the unstated reason for his inclusion in the IMF's schedule in that early fall of 1999, if only culture – what Soyinka equated to "a continuing process of creative participation" – was made the central consideration for human development and thus the liberation of Africa's peoples. Using other yardsticks or instruments to measure human progress will never be adequate, or even appropriate because, Soyinka insisted, "The program of creative liberation is the profoundest of any form of investment in Humanity, and humanity is the sole end and purpose of the project of material development within any society" (p. 116).

Meaningful change starts from within, and it necessarily requires self-awareness, a willingness to embrace truth, and a proclivity toward community service and participation. Culture is at the heart of these considerations and both Matthew Arnold and Wole Soyinka, men of different eras, ethnicities and nationalities, and socio-economic backgrounds, used their platforms to share the same message with their respective societies. The authors' shared perspective on the value of culture is deeply relevant to Africa because of the similarities between what prevailed in England and Palermo, Sicily during the time of their writings and what prevails in African countries today. People on the African continent are making the choice to "do as they like" (as Arnold might have said) and, in turn, debasing the very mechanism (culture) that can help them unite and engage in "creative participation" (as Soyinka might have said) for social mobilization.

SOCIAL PROCESS OF LEADERSHIP

Soyinka's creative participation reference is another way of identifying the social process of leadership, the human element of engagement that produces change. This social process of leadership, as we are now familiar through a reading of Barker (1997), demands training, development, and education in career skills and pertinent social realities that cultivates awareness and responsibility through a focus on choice (decision-making/agency) and the consolidation of an enabling culture – the very human factor that both Mathew Arnold (1869) and Wole Soyinka (2000), in the foregoing paragraphs, contended aligns thinking and behavior toward growth and service to others.

CONCLUSION

The external and internal impediments for Africa's underdevelopment highlighted in the literature exposed "the bidirectional influence process" of environmental sources of control and personal control; the "reciprocal interaction" of outside forces coupled with personal or internal forces. A deductive analysis of the literature uncovered the extent or outcome of this reciprocal interaction between the external and internal impediments: the confluence of choice (decision-making) and culture, what can be called the nexus of the impediments to socio-economic development in Africa.

This nexus, the need to study it further, represents the gap in the literature because there is simply no concrete evidence in the latter of the influence of the interplay of choice and culture in the lives of Africans as it relates to socio-economic development considerations on the continent.

There exists, therefore, an imperative and timely need to consider a research study that seeks to leverage narrative inquiry and case study design to describe the relationship between the lived experience of everyday Africans and the challenges of socio-economic development in African countries. This relationship can be explored through investigation of research questions that focus on how everyday Africans describe their lived experience in pursuit of socio-economic development; how choice (decision-making) and culture (environment) influence everyday Africans' ability to develop socio-economically; and how the lived experience of everyday Africans inform understanding about achieving social transformation? The answers to these questions will illuminate the intersectionality between the variables of choice (personal control), culture (environmental sources of control), and socio-economic development (human accomplishments), which is a conceptual framework that is rooted in the established ideas of social learning theory, leadership as a social process, and choice and culture as the catalyst for change in society.

Chapter 4 provides an extensive overview of the present study's methodology, to include information on positionality, research design, participants and setting, sources of data, and validity and trustworthiness.

REFERENCES

Acemoglu, D., & Robinson, J. A. (2013). *Why nations fail: The origins of power, prosperity, and poverty (Pbk* (C. Business, Ed.).

Achebe, C. (1994). *Things fall apart.* Anchor Books.

Achebe, C. (1998). *The trouble with Nigeria.* Fourth Dimension Publishing.

Ajah, A. (2014). On Truthful narrative-identity and a development model for Nigeria. *Open Journal of Philosophy*, *4*(4), 531–540. doi:10.4236/ojpp.2014.44055

Ake, C. (1996). *Democracy and development in Africa.* Brookings Institution.

Arendt, H. (1958). *The human condition.* The University of Chicago Press.

Arnold, M. (1869). *Culture and anarchy: An essay in political and social criticism*. Macmillan.

Ayittey, G. (1998). *Africa in chaos*. St. Martin's Press.

Bandura, A. (1974). Behavior theory and the models of man. *The American Psychologist*, *29*(12), 859–869. doi:10.1037/h0037514

Bandura, A. (1977). *Social learning theory*. Prentice Hall.

Barker, R. A. (1997). How can we train leaders if we do not know what leadership is? *Human Relations*, *50*(4), 343–362. doi:10.1177/001872679705000402

Bolden, R., & Kirk, P. (2006). Transforming communities through leadership development: A Pan-African example. *British Academy of Management Conference*. British Academy of Management.

Bonsu, O. K. (2002). *Leadership: The missing variable in the economic development of sub-Saharan Africa*. ProQuest Dissertations Publishing.

Bruijn, D. R. & Gewald, J.B. (2007). Strength beyond structure social and historical trajectories of agency in Africa. Brill.

Camilli, E. P. B., & Green, J. L. (2006). Handbook of complementary methods in education research. Lawrence Erlbaum Associates.

Cappelen, A., Fest, S., Sørensen, E. Ø., & Tungodden, B. (2022). Choice and Personal Responsibility: What Is a Morally Relevant Choice? *The Review of Economics and Statistics*, *104*(5), 1110–1119. doi:10.1162/rest_a_01010

Castaneda Dower, P., Gokmen, G., Le Breton, M., & Weber, S. (2021). Did the Cold War Produce Development Clusters in Africa? *IDEAS Working Paper Series from RePEc*.

Chapman, G. (1992). *The 5 love languages: The secret to love that lasts*. Northfield Publishing.

Dieckmann, O. (1996). Cultural determinants of economic growth: Theory and evidence. *Journal of Cultural Economics*, *20*(4), 297–320. http://dx.doi.org.proxymu.wrlc.org/10.1007/s10824-005-7320-0. doi:10.1007/s10824-005-7320-0

Ekeh, P. (1986). Development theory and theAfrican predicament. *Africa Development. Afrique et Developpement*, *11*(4), 1–40. https://www.jstor.org/stable/24486618

Fanon, F. (1963). *The wretched of the earth*. Grove Press.

Forsyth, F. (1969). *The Biafra story: The making of anAfrican legend*. Penguin Books.

French, H. (2015). *China's second continent: How a million migrants are building a new empire in Africa*. Vintage Books.

Gemmill, G., & Oakley, J. (1992). Leadership: An alienating social myth? *Human Relations*, *45*(2), 113–129. doi:10.1177/001872679204500201

Goldin, I. (2018). *Development: A very short introduction*. Oxford University Press. doi:10.1093/actrade/9780198736257.001.0001

Hammarlund, C., & Andersson, A. (2019). What's in it for Africa? European Union fishing access agreements and fishery exports from developing countries. *World Development*, *113*, 172–185. doi:10.1016/j.worlddev.2018.09.010

Haugen, D. M., & Musser, S. (2012). *Africa*. Greenhaven Press.

Johnson, C. (2021). *Meeting the ethical challenges of leadership: Casting light or shadow* (7th ed.). Sage Publications.

Johnson, R. B., & Christensen, L. (2020). *Educational research: Quantitative, qualitative, and mixed approaches* (7th ed.). Sage Publications.

Juma, T. O., & Oluoch, K. K. (2013). System failure causes of conflict in Africa as a social transformation. *International Affairs and Global Strategy*, *17*, 2013.

Kincaid, J. (1988). *A small place*. Penguin.

Kuada, J. (2010). Culture and leadership in Africa: A conceptual model and research agenda. *African Journal of Economic and Management Studies*, *1*(1), 9–24. doi:10.1108/20400701011028130

Leotti, L. A., Iyengar, S. S., & Ochsner, K. N. (2010). Born to choose: The origins and value of the need for control. *Trends in Cognitive Sciences*, *14*(10), 457–463. doi:10.1016/j.tics.2010.08.001 PMID:20817592

Lin, J. Y. (2014). *The Quest for prosperity: How developing economies can take off*. Princeton University Press.

Mawere, M., & Mwanaka, T. R. (2015). Democracy, good governance and development in Africa (Mawere & T. R. Mwanaka, Eds.). Langaa Research & Publishing CIG.

Meredith, M. (2006). *The state of Africa: A history of fifty years of independence*. Free Press.

Müller, H., Mekgwe, P., & Mhloyi, M. (2013). *Values and development in Southern Africa*. Council for the Development of Social Science Research in Africa. doi:10.2307/j.ctvk8vz4z

Mutiiria, O. M., Ju, Q., & Dumor, K. (2020). Infrastructure and inclusive growth in Africa: An empirical analysis. *Progress in Development Studies*, *20*(3), 187–207. doi:10.1177/1464993420927507

Njoh, A. J. (2006). *Tradition, culture and development in Africa: Historical lessons for modern development planning*. Ashgate Publishing.

Nugent, T. (1949). *The spirit of the laws (trans.)*. MacMillan.

Nyerere, J. (1985). Africa and the debt crisis. *African Affairs (London), 84*, 337.

Odhiambo, N. M. (2021). Health expenditure and economic growth in Africa: An empirical investigation. *Development Studies Research*, *8*(1), 73–81. doi:10.1080/21665095.2021.1892500

Olopade, D. (2014). *The bright continent: breaking rules and making change in modern Africa*. Houghton Mifflin Harcourt.

Powell, J., & Thyne, C. (2011). Global Instances of Coups from 1950-Present. *Journal of Peace Research*, *48*(2), 249–259. doi:10.1177/0022343310397436

Proxy Wars During the Cold War. (2018). Atomic Heritage Foundation. https://www.atomicheritage.org/history/proxy-wars-during-cold-war-africa

Riddell, J. (1992). Things fall apart again: Structural adjustment programs in Africa. *The Journal of Modern African Studies*, *30*(1), 53–68. doi:10.1017/S0022278X00007722

Sachs, J. B. (2006). *The end of poverty: Economic possibilities for our time*. Penguin.

Scanlon, T. M. (1986). The significance of choice. *The Tanner Lectures on Human Values*, *7*, 149–216.

Settles, J. D. (1996). *The impact of colonialism on African economic development*. Chancellor's Honors Program Projects. https://trace.tennessee.edu/utk_chanhonoproj/182

Soyinka, W. (1975). *Death and the king's horseman*. Hill and Wang.

Soyinka, W. (1976). *Myth, literature and theAfrican world*. Cambridge University Press.

Soyinka, W. (2000). Culture, democracy and renewal. *Trends in Organized Crime*, *5*(3), 110–117. doi:10.1007/s12117-000-1039-2

Chapter 4
Design for Action

ABSTRACT

Qualitative research, the methodology of the present study, is a comprehensive and interpretive approach to studying and understanding the experiences of human beings. The research approach allows for a study of an exploratory nature to investigate "human choice and behavior as it occurs naturally in all of its detail" (Johnson and Christensen). In this study, the qualitative research approach provides a pathway, through evidence in the form of a qualitative questionnaire, interviews, research documents, and field notes, to explore, describe, and analyze the relationship between the lived experience of everyday Africans and the challenges of socio-economic development that impede social transformation in African countries. This chapter begins with an exploration of the researcher's positionality and the philosophical assumptions that influence use of the study's methods. The chapter provides an overview of the research design, participants and setting, sources of data, validity, and trustworthiness.

INTRODUCTION

In narrative inquiry, the researcher has to attend to three justifications: personal, practical, and social and/or theoretical (Johnson and Christensen, 2020). Personal justification entails the researcher justifying the narrative inquiry in the context of his/her own life experiences and personal inquiry puzzles. The absence of lasting social transformation in African countries has troubled me for years. While a citizen of the United States, I spent the formidable years of my life growing up and working on the African continent. I lived through unimaginable poverty, as a child reared by his Grandmother,

DOI: 10.4018/979-8-3693-2403-5.ch004

owing to deteriorating conditions in Sierra Leone that only seemed to worsen as time passed in the decade I lived in the country. I was again confronted with the same poor material and living conditions in Africa when I returned to the continent years later for work as a Foreign Service Officer.

Being an eye-witness to the manifestations of the poor state of affairs in so many African countries and the reasons for them both at the local and national level was motivation for me to better understand the problem and assess what measures can be taken to address the problem. This study was thus born out of a need to help people in their life struggles – to help improve the lives of those from whom I originate and whose land is also my ancestral home.

Practical justification requires justification of narrative inquiry in practical terms, i.e. attending to the possible need for a change in current practices. The study of Africa's socio-economic struggles is replete with observations on the root causes that are based on structural or theoretical arguments about development. For many, the problem lies with historical factors, globalization, or the internal systems and institutions of these countries. The present study aims to diverge from this traditional approach. At the core of the effort is an attempt to understand the phenomenon through the lens of the people themselves, through examination of the lives we live and arch of our experiences with making choices to navigate life, as well as gaining a better understanding of the culture that shapes and influences the decisions we make. The goal is not only to understand and describe the phenomenon, but to do so in a way that might inform the change in society that is needed to affect social transformation.

Social and/or theoretical justification demands attention to social action and policy justifications, notably concerns about social justice. My aim is to leverage the findings to educate and broaden understanding about a phenomenon that has troubled people for generations. While participants might benefit from the application of the findings in their own lives, the entire continent (and outside observers with keen interest) might consider giving greater attention to improving the conditions that will help individuals better navigate their lives and, in so doing, set the stage for them to contribute in the advancement of the common good of their communities and nation-states.

RESEARCH DESIGN

The study was grounded in the qualitative research methods of narrative inquiry and case study of everyday men and women from select countries in Africa, namely Ghana, Tanzania, South Africa, and Sierra Leone. It began with a deductive analysis of the established literature on what has been identified as impediments to development in this part of the world. The study then explored, through narrative inquiry and case study (a) how everyday Africans describe their lived experience in pursuit of socio-economic development; and (2) how choice (decision-making) and culture (environment) influence everyday Africans' ability to develop socio-economically. This inquiry and study, enabled by an open-ended qualitative questionnaire, semi-structured interviews, and field notes, provided evidence of (3) how the lived experience of everyday Africans inform understanding about achieving social transformation.

The case study portion of the research focused on the participants' home countries within the context of and in parallel with two participant narratives. The purpose of these specific case or country examinations was to offer environmental context for the narratives of some of the participants. This collective case study design was conducted instrumentally. The goal was to learn broader lessons, as Johnson and Christensen (2020) observed about the aim of instrumental case study designs – to understand the challenges in these nation states and the universal nature of their socio-economic struggles. It was an effort to provide "a detailed account of the characteristics and dynamics present" in the countries being examined through participant narratives (Johnson and Christensen, 2020, p. 412).

Narrative inquiry was used in conjunction with case study because of the methodology's capacity to reveal the meanings we attach to our lives and the relationships and communities that we build. Connerly and Clandinin (2006) observed in their analysis of narrative inquiry as a research methodology that people construct and give meaning to our lives and others through storytelling about our experiences. "Narrative inquiry, the study of experience as story, then is first and foremost a way of thinking about experience. Narrative inquiry as a methodology entails a view of the phenomenon. To use narrative inquiry methodology is to adopt a particular view of experience as a phenomenon" (p. 375).

Use of narrative inquiry to explore the socio-economic challenges in Africa offered a unique way to broaden understanding of the phenomenon through the telling of true life stories of Africans. The endeavor's central focus," as Clandinin and Rosiek (2007) reminded us, "is not only on an individual's experience but also on the social, cultural, and institutional narratives within which individuals' experiences are constituted, shaped, expressed, and enacted. Narrative inquirers study the individual's experience in the world, an experience that is storied both in the living and telling and that can be studied by listening, observing, living alongside another, and writing and interpreting texts" (p. 35).

The use of narrative inquiry in the study also offered a contrast to the traditional reliance on theories and structural arguments about the continent's geography, history, and politics to explain the root causes of Africa's socio-economic challenges. This contrast in methodology tapped into lessons about story, its impact on human evolution, as well as the reason usage of narrative inquiry to explore the phenomenon under study is compelling. Stories and storytelling have been the ways in which human beings communicate about and make meaning of our living conditions. They are the well-spring of information, the rich sources of data, that explain and amplify the human condition as it is experienced and recorded for posterity.

Will Storr (2020) related the origins and significance of storytelling brilliantly in *The science of storytelling*. Early humans, his research showed, used storytelling for survival, to influence and control the self-interested behaviors of tribe members for the preservation of the tribe. When the stories told about individual tribe members were positive, listeners experienced positive emotions and felt compelled to "celebrate them." When the stories were negative, listeners were morally outraged and "motivated to act – to punish" the wrong doers to the extent of banishment from the tribe (p. 138). There were other driving forces behind storytelling, however. People wanted (and still do today) to "get along with people" but also to "get ahead of them" (gaining status) (p. 143). These sometimes incompatible motivations "haunt human lives and stories" (p. 145). They inform our efforts to make meaning of our behaviors and the actions we take to navigate our lives. They provide the tapestry of our storytelling about life as we know it to be.

Hutson and Johson (2016) offered a more immediate rationale for storytelling's usefulness to humans. In times of crisis, the authors observed, storytelling is an imperative, especially for leaders. "In chaos or calamity, the greatest loss an organization [or a people] can experience is the loss of meaning. When meaning is disrupted, we feel unsafe, out of control, baffled, or dazed. Without meaning, we don't trust our ability to understand what is going on or to imagine what could happen next. We need coherence. We need a story" (p. 3). African countries' experience with socio-economic development qualifies, at least for those enduring it, as chaotic and cataclysmic. So what better way to explore the reasons for the chaos and calamity than a narrative inquiry of the storied experience of some of the very people who have suffered through the chaos and calamity?

PARTICIPANTS AND SETTING

Four candidates were selected to participate in the study through use of a purposive sampling approach, notably convenience sampling and critical-case sampling (Johnson and Christensen, 2020). This approach allowed the examination of cases that were particularly important and relevant to the constructs under study (Johnson and Christensen, 2020). The target population of the participants was adult males and females who are citizens of Africa's core regions. The participants varied in age and included a multi-generational make-up of Baby boomers, Generation X, and Millennials – the core generations that have lived through African countries' socio-economic development struggles since the first nation (Ghana) gained its independence in 1957.

The participants selected shared the commonality of a lived experience and a struggle to overcome personal challenges in similar social, cultural, and political environments in Africa, including Ghana, Tanzania, South Africa, and Sierra Leone. These countries are representative of the core regions of Africa. They are also representative of the countries for which the researcher used existing data for analysis.

The participants informed the study through provision of data about their personal lives, the choices they made and how they navigated cultural expectations. This data enabled examination of the constructs under study, namely choice (decision-making) and culture on individual development and the connection of the same to Africa's struggles with achieving lasting social transformation.

The participants were recruited through a formal email invitation (Appendix A) that outlined the purpose and methodology of the planned study, including specificity for their participation in personal interviews (via an internet platform such as Zoom and Whatsapp) and the completion of an open-ended qualitative questionnaire. The emails were obtained through informal online solicitation of candidates, many of whom belonged to online social media platforms.

The study took place online, specifically on the Zoom and Whatsapp social media platforms. One of the participants of the study was located in the United States. Three of the participants were located in their home countries. All of the participants signed an informed consent form (Appendix B) prior to participation in the study. Data collection began with completion of the six question open-ended qualitative questionnaire and it continued with the conduct of semi-structured interviews with participants. The questionnaire and interviews were arranged electronically (email) and through telephone and conducted through Zoom and Whatsapp.

SOURCES OF DATA

The study made use of multiple data sources, to include an open-ended qualitative questionnaire, semi-structured interviews, research documentation and field notes. Usage of these various data sources enabled data triangulation to improve data credibility and strengthen trustworthiness within the study (Johnson and Christensen, 2020). An interview protocol and an open-ended qualitative questionnaire were instruments that enabled effective study of a social phenomenon, specifically gaining understanding of people's storied experiences through narrative inquiry and case study (Johnson and Christensen, 2020). This study approach implied talking with people, getting to know them and their experiences, and having the ability to deeply understand the conditions and contexts underpinning those experiences. The questionnaire and semi-structured interviews provided the time, access, and flexibility to conduct this exploratory work.

Data collected from both interviews and survey questionnaires were analyzed to inform understanding of the influence of choice (decision-making) and culture on participants' ability to advance socio-economically. This analysis was examined to explore broader questions about national development, including how the findings uncovered through the study of the participants' lives informs our understanding of the study's research questions: (a) how do everyday Africans describe their lived experience in pursuit of socio-economic development; (b) how does choice (decision-making) and culture (environment) influence everyday Africans' ability to develop socio-economically; and (c) how does the lived experience of everyday Africans inform understanding about achieving social transformation?

Semi-Structured Interview Protocol

The interview protocol (Appendix C) addressed all three research questions of the study. The protocol included ten open-ended questions in a semi-structured format. The first segment focused on the participants' coming of age narrative and the events in their lives that had the most impact. The second segment explored the participants' adulthood narrative, including their professional career and the conditions (social, economic, cultural, and political) that shaped or determined their professional lives. The final, third segment focused on the participants' social experience, including the personal life choices they made as they attended to their community's cultural expectations.

Open-Ended Qualitative Questionnaire

The open-ended qualitative questionnaire (Appendix D) addressed research question two: how does choice (decision-making) and culture (environment) influence everyday Africans' ability to develop socio-economically? The six question survey, which invited responses in narrative format, focused on three areas: participants' views of their personal locus of control; the role of choice (decision-making) and culture in participants' lives; and participants' views on locus of control as it pertains to events in their home countries.

Research Documentation and Field Notes

The research documentation and field notes addressed the three research questions of the study. The data provided greater depth and granularity for the narrative inquiry and case study conducted for Ghana, Sierra Leone, Tanzania, and South Africa and their citizen participants. The data provided an on-the-ground, contemporary perspective on the developments in these countries and their effect on the lives of the participants who shared their lived experiences. It included information on some of the social, cultural, economic, and political events that shaped the direction of the participants' nations from 2004 to 2016. The researcher authored the field notes during his work as a Foreign Service Officer.

Validity and Trustworthiness

Trustworthiness of the data collected was established through several methods. Among the methods was a review of the interview protocol and survey questionnaire by two Ph.D. scholars and academic advisors. These reviewers assessed the strength of the questions, language usage and overall effectiveness. The protocols were then pilot-tested by two candidates who shared demographic commonalities with the target sample population to assess the quality or soundness of the instruments. Data triangulation was then employed to cross-check information and conclusions from the survey with those from the interviews conducted with participants. The survey was conducted several weeks prior to the semi-structured interviews with the participants in order to get a baseline understanding of the participants' perspectives on the constructs under study (choice and culture). This baseline perspective thus enabled comparison of the participants' views on the constructs and (from the interviews) how the constructs actually manifested in their lives. There was a convergence in both data sets, with participants largely providing evidence of choice and culture playing an integral role in their pursuit of socio-economic development.

Reflexivity was another strategy used to promote validity because researcher bias was a potential threat. As Darawsheh (2014) observed, "Reflexivity enables researchers to gain awareness of personal attributes that may influence the research process" (p. 562). This self awareness lays the foundation for identification and implementation of effective mitigating strategies. The researcher for this study has lived with and worked on aspects of the research questions for the majority of his life. The researcher grew up in Sierra Leone from age two to 11. He worked on the continent as a Foreign Service Officer for over a decade, residing in or visiting over 35 African nations. The researcher also worked alongside Africans at the United Nations in New York during the course of two separate two-year assignments. The understanding and relationships developed from these experiences made it difficult for the researcher not to have a view on the research question.

The researcher hypothesized that there would be credible links between the constructs under study and their effect on African countries' struggle to achieve lasting social transformation. This view (and the researcher's sheer passion for his ancestral home and people) was largely the reason the researcher committed to conducting this study. Along with the gaps revealed in the literature review, this view guided the application of the research, notably the selection of the methodology and accompanying data collection instruments. The above notwithstanding, the researcher had to restrain his views when it came to the collection of data and data analysis in this study, as these processes drove the answers to the research questions.

The researcher applied restraint by acknowledging his bias, then made a concerted effort to ask questions objectively of the participants. The researcher was careful about the accuracy of describing and interpreting the lived experience of the participants. This was a point of emphasis in the literature for many methodologists, who identified in their works mitigation strategies for addressing the issue of when the researcher is close to what is being studied. Noble and Smith (2015) concluded, for example, that "Including rich and thick verbatim descriptions of participants' accounts to support findings" was among the best strategies researchers could employ to ensure trustworthiness of findings (p. 34). Slevin and Sines (2000) also identified this strategy as a best practice. Ensuring such descriptive validity required deep, active listening and the use of related listening tools to ensure understanding of what the participants conveyed. While the researcher did not have access to multiple investigators, he used hand-written notes and recording devices (audio and online platforms) to document interviews for later retrieval, transcription, and analysis.

Reflexivity was also useful in addressing the potential bias emanating from use of the researcher's own field notes. To mitigate his personal views and judgements in the case study portion of the study, the researcher only included from his field notes the occurrence of relevant events that unfolded in the public domain, the energy crisis in Tanzania in 2005-2006 and the xenophobic uprisings in South Africa in 2008, for example. The researcher also ensured to cross-check and verify the validity of his notes on the said events with information reported by other authors and news outlets about the events when they took place.

One additional strategy used to promote validity in the study was negative-case sampling. The researcher looked purposefully for "examples that disconfirm [his] expectations and generalizations" about the study, as Johnson and Christensen (2020) advised about the strategy in their seminal work (p. 283). For example, the researcher juxtaposed one example of the impediments to socio-economic development revealed in the literature review, (politics, institutions and economic policies), with examples found in the participants' narratives, namely Zahra's decision to avoid political participation in Tanzania because of the nature of the politics in her country, and Amie's inability to fully participate in the economic life of her country, Sierra Leone, for the same reason. In both examples, the toxic and incendiary nature of political discourse and system, wherein those in power and their supporters ostracize those left out of power, as well as the access (or lack thereof) to political participation that this system allows, proved to be obstacles for the participants.

Yet, in examining the participants' lived experience, we learned that the nature of politics in their countries was not the only impediment to their development or to that of their nation-states. Participants were challenged with other internal considerations, namely family pressures, community expectations, and inadequate infrastructure for social services that compelled participants to seek socio-economic development outside of their homelands. Their departures negated their participation in the political and economic life of their nations, which in turn robbed their nations of the kind and level of citizenry participation required for nation building. Further illustrating the limits of politics, institutions, and economic policies as a sole reason for African countries' development was the fact that despite the toxic nature of politics in their countries, participants either returned home from abroad to get involved in their nations, or they stayed home, participated and then elected to discontinue participation for various personal reasons. Thus, the bidirectional influence of participants' environment and their choices amplified the effect of the confluence of the external and internal impediments to development that the literature identified on both personal development and national advancement in Africa.

DATA COLLECTION AND MANAGEMENT

The study began with a deductive analysis of the established literature. This review and analysis explored what has been written about the impediments that have prevented African nations from achieving socio-economic development. The goal was to outline the root-causes that have been identified, then analyze whether or not they offered a satisfactory explanation. This deductive analysis was informed by the study's theoretical and conceptual framework, as well as the study purpose and research questions. Specifically, the analysis focused on what the research has identified as external and internal factors that influence development in Africa. This exploration aligned with Albert Bandura's (1977) explanation of human behavior and achievement being determined by "the bidirectional influence process" of environmental sources of control and personal control.

The study's conceptual framework, the relationship between choice and culture and how they yield the social process (leadership) that leads to collective engagement for socio-economic development (Arendt, 1958; Arnold, 1869; Bandura, 1977; Barker, 1997; Gemmill and Oakley, 1992; Soyinka, 2000), was reflected in the research's identification of these constructs as the nexus – the central and most important considerations – in this exploratory work. This nexus of choice and culture within the broader consideration of factors that influence social transformation informed the purpose of this study and it illuminated a credible basis for examination of the research questions: (a) how do everyday Africans describe their lived experience in pursuit of socio-economic development; (b) how does choice (decision-making) and culture (environment) influence everyday Africans' ability to develop socio-economically; and (c) how does the lived experience of everyday Africans inform understanding about achieving social transformation?

Data collection began with completion of the six question open-ended qualitative questionnaire. Each participant was asked to complete the 20 minutes survey either in-person or electronically. Participants provided answers in narrative form to questions keyed to (a) personal locus of control, (b) the impact of choice (decision-making) on participants' lives, (c) the impact of culture on participants' life decisions, and (d) participants' views on locus of control as it pertains to events in their home countries.

Data collection continued with the conduct of semi-structured interviews with the participants. The interviews were arranged electronically (email) and through telephone. The interviews were conducted over the online platforms Zoom and whatsapp. Interviews were 60-90 minutes in duration, and they focused on important milestones in participants' lives – with questions keyed to how choice and culture influenced these milestones.

Data was collected and stored in Google Forms, a survey administration software provided by Google. The software is part of the web-based Google Docs Editors suite. The software permits the creation and analysis of surveys through a mobile or a web-browser, including charts and graphs. The data collected, both through the survey questionnaire and the interview protocol, were stored securely on Google's cloud platform. The researcher downloaded the data onto his personal laptop and the Delve CAQDAS software for coding and analysis. The researcher assumed responsibility for ensuring security and made certain that the privacy of the data was maintained through use of strong passwords and restriction on usage of the laptop.

DATA ANALYSIS PROCEDURES

Thematic analysis was the primary mechanism for analyzing the data collected for the study. Braun and Clark (2006) defined thematic analysis as "a method for identifying, analyzing and reporting patterns (themes) within data. It minimally organizes and describes your data set in (rich) detail" (p. 79). The method trains the researcher's focus on establishing recurring patterns within a data set and interpreting the patterns, for presentation, in the selection of codes and the formation of themes. From an epistemology standpoint, thematic analysis enables the researcher to "report experiences, meanings and the reality of participants, or to [examine] the ways in which events, realities, meanings, experiences and so on are the effects of a range of discourses operating within society… It can also be a 'contextualist' method…Therefore, thematic analysis can be a method that works both to reflect reality and to unpick or unravel the surface of 'reality' (Braun and Clark, 2006, p. 81).

The contextualist method of thematic analysis was the focus of analysis for this study. The researcher made an effort to blend the realist and constructionist epistemologies through a focus on the ways participants made meaning of their experience and how the broader social context in which they lived influenced the meaning they made of their experience. The transcribed interviews and open-ended qualitative questionnaire were uploaded into the Delve CAQDAS software. Data analysis was conducted through implementation of the six phases of thematic analysis (Braun and Clark, 2006). In phase one, the researcher familiarized himself with the data through multiple readings and transcription. This effort resulted in a deeper understanding of the participants' narratives and the initial formation of commonalities across the data set. Phase two involved the assignment of preliminary codes to the data in order to describe the data content. Preliminary codes focused on the participants' description of their childhood, adolescent milestones (coming of age), adult experience, and social/environmental influences.

Phase three of the analysis was the process of the researcher searching for patterns or themes in the codes across the data provided by each participant. The early patterns were highlighted by events or experiences at home, within the community, and outside in educational or professional settings that touched the participants in a searing manner, to a degree that the participants' outlook on life was changed or confirmed. Developments within the family, community mores, conditions of their countries, trauma such as the sudden passing of a loved one, and leaving of the nest (transition from home) all proved to be defining commonalities among the participants. Phase four of the analysis required the researcher to review the themes discovered and ensure their applicability across the data set. In confirming the themes, the researcher settled on development of the same at the latent level, which compelled analysis beyond the surface or semantics of the participants' descriptions. As Braun and Clark (2006), explained in their research on the methodology, "a thematic analysis at the latent level goes beyond the semantic content of the data, and starts to identify or examine the underlying ideas, assumptions, and conceptualizations / and ideologies / that are theorized as shaping or informing the semantic content of the data" (p. 84). Thus the theme 'lived experience as storytelling' and the sub-theme 'trajectory of development' (for research question #1) sought to explain the underlying ideas of the participants' life narratives and their pattern of describing how they embarked on their socio-economic development journey.

Phase five of the analysis involved the task of defining and naming the themes. This was done through a close reading of the data and the juxtaposition of the research questions in order to drive the process with a particular analytical frame. For example, the theme "lived experience as storytelling" was a byproduct of participants' common descriptive narratives about their childhood, adolescents and adult life coupled with one of the study's endeavors to understand how participants describe their lives as they pursued socio-economic development. What counted as a theme and the prevalence of each theme across the data set were instrumental considerations that were addressed through careful and recurrent reading of the data coupled with reference to the pertinent analytical questions of the study. Phase six of the analysis was report production. The researcher outlined the themes, keyed to each research question, and provided a table representation and narrative analysis of each of them. In so doing, the researcher focused on drawing out a contextualist epistemology (how participants made meaning of their experiences and the influence of the broader social context on those meanings), as well as on usage of a theoretical thematic analysis, which enabled the researcher to focus on the areas of his analytical interest (Braun and Clark, 2006).

CONCLUSION

Qualitative research was the study's methodology/design for action. Through the narrative inquiry and case study approach, an examination of the lived experience of everyday Africans, the study aimed to fill the gap in the literature concerning understanding about Africa's struggles with socio-economic development. The area studied in particular was how everyday Africans describe their lived experiences in our individual pursuit toward socio-economic advancement, as well the role of our choices (decision-making) and culture on our pursuit of individual development and national advancement. The researcher attended to personal, practical, and social/theoretical justifications in conducting the study to define his positionality. The researcher also outlined considerations for the study's trustworthiness to address overarching questions about objectivity and validity.

Chapter 5, to which we now turn, provides an analysis of the data from the qualitative survey questionnaire and semi-structured interviews of the study participants.

REFERENCES

Arendt, H. (1958). *The human condition.* The University of Chicago Press.

Arnold, M. (1869). *Culture and anarchy: An essay in political and social criticism.* Macmillan.

Bandura, A. (1974). Behavior theory and the models of man. *The American Psychologist, 29*(12), 859–869. doi:10.1037/h0037514

Bandura, A. (1977). *Social learning theory*. Prentice Hall.

Barker, R. A. (1997). How can we train leaders if we do not know what leadership is? *Human Relations*, *50*(4), 343–362. doi:10.1177/001872679705000402

Barrett, M. S., & Stauffer, S. L. (2009). *Narrative inquiry in music education: Troubling certainty*. Springer. doi:10.1007/978-1-4020-9862-8

Bengtsson, M. (2016). How to plan and perform a qualitative study using content analysis. *NursingPlus Open*, *2*, 8–14. doi:10.1016/j.npls.2016.01.001

Braun, V., & Clarke, V. (2006). Using thematic analysis in psychology. *Qualitative Research in Psychology*, *3*(2), 77–101. doi:10.1191/1478088706qp063oa

Camilli, E. P. B., & Green, J. L. (2006). Handbook of complementary methods in education research. Lawrence Erlbaum Associates.

Clandinin, D. J., & Rosiek, J. (2007). Mapping a landscape of narrative inquiry: Borderland spaces and tensions. In D. J. Clandinin (Ed.), *Handbook of narrative inquiry: mapping a methodology* (pp. 35–75). Sage. doi:10.4135/9781452226552.n2

Collier, D., & Mahoney, J. (1996). Insights and pitfalls: Selection bias in qualitative research. *World Politics*, *49*(1), 56–91. doi:10.1353/wp.1996.0023

Connelly, F. M., & Clandinin, D. J. (1990). Stories of Experience and Narrative Inquiry. *Educational Researcher*, *19*(5), 2–14. doi:10.2307/1176100

Darawsheh, W. (2014). Reflexivity in research: Promoting rigor, reliability and validity in qualitative research. *International Journal of Therapy and Rehabilitation, 21*(12), 560– . doi:10.12968/ijtr.2014.21.12.560

Denny, E., & Weckesser, A. (2019). Qualitative research: What it is and what it is not: Study design: qualitative research. *BJOG*, *126*(3), 369–369. doi:10.1111/1471-0528.15198 PMID:29916201

Gemmill, G., & Oakley, J. (1992). Leadership: An alienating social myth? *Human Relations*, *45*(2), 113–129. doi:10.1177/001872679204500201

Guenther, J., & Falk, I. (2019). Generalizing from Qualitative Research (GQR): A New Old Approach. *The Qualitative Report*, *24*(5), 1012–1033. doi:10.46743/2160-3715/2019.3478

Hutson, H., and Johnson, M. (2016, May 2). *To recover from a crisis, retell your company's story*. Harvard Business Review Digital Archives.

Jackson, R. L. II, Drummond, D. K., & Camara, S. (2007). What Is Qualitative Research? *Qualitative Research Reports in Communication*, *8*(1), 21–28. doi:10.1080/17459430701617879

Johnson, R. B., & Christensen, L. (2020). *Educational research: Quantitative, qualitative, and mixed approaches* (7th ed.). Sage Publications.

Marshall, B., Cardon, P., Poddar, A., & Fontenot, R. (2013). Does Sample Size Matter in Qualitative Research?: A Review of Qualitative Interviews in Research. *Journal of Computer Information Systems*, *54*(1), 11–22. doi:10.1080/08874417.2013.11645667

Noble, H., & Smith, J. (2015). Issues of validity and reliability in qualitative research. *Evidence-Based Nursing*, *18*(2), 34–35. doi:10.1136/eb-2015-102054 PMID:25653237

Oakes, J.M., and Rossi, P. H. (2003). The measurement of SES in health research: current practice and steps toward a new approach. *Social Science & Medicine (1982)*, *56*(4), 769–784. . doi:10.1016/S0277-9536(02)00073-4

Polit, D. F., & Beck, C. T. (2010). Generalization in quantitative and qualitative research: Myths and strategies. *International Journal of Nursing Studies*, *47*(11), 1451–1458. doi:10.1016/j.ijnurstu.2010.06.004 PMID:20598692

Shadish, W. R. (2011). Randomized Controlled Studies and Alternative Designs in Outcome Studies: Challenges and Opportunities. *Research on Social Work Practice*, *21*(6), 636–643. doi:10.1177/1049731511403324

Slevin, E., & Sines, D. (2000). Enhancing the truthfulness, consistency and transferability of a qualitative study: Utilizing a manifold of approaches. *Nurse Researcher*, *7*(2), 79–98. doi:10.7748/nr2000.01.7.2.79.c6113

Soyinka, W. (2000). Culture, democracy and renewal. *Trends in Organized Crime*, *5*(3), 110–117. doi:10.1007/s12117-000-1039-2

Storr, W. (2020). *The science of storytelling: Why stories make us human and how to tell them better*. Abrams Press.

Section 2
The Data and Analysis

Chapter 5
Questionnaire and Interviews

ABSTRACT

This chapter presents the findings from the data collected and analyzed from the qualitative questionnaire and semi-structured interviews, which endeavored to answer three primary questions: (1) How do everyday Africans describe their lived experience in pursuit of socio-economic development; (2) How does choice (decision-making) and culture (environment) influence everyday Africans' ability to develop socio-economically; and (3) How does the lived experience of everyday Africans inform understanding about achieving social transformation? These questions shed light on the intersectionality of choice (personal control), culture (environmental sources of control), and socio-economic development (human achievements) – social constructs that are germane to the endeavors of human development according to this study's theoretical and conceptual frameworks and a close reading of the literature. The chapter details the preparation of the raw data for analysis and descriptive data as well as the research findings.

PREPARATION OF RAW DATA FOR ANALYSIS AND DESCRIPTIVE DATA

Research Participants

The study engaged four citizens from four African countries as participants for data collection. Table 1 provides the participants pseudonyms, professional fields, and nationalities, and is followed by a brief narrative introduction of each participant.

DOI: 10.4018/979-8-3693-2403-5.ch005

Table 1. Participants of the study

	Participants		
Pseudonyms	**Professional Field**	**Country of Origin**	**Region of Africa**
Osie	Telecommunications	Ghana	Western Africa
Zahra	Music	Tanzania	Eastern Africa
Siya	Government	South Africa	Southern Africa
Amie	Business Development	Sierra Leone	Western Africa

Note: All names of the participants are pseudonyms.

Osie From Ghana

Osie, an approximately 48 year old male, was born and raised in Ghana, West Africa. He grew up in a middle class home before spending parts of his childhood and adolescent years overseas with his mother, who worked for the Ghanaian government. Osie was educated abroad, returned to Ghana for a few years and, due to conditions in Ghana, eventually immigrated to the United States. A 90 minutes interview with Osie was conducted over the Whatsapp online platform during the course of several days, beginning on September 14, 2022.

Zahra From Tanzania

Zahra, an approximately 39 year old female, was born and raised in Tanzania, East Africa. She grew up in a lower-middle class home before spending parts of her adolescent years in Nairobi, Kenya, where her parents traded gemstones. She was educated in Kenya and Tanzania. She returned to Tanzania after her parents were diagnosed with HIV. Zahra served as caretaker for her younger siblings in the capital city, Dar es Salaam, and eventually pursued a career in music. A 90 minutes interview with Zahra was conducted over the Whatsapp online platform during the course of two days, beginning on January 11, 2023.

Siya From South Africa

Siya, an approximately 60 year old male, was born to illiterate parents and raised in a Township in South Africa. He grew up in a materially impoverished home with several siblings, many of whom did not survive. The impoverished conditions of his home, rooted in the country's struggle against apartheid, proved a catalyst for Siya to educate himself in South Africa while he also participated in the struggle for liberation. Siya eventually joined the South African foreign service corps and worked overseas for several years before returning home to pursue business interests. A 90 minutes interview with Siya was conducted over the Zoom online platform during the course of two days, beginning on September 14, 2022.

Amie From Sierra Leone

Amie, an approximately 35 year old female, was born and raised in a village in the northern province of Sierra Leone. She grew up in a materially impoverished home and, as a daughter to the Village Chief in a traditionalist society, shouldered remodel responsibilities. The passing of her father forced Amie's relocation to the capital city, Freetown, where conditions compelled yet another relocation to the United States. Amie received her education and embarked on a professional career in the United States before making a decision to return to Sierra Leone. A 90 minutes interview with Amie was conducted over the Whatsapp online platform on January 6, 2023.

RESEARCH FINDINGS

Qualitative Questionnaire

The qualitative questionnaire addressed research question number two: how does choice (decision-making) and culture (environment) influence everyday Africans' ability to develop socio-economically? The survey was conducted several weeks prior to the semi-structured interviews with the participants in order to get a baseline understanding of the participants' perspectives on the constructs under study (choice and culture). This baseline perspective thus enabled comparison of the participants' views on the constructs and (from the interviews) how the constructs actually manifested in their lives.

The six question survey focused on three areas: participants' views of their personal locus of control; the influence of choice (decision-making) and culture (environment) on participants' lives; and participants' views on locus of control as it pertains to events in their home countries. Figure 1 displays the four participant responses to the six survey questions. All of the names used to identify participants in the study (Osie, Zahra, Siya, and Amie) are pseudonyms.

Figure 1. How does choice (decision-making) and culture (environment) influence socio-economic development?

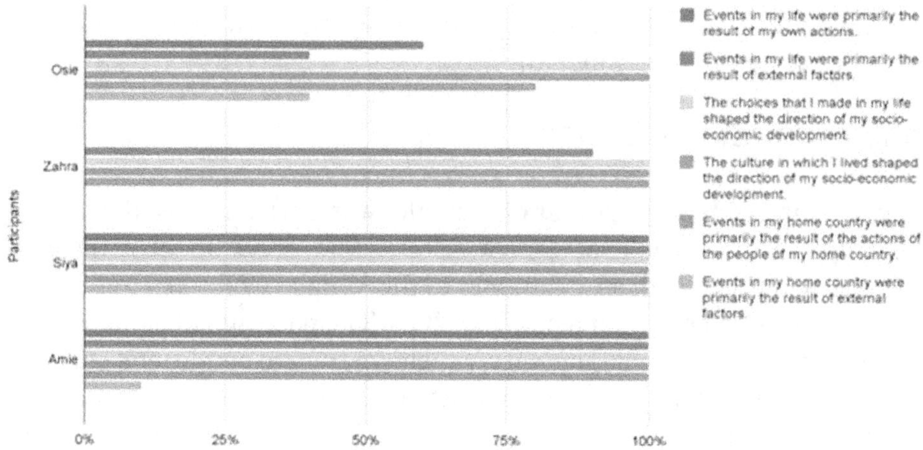

Personal Locus of Control

In the first area of the questionnaire, participants' views on their personal locus of control (in blue and red), 65 percent of the participants indicated that the statement, events in my life were primarily the result of my own actions, was accurate. Osie from Ghana indicated that the statement was 60 percent accurate. Zahra from Tanzania indicated that the statement was 0 percent accurate, which made the marking of her response (blue line) not appear on the chart. In response to the statement, events in my life were primarily the result of external factors, 83 percent of the participants indicated that the statement was accurate. Osie from Ghana indicated that the statement was 40 percent accurate. Zahra from Tanzania indicated that the same statement was 90 percent accurate. The findings for personal locus of control for each participant are further delineated in Figure 2 below.

Influence of Choice and Culture

In the second area of the questionnaire, the influence of choice (decision-making) and culture (environment) on participants' lives (in yellow and green), 100 percent of the participants indicated that the statement, the choices that I made in my life shaped the direction of my socio-economic development, was accurate. In response to the statement, the culture in which

I lived shaped the direction of my socio-economic development, 100 percent of the participants indicated that this statement was accurate. The findings for influence of choice and culture for each participant are further delineated in Figure 3 below.

Figure 2. Personal locus of control

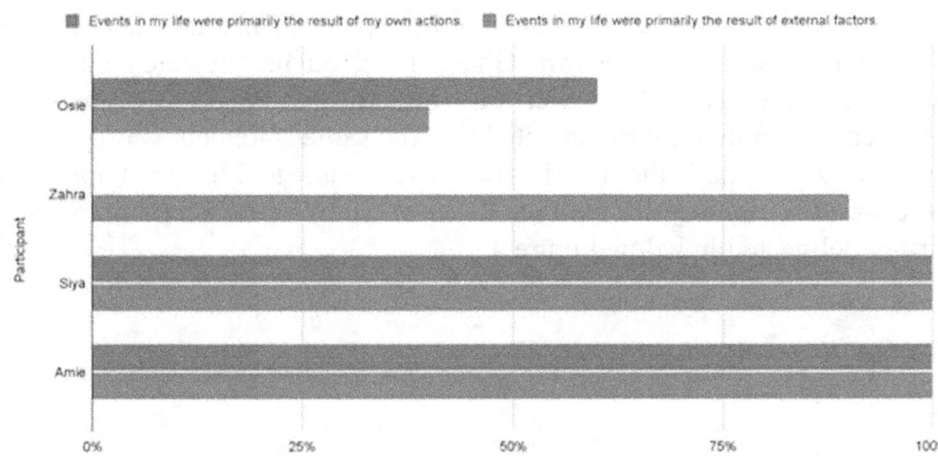

Figure 3. Influence of choice and culture

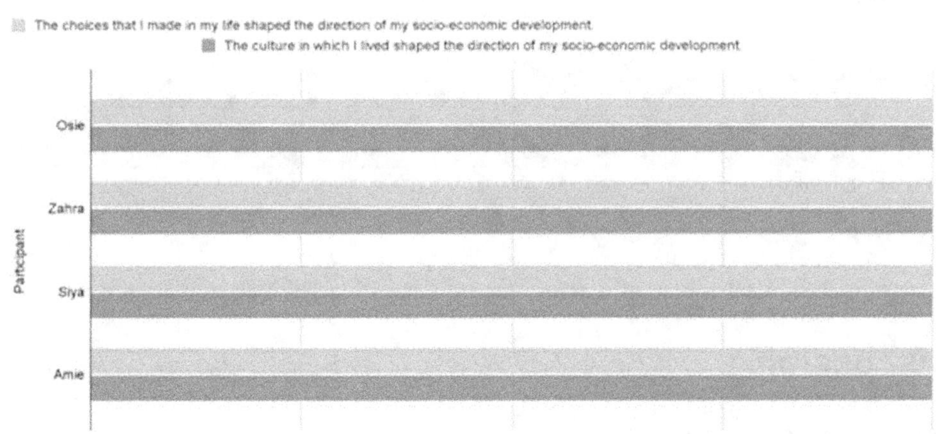

National Locus of Control

In the third area of the questionnaire, participants' views on locus of control concerning events in their home countries (orange and teal), 95 percent of the participants indicated that the statement, events in my home country were primarily the result of the actions of the people of my home country, was accurate. Osie from Ghana indicated that the statement was 80 percent accurate. In response to the statement, events in my home country were primarily the result of external factors, 37.5 percent of the participants indicated that this statement was accurate. Osie from Ghana indicated that the statement was 40 percent accurate. Amie from Sierra Leone indicated that the statement was 10 percent accurate. Zahra indicated that the same statement was 0 percent accurate, which made the marking of her response (teal line) not appear on the chart. The findings for national locus of control for each participant are further delineated in below Figure 4.

Figure 4. National locus of control

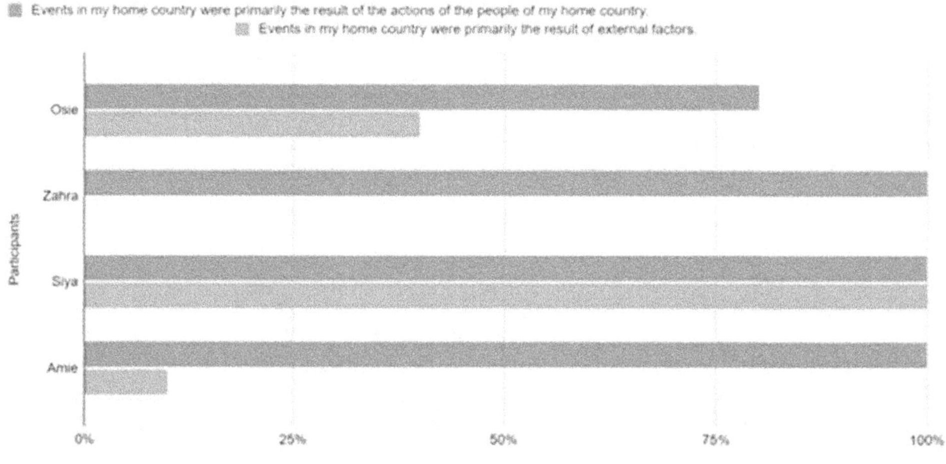

Discussion

How does choice (decision-making) and culture (environment) influence everyday Africans' ability to develop socio-economically?

The majority of the participants believed that choice and culture played a profound role in their ability to develop socio-economically. This evidence was demonstrated in the second area of the survey, in which participants were asked to respond to the influence of choice and culture in their lives. All the participants (100 percent of them) indicated that the choices they made and the culture in which they lived shaped the direction of their socio-economic development. This baseline perspective of the participants on the role of choice and culture in their lives offered surface evidence or initial validation of the study's theoretical framework: social learning theory.

According to the theory, human beings learn by observing and imitating others. We act to influence our environment. Internal factors (including cognition) influence how we act in given situations. Our behavior is thus subject to what Bandura (1974) termed "the bidirectional influence process" of environmental sources of control and personal control (p. 867). Our accomplishments result from "reciprocal interaction" of outside forces coupled with personal or internal forces of control. The participants recognized, with just a cursory reflection on the experiences that have shaped their lives, that their agency had just as much to do with how they evolved into the human beings they are as the culture in which they each exercised their agency.

The participants also recognized, with a great deal of convergence, that events in their lives were largely the result of internal and external factors. The participants further recognized, with some variation, that events in their home country were primarily the result of the actions of the people of their home country. All the participants believed that the latter statement was largely true, but at least three of participants also believed that external factors were 40 to 0 percent (a combined 16.6 percent) responsible for events in their home country.

Participants' recognition or identification of the locus of control pertaining to the outcome of their lives and the events that have unfolded in their home countries was crucial because we have learned, from a reading of the literature, that choice and culture (including external environmental sources of control) are critical considerations in the exploration of the phenomenon of socio-economic development and lasting social transformation. We turn now to the findings from the exploration of the lives of the participants through semi-structured interviews.

SEMI-STRUCTURED INTERVIEW PROTOCOL

The interview protocol addressed all three of the research questions. The protocol featured ten open-ended questions in a semi-structured format. The first segment of the interview focused on the participants' coming of age narrative and the events in their lives that had the most influence. The second segment of the interview explored the participants' adulthood, including their professional career and the conditions (social, economic, cultural, and political) that shaped or determined their professional lives. The third segment of the interview focused on the participants' social experience, including the personal life choices they made as they attended to their community's cultural expectations. All of the names used to identify participants in the study (Osie, Zahra, Siya, and Amie) are pseudonyms.

Research Question One

How do everyday Africans describe their lived experience in pursuit of socio-economic development?

The following are the theme and sub-themes from the above research question.

Table 2. Themes and sub-themes concerning lived experience in pursuit of socio-economic development

	Lived Experience	
Theme	**Sub-Theme**	**Issues Raised**
Lived experience as storytelling	Trajectory of Development	Childhood Family/Community behaviors Coming of Age/Awareness Traumatic experience
	Personal Agency/Action	Personal development Transition/Relocation Choice/Decision-making
	Social Influence	Achievements Condition of country Culture/Environment

Source: Field work 2022-2023

Sub-Theme One: Trajectory of Development

All of the participants used storytelling to share the trajectory of their development. Each reflected on this consideration through a retelling of the experiences and milestones that shaped the direction of their childhood and adolescent years. Each focused their storytelling on how they were influenced and how their outlook on life changed. The common factors of these changes were observations of family and community behaviors as well as enduring a traumatic experience that raised awareness and ushered in their coming of age in challenging socio-economic environments.

Sub-Theme Two: Personal Agency/Action

All of the participants raised their embrace of personal agency and action through descriptive narratives about their journey toward personal development and a professional career. All participants engaged in some degree of transition or relocation from their homeland to another country. The reasons for the transitions varied, but each was rooted in a personal choice to develop socio-economically, notably through the acquisition of formal education, professional training, and/or employment.

Sub-Theme Three: Social Influence

All of the participants raised the specter of social (family and community) influence in their respective journeys toward socio-economic development. Family members, namely parents, were particularly influential in participants embracing the discipline required to get a formal education, which they believed would lead to a good paying job. Participants' communities were equally influential, as they established and generally enforced through social pressure accepted standards for children and other group members. Also common among the participants was their discussion about the poor socio-economic conditions of their countries, which motivated them to seek a better life either internally or elsewhere. The effect of culture and the environment was top of mind for the participants.

The following were the exemplary narrative inquiry and case study findings from each participant.

Osie From Ghana

Osie from Ghana had fond memories of his childhood until he was uprooted from home. His mother's diplomatic career triggered the family's relocation to North America and beyond, where the family, without Dad who stayed home to focus on his own career, spent years in what Osie described as the cultural antithesis of all that they had known. Ghana was communal. Education and religion were paramount concerns there, as was having the discipline to focus on achievements while still enjoying the fruits of meaningful relationships. Osie's initial transition to Canada upended the lifestyle to which he was accustomed. It was a "culture shock," he shared. "I tried to fit in, so I lied, performed poorly in school on purpose because it was not cool to be a smart kid" (Osie, personal interview, October 20, 2022). Osie shunned academics and emulated the bad behaviors of his peers just so he would be accepted.

Following similar stays in the US and Europe, Osie returned home to Ghana years later with the perspective of a changed young man. He was ambitious about sports, far less interested in academics and yet academics was exactly where he was compelled to focus. His Dad pressured him, as did the expectations of his society, which both discouraged the pursuit of sports as a profession and lacked the physical infrastructure to support sports training. Underlying this parental and social pressure is a theme that permeated Osie's life: the propensity for him to be a follower and to allow others to frame his ambitions. His willingness to follow the crowd in Canada, to embrace religion in Ghana, to settle on engineering for his academic degree and career choice, and to marry a Ghanaian woman all reflect this propensity. Osie's lived experience was thus a culmination of environmental factors influencing his agency to shape the direction and scope of his socio-economic development.

Zahra From Tanzania

Zahra's early life was also spent in transition, with her family balancing life between homes in Arusha, Tanzania and Nairobi, Kenya because of her parents' involvement in the Tanzanite trade. The rare stone was sourced in Tanzania and yet the market for it was more robust in Kenya. Zahra too experienced a cultural immersion of sorts, but hers was a pleasant introduction to education that encouraged children to pursue their passions. In Tanzania, she and her siblings were compelled to focus on conventional disciplines (law, science, math or engineering). The arts were not encouraged or supported. There was a focus on the conventional disciplines in Kenya, but the Kenyan society also supported and provided infrastructure for involvement in extracurricular activities, including music and the arts. Zahra thus embraced music, which, despite opposition from her Dad and community in Tanzania, would pave the way for a transformational career.

Long before the years of her transformational career, however, Zahra observed behaviors and had experiences at home that forever changed her outlook on life. Zahra recalled the challenges:

My parents were strict, but Dad was even more so than Mom. He would always remind us that he did not bring us to Kenya to play around. His presence in the home would always make us afraid and we would run away and hide whenever he returned from Arusha, where he was based. The times he was not around were the best for us. But Mom drank heavily and she suffered from his abuse. Dad would often beat her and abuse her emotionally. This violence scarred me for life. It led me to select men in my life who were not good for me. I saw myself as being needy and thus sought needy relationships (Zahra, personal interview, January 11, 2023).

Compounding this difficult home life for Zahra was the news of her Dad contracting the HIV virus in the early 2000s. Her dad transmitted the virus to her mother. Her mother gave the virus to their unborn child. This revelation was made only to Zahra at the time she was barely 18 years old. Her parents believed that she could handle the news because she was the eldest child. Zahra carried this knowledge with her, recognizing that the lifestyle they had grown accustomed to was gradually disappearing. Zahra was thrusted into the position of caregiver for herself and her younger siblings.

Zahra's lived experience, in pursuit of socio-economic development, was thus a compelling need to balance family and community interests with those of her own. Even before Zahra could take the steps necessary to embark on her career, she was saddled with opposition and lack of support from family and community for what she wanted to pursue (music) and was also compelled to prioritize the welfare of her siblings due to the health of her parents. These extenuating circumstances greatly influenced when, how and to what degree Zahra pursued and attained socio-economic development.

Siya From South Africa

Born to illiterate parents in a South African township suffering under the weight of apartheid in the 1960s, Siya quickly embraced the responsibility to "extricate" his family from poverty. His bad behavior and indiscipline as an adolescent put the achievement of this objective in jeopardy. Siya was arrested and sent to prison at the tender age of 16. "I would describe the experience as being in the wrong place at the wrong time – a common refrain for many young people in my day," Siya recalled. "Going to prison fundamentally changed my perspective. It was a wake-up call. I realized that I had to change my ways if I wanted to survive, let alone make good on my promise to extricate my family from poverty" (Siya, personal interview, September 14, 2022).

Prison more closely oriented Siya to the reasons behind the abject living conditions of his people: apartheid. Their material poverty was made worse by a lack of freedom and the rampant extrajudicial killing and dislocation of family, friends, and neighbors. Siya grew convinced that his own survival depended on what happened to his people. He turned his focus to personal development through education with a fervor that could not be diminished. But just as he sought an opening through acquisition of a degree in law, his environment intervened once more. "My dream was to study law, but I was made to forgo this because of guidance from a professor…He advised me not to train and work to interpret laws that violated the rights of the South African majority while the same laws helped the minority retain its grip on power. I therefore pursued a degree in the social sciences" (Siya, personal interview, September 14, 2022).

Siya was disappointed about not studying law but his hunger for activism remained. He found a way to fight as an activist student leader at his university during what he described as the height of the liberation struggle in the late 1980s. The University of the North was to become the hotbed of the liberation struggle. The school was under a state of emergency law, rendering it vulnerable to years of occupation by soldiers and policemen. Siya assumed leadership of the liberation struggle movement on campus by way of his oratory skills and his ability to organize. "On a memorable occasion," he shared, "I led student protests with a speech in which I conveyed to the authorities that we are not going to class until our leaders were released. Nearly 3,000 students heard me speak that day. The scene was unreal. We had the police and the military all around us, threatening to strike us down. We were ready to die in pursuit of what we believed was just" (Siya, personal interview, September 14, 2022).

Siya's involvement in the struggle and membership of the African National Congress (ANC) youth league ultimately paved the way for his entry into public service once the ANC was elected in 1994 to form the country's first democratic government. Siya would go on to enjoy a long and successful professional career in government and in business, which assured the upward trajectory of his socio-economic development.

Amie From Sierra Leone

Amie was the daughter of a Chief in a small and materially poor village whose people survived mostly on subsistence farming and fishing. Amie felt the pressure to excel, as the Chief's daughter, and to behave according to the dictates of her conservative community. She had to be a role model and assume leadership at an early age. These responsibilities were further pronounced when she underwent, at the age of six, her community's rite of passage ceremony for young girls to become women – what is commonly known as female circumcision. Amie was the youngest in the group and she said she "felt a sense of accomplishment" afterward. She explained that "the experience changed how I viewed myself and also how people in the village viewed me. I had become a woman and could no longer be mocked in the village as being a young girl. I felt a sense of belonging" (Amie, personal interview, January 6, 2023).

Amie felt the same pride from the formal education she was allowed to receive. Most girls in her village were discouraged or even prevented from going to school. But Amie's mother, a trader and the breadwinner of the family, insisted that her daughters learn in the classroom. The learning and exposure to the Peace Corps volunteers who ran the school she attended seared in her mind the value of personal development. "I felt empowered," she declared, and this empowerment enabled Amie to envision a life that was far different from what her peers in her village envisioned for themselves. For one, women in her village were subservient to men. They had no voice and were expected to take a back-seat to their male counterparts. Later experiences in the United States would lead her to challenge these gender roles, but exposure to them in her village left an indelible mark to such a degree that Amie shared "I still subscribe to the idea that women should be subservient at home – even if I believe otherwise and I act differently in the workplace" (Amie, personal interview, January 6, 2023).

Tragedy struck the family when Amie was 10 years old. Her father died unexpectedly, forcing Amie and her older sister to relocate to Freetown, where their mother ran her trading business. It was a shocking transition. The communal life and safe environment she knew in her village gave way to a filthy urban setting, where people barely tolerated each other as they pursued their interests. The living conditions in Freetown were such that anyone who could find a way out of the country did just that. And so it was for Amie. Their eldest sister had earlier immigrated to the United States. Amie joined her sister in Northern Virginia in 1990, beginning a journey that forever changed the trajectory of her socio-economic development.

Discussion

Lived Experience as Storytelling

Storytelling was the format the participants used to describe their lived experience. They each shared how their lives unfolded through a retelling of stories about events and milestones that shaped the direction of their lives. Osie shared fond memories of life in Ghana and the stories behind his relocation to North America. Zhara described growing up in Kenya and juxtaposing the experience with life in her native Tanzania, where she embarked on a transformational career in music and endured setbacks. Siya shared stories of his activism against apartheid and his eventual foray into diplomacy and business. Amie recounted her experience as a village Chief's daughter, who weathered the expectations of her traditional society to make a life for herself outside of her homeland.

In the retelling of their storied experiences, the trajectory of development, personal agency/action, and social influence were consistent themes that emerged. These themes brought to light the convergence of personal choices and environmental circumstances that manifested in each of the participants' lives. For example, the participants' choices or decision-making, related to major and minor life decisions, were greatly influenced by their observations of family and community behaviors, by enduring a traumatic experience, or experiencing a physical relocation from home to another land. The participants' observations of family and community behaviors influenced their perceptions of what was possible for them to achieve. Experiencing trauma or relocating to another land had a similar life altering effect – either helping to set the stage upon which the participants' lives could unfold, forcing the participants to defer their dreams, or stifling the participants' dreams altogether.

The participants' storytelling demonstrated how each of them made meaning of their lives through stories. Their stories were not only about their individual experience, as Clandinin and Rosiek (2007) observed when discussing the importance of narrative inquiry as a research methodology, "but also [about] the social, cultural, and institutional narratives within which individuals' experiences are constituted, shaped, expressed, and enacted" (p. 35). The participants' storytelling provided a well-spring of information, rich data that explained and amplified the human conditions they experienced. The sum total of their experiences was a confluence or convergence of personal choices and environmental circumstances. This overarching theme underscored the baseline theory of social learning: that personal source of control and environmental sources of control – the interplay of the two in the lives of human beings – determines human behavior and ultimately dictates the achievement of human accomplishments (Bandura, 1974).

Research Question Two

How does choice (decision-making) and culture (environment) influence everyday Africans' ability to develop socio-economically?

The following are the theme and sub-themes from the above research question.

Table 3. How choice (decision-making) and culture (environment) influence socio-economic development

	Choice and Culture	
Theme	**Sub-Theme**	**Issues Raised**
Confluence of choice and culture on development	Educational Pursuit	Personal interests Parental involvement Community expectations Educational standards
	Professional Pursuit	Personal interest Parental involvement Community expectations Professional opportunities
	Personal/Social Life	Family experience Community expectations Outside influence

Source: Field work 2022-2023

Sub-Theme One: Educational Pursuit

All of the participants raised formal education and the acquisition of the same as significant considerations for their development, considerations that were consistently espoused by participants' parents and inculcated in the expectations of their communities. Parental involvement, specifically, parents' demands for participants to study conventional or traditional fields such as engineering or law greatly influenced the participants. Participants' personal interests in subject matters that were different from those which were favored by their parents or influential adults in their lives also featured prominently in the participants' narratives about the role choice and culture played in their lived experience. The educational standards in the locations in which the participants obtained their education also proved instrumental in participants' choice and culture considerations. For example, all the participants, with the exception of Siya from South Africa, primarily secured higher learning at the University level outside of their respective homelands because of concerns about inadequate infrastructure and resources in their home countries.

Sub-Theme Two: Professional Pursuit

All of the participants raised employment at the professional level as the end goal of their developmental efforts and a consideration that depended on choice and culture. Each had an area of particular interest, but parental involvement and/or community expectations influenced their decisions to pursue, delay pursuit of, or abandon their personal interests. Also common among the participants was consideration for the opportunities available to them at the professional level within the countries of their birth. The participants generally viewed their homelands as lacking adequate opportunities for employment, particularly employment that allowed them to develop and grow in terms of promotions and assignments. The lack of adequate professional opportunities weighed on their minds as participants contemplated their careers and the locations in which to attain the said careers. Siya from South Africa was an exception, as he joined his country's foreign service and traveled for work overseas before returning home to find work in the private sector.

Sub-Theme Three: Personal/Social Life

All of the participants raised their personal and social life as areas that were also influenced by choice and culture. Participants cited family history and experience and community expectations, such as domestic violence or traditional gender role expectations within the community, as factors that impressed upon them the values they should embrace or the outlook they should have. These same experiences and expectations also served to underpin the participants' psychological disposition about romantic relationships, especially as it related to the kind of people whom they should date or marry. Outside influences, notably exposure to western society and customs, figured prominently in the participants' considerations.

The following were the exemplary narrative inquiry and case study findings from each participant.

Osie From Ghana

Osie from Ghana was not encouraged or allowed to pursue his interests in sports. His Dad was a particular stumbling block in this area. Father and son did not connect emotionally and Osie felt unsupported in following his true passion. This lack of support led Osie to focus on academics and engineering, the areas others around him valued most. He made the conscious decision as an adult to obtain an engineering degree in Canada. Osie was knowledgeable in this field and believed he could fashion a desirable career out of the academic training he had received in it. Osie could not secure employment in Canada after graduating, however, despite his earnest interest and efforts in doing so. His foreign national status and what he described as "a lack of opportunities" were hurdles he just could not overcome.

So, Osie returned home to Ghana with the promise of a contract with an American energy company constructing a thermal plant in the country. This contract fell-through before it ever started, leading to some "lean" years for Osie in Ghana. Osie eventually gained employment as an engineer with local companies, but these jobs offered low pay and limited growth opportunities. Osie had to once again look outside of Ghana by way of immigration to the United States, where his brother had been born and was a citizen. "I knew that I wanted to immigrate to the United States, even as I worked in Ghana," Osie explained. Professional development was important to him and "I wanted a better quality of life. The [socio-economic] conditions in Ghana did not permit me to consider staying in Ghana" (Osie, personal interview, October 20, 2022).

A better life is precisely what Osie secured in moving to the US in 2011. Gainful employment with better pay enabled him to resettle his wife and child in the US, to purchase a home, and to pursue a Masters degree in Business Administration, which further increased his earning potential. By 2017, Osie and family were living the American Dream as middle-class homeowners in a suburb in the American South. But even as his fortunes changed for the better, Osie could not escape the interplay of choice and culture (environment) in his life. He experienced discrimination at work on account of his African identity, preventing him from advancing in his career as he had envisioned. The onset of the 2020 health pandemic and economic downtown further rendered him expendable in the company. Osie was laid off. Environmental factors were at play, Osie reflected. But, he continued, "I likely could have prepared for the job loss by hedging toward something else. I could have made better decisions, anticipated the likely changes in my industry and the job market. But I did not. I did not seek out new job opportunities in a proactive fashion" (Osie, personal interview, October 20, 2022). Osie would learn from the impact of his environment and his own choices and seek to better himself for an eventual return home.

Zahra From Tanzania

Zahra made the conscious decision to embrace music and become a singer because her cultural environment in Kenya, where arts was encouraged, made this possible. Yet it would take Zahra years to make a career out of music because her cultural environment in Tanzania, where the family returned in the early 2000s after her parents' HIV diagnosis, did not promote the arts as a professional calling. The Tanzanian community "demonized" music. Families went to great lengths to prevent their children from getting involved, she explained, much like Zahra's uncle did when he told her to stop singing and threatened to tell her father after Zahra had latched onto a local group in Dar es Salam as a background singer.

With her parents sick and music on the backburner, Zahra focused attention on taking care of her siblings. She leaned on boyfriends, including an older, married man to help meet her needs. It was an experience – having romantic relationships based on need – that she connected to both circumstance and childhood memories of her parents' relationship. Choice and culture were again at play, much like in the trajectory of her music career. The lack of cultural environment support for music had led Zahra to study political science and communication, the "anything but music" option that her Dad forced upon her during Zahra's university years. Yet music had remained a passion. She rebelled by skipping classes and instead going to Nairobi's national theater to look for roles in music and acting projects. Zahra was deliberate and persistent in her choice to become a singer despite the challenges of her community.

She entered the Tanzanian and Southern African music scene in 2008 after an appearance on a television series that highlighted her talents. With the financial support of a new lover, Zahra recorded her first album and filmed a video for a hit single. "The stars were aligning at that point. I was singing, traveling all across Africa and Europe and making money. I had achieved the [professional heights] that I'd long dreamed of attaining" (Zahra, personal interview, January 11, 2023). Zahra went on to leverage her fame and stardome for acceptance into Tanzanian high society. She rubbed shoulders with famous people, influence makers, and even politicians. Her persistence and resilience to sing had paid off. But where she succeeded in music, she would soon fail in relationships on account of choices and her cultural environment.

The years 2009-2010 ushered in changes. Insecurities brought on by her fame led her new lover to have an affair because he suspected (wrongly) that she had done the same thing. Hurt and humiliated, Zahra retaliated by having her own affair. Their relationship never recovered from that point. Zahra was faced with the prospect of seeing him around town with other women. She could not bear the experience because she was deeply in love with him. So, Zahra made the decision to relocate from the base of her music career in Dar es Salaam to another city. And that was when her troubles truly began.

In 2010-2011, Zahra met a man. She explained that he "was supposed to be a rebound, and while many of my friends told me to ditch the relationship for reasons obvious to them, I insisted on continuing it. The sex was great, I admit, and the romance quickly developed into a deeply intimate relationship. What I didn't count on was the relationship being toxic. The man abused me" (Zahra, personal interview, January 11, 2023). Beatings and emotionally abusive exchanges were commonplace. Zahra elected to stay through it all. In fact, she doubled-down on this decision by conceiving a child with the man. She felt "the weight" of her culture bearing down on her at the age of 30, many years beyond the age women in her society were expected to marry and have children. Zahra elaborated:

He was more like my father, very domineering. He slapped me for talking back, talking to other men, for not coming home at a certain time. I tried to rationalize the behavior. I needed him. I needed to be loved, to belong to someone, to be validated, to have someone to show-off and be seen as having someone…my parents' [relationship] likely contributed to me rationalizing the behavior (Zahra, personal interview, January 11, 2023).

Zahra was also fearful that the fame she had garnered from music would render her vulnerable to being blamed. So, she kept quiet and endured the pain. Depression set in, as she looked around and realized that she had lost the father of her child to another woman with whom he had also fathered another child. Depression deepened, as she realized that she was far removed from the music career she had in Dar es Salaam. Depression overwhelmed, as Zahra realized that her savings had run-out. She had reached a breaking point. Zahra was literally and figuratively flat broke. So, she did and thought of little else but to end her own life.

Siya From South Africa

Choice and culture permeated Siya's adolescent and adult years. "For me and many others like me," he confided, "those years were a time to resist and a time to build. These twin motivations led me to balance my choices with the cultural expectations of my community" (Siya, personal interview, September 14, 2022). Siya was addressing, in the above comments, his decision to educate himself and concurrently participate in the struggle against apartheid. His choice to do so was influenced by both internal and external factors.

Education was important because he saw it as the gateway to a better life, a way to escape the impoverished conditions of his home. Getting a formal education and the accompanying success became a devotion, a "black tax" successful children from poor families had to pay by taking care of their family and community. And this was so, Siya explained, because one's success was not his alone. It also belonged to the community. Regarding the struggle movement, joining it appealed to Siya's disposition. He was an agitator, evidenced by his troubled childhood and imprisonment, as well as his instincts to study law in university.

Siya's choice to educate himself and join the struggle was also culture or environment driven. Apartheid created the material poverty and lack of freedoms South Africa's majority endured. Apartheid made him think that he could only aspire to be a laborer because that was what he saw around him and that was what the system permitted for Africans. Siya saw a way out, or at least a way to exercise some degree of agency and control, through education. As he worked on getting his degree, Siya capitalized on the chance to fight the system directly. He organized and led student protests in university, then worked underground as an ANC youth league activist to counter the apartheid regime.

His education in social sciences, activism, and the environmental conditions that proved influential coincided with a period of political opening in South Africa in 1994. South Africans gained the right to political self-determination and, with it, the ability to form institutions that required the education and talents of people like Siya. He was in the right place at the right time when candidates were needed to fill openings in South Africa's foreign affairs department. Siya went on to work as a diplomat at the United Nations in New York and in another country in Africa. He also served as an advisor to the Foreign Minister for many years. Siya not only traveled the world and gained a wealth of experience during those years, but also played an instrumental role in shaping South Africa's foreign policy and relationship with key allies. Siya's choice and culture had made all of this possible. By the mid-2000s, choice and culture would once again compel a transition for Siya into business because of prevailing politics in South Africa.

Amie From Sierra Leone

Amie's socio-economic development was influenced by choice and culture from the onset of her childhood. Her status as the child of a Chief and decision to be a role model, her rite of passage into womanhood, and her relocation to Freetown after her father's passing were all a confluence of choice and culture – Amie's young age at the time notwithstanding. But it was her transition from Freetown to the US that forever changed the course of her development. She and family elected to leave Sierra Leone in 1990 because the country had deteriorated to such a degree that it could no longer provide opportunities for social mobility for her people. A rebel war would break-out in the country just months after Amie's departure for the same reasons.

Despite the challenges of integrating into the cultural fabric of the US, where the idea of community was different and children poked fun at her for being African and for speaking English with an accent, Amie thrived in the Northern Virginia suburb she and her sisters settled. Food and material resources were plenty, as was access to quality education. Amie leaned on the self-discipline she learned in her village to not only overcome the communal challenges of her new life in the US but to also focus on achievement. She explained,

The US did not offer a communal setting where people genuinely looked after each other…The flip side [of this lack of community] was a focus on individualism that provoked ambition. I became motivated to achieve at a high level. The choice to move to the US gave me confidence, freedom, and a voice. It was not my choice alone, given my young age at the time, but I welcomed it and knew what it would do for my education to support my material development (Amie, personal interview, January 6, 2023).

Amie carried this ambition to university in Southern Virginia, joining a sorority there and taking leadership positions that cemented her transition and transformation from the impoverished life she lived in Sierra Leone just several years earlier. But her journey would not proceed without challenges. Amie fell pregnant at the start of her senior year in university. She was not in a committed relationship with the father. Amie struggled with the decision but ultimately decided to have her baby while finishing her last year of school. "My value system, more than anything else, compelled me to keep the pregnancy," she confided (Amie, personal interview, January 6, 2023).

The same values that had kept her oriented and focused when she first arrived in the US were again being put to the test. Amie's cultural environment in the US, the support she had and the learning she obtained that enabled her to establish a future for herself, rendered Amie capable of adhering and living up to her values. She gave life to a beautiful baby girl and, with a business degree in hand in 2002, embarked on a successful career in the corporate world. Choice and culture had been instrumental through it all. They would intervene once more to play a role in Amie's return to Sierra Leone.

Discussion

How choice (decision-making) and culture (environment) influence socio-economic development

Choice and culture were instrumental in the socio-economic development process of the participants. Each had experiences in choice and culture operating interdependently to alter – for better or worse – the path of the participants' development. Common among all participants was the fact that (1) choice was often influenced by culture or the environment; (2) culture or the environment often influenced choice; and (3) choice and culture influenced minor and major life decisions such as schooling, residence, career path, relationships, and community/political participation.

Choice and culture was evident in each of the participants' socio-economic development journey, especially in their acquisition of formal education, professional training and employment, and their personal/social life. Osie struggled through his Dad and community's influence to settle on engineering as an education and career path. He then left Ghana for the US in pursuit of social mobility, only to be challenged by discrimination, a global pandemic, and his choice not to actively prepare for the job loss he eventually suffered. Zahra overcame the resistance of family and community to embrace a transformational career in music, only to lose this career to choices in relationships and efforts to meet her society's expectations. Siya blazed a trail of political activism while attaining an academic degree in social sciences that he did not plan to acquire. This background and South Africa's political opening in the early 1990s were the catalyst for Siya's successful career in diplomacy, which he eventually left to pursue a career in business. Amie leveraged her humble beginnings in Sierra Leone to harness values and a discipline that would enable her to thrive in the different and enabling environment in the US. Decisions, including whether to keep an unexpected pregnancy, were forced upon her. She responded with determination and, in doing so, amplified how choice and culture can combine to shape the direction of one's life.

Evidence from the exploration of the participants' lives aligned with Bandura's (1974) theory about human behavior, specifically the interplay between or the "bidirectional influence" of personal control and environmental sources of control. What each of the participants were able to accomplish or not accomplish "[resulted] from reciprocal interaction of external circumstances with a host of personal determinants including endowed potentialities, acquired competencies, reflective thought, and a high level of self-initiative" (p. 867). This interdependency of choice and culture proves significant when the consideration is social development.

To be sure, choice and culture, as established in the literature, are prerequisites for individual and societal transformation (Arendt, 1958; Arnold, 1869; Bandura, 1977; Barker, 1997; Gemmill and Oakley, 1992; Soyinka, 2000). They make change possible through leadership, the type and kind Barker (1997) instructed had to be different from our traditional concept of the construct: a man in a position of authority or one with traits that can turn around a struggling enterprise. Barker (1997) employed us to define leadership as a social process if our goal is freedom, education, or social development – human endeavors that require the navigation of complex social and political processes.

Freedom, education, and social development were precisely what the participants of the study were after. Their achievement of these goals depended on choice (their decision-making). Their achievement of these goals was also predicated on the culture (environmental circumstances or sources of control) they experienced. The resulting "bidirectional influence process" of the two dictated or shaped the course of the lives of each participant. Their individual examples underscored the significance of the conceptual framework assumption that if people are empowered to make good choices about our life pursuits, and we are supported, rather than hindered, by our cultural environment, we might be better equipped to navigate the conditions that influence our socio-economic development.

Research Question Three

How does the lived experience of everyday Africans inform understanding about achieving social transformation?

The following are the theme and sub-themes from the above research question.

Table 4. How participants' lived experience informs understanding about achieving social transformation

	Achieving Social Transformation	
Theme	**Sub-Theme**	**Issues Raised**
Lived experience informing social transformation	Choice of residence	School Career Opportunities
	Path of career	Opportunities Advancement and growth Organizational affiliation
	Condition of country	Lack of opportunities Infrastructure Politics

Source: Field work 2022-2023

Sub-Theme One: Choice of Residence

The choice or election of where to pursue socio-economic development was a common consideration for the participants. In the exploration of how participants' lived experience informs understanding about achieving social transformation, the researcher discovered that each participant carefully considered the level of education they required to attain the careers they envisioned for themselves. This calculation followed another careful consideration about their prevailing environment, notably available job opportunities and political stability. The considerations, including those enabled by family members, led participants to leave their homelands in pursuit of socio-economic development elsewhere in the world. Siya from South Africa was the one participant who received higher education in his home country.

Sub-Theme Two: Path of Career

The path of career taken by the participants in pursuit of socio-economic development was a common consideration among the participants. In the exploration of how participants' lived experience informs understanding about achieving social transformation, the researcher discovered that the career paths selected by the participants contributed to their decisions to leave their homelands. Participants were in search of professional opportunities, advancement and growth, all of which existed in limited supply at home. Organizational affiliation was also instrumental, as participants became attached to enterprises with presence and reach outside of their respective homelands. Siya from South Africa had a slightly different experience, as he obtained employment in South Africa with his government and yet worked outside of South Africa with his foreign service. Zahra from Tanzania also found employment in Tanzania as a musician after struggling to find employment in more traditional fields.

Sub-Theme Three: Condition of Country

The condition of their respective countries was an important point of consideration among the participants. In the exploration of how participants' lived experience informs understanding about achieving social transformation, the researcher discovered that participants placed great stock in the economic and political environment of their nations. Participants examined their nations for opportunities, quality of infrastructure, and the nature of politics and they weighed their decision to pursue self development in their nations and whether to participate in the life of their nations against these important considerations. Siya from South Africa gained employment with his government in South Africa, but worked outside of South Africa for years until his return to pursue a career in business when his environment permitted such a transition.

The following were the exemplary narrative inquiry and case study findings from each participant.

Osie From Ghana

Osie from Ghana learned from losing his job that he had to constantly prepare for what might be next and this preparation required deliberate decision-making to anticipate change in uncertain environments. His previous life experiences had demonstrated this much. To be sure, Osie developed himself outside of Ghana's unstable environment because his middle-class Ghanaian parents had the means to send him to a more stable environment in Canada for an engineering degree. He elected to remain in Canada after graduating, but he could not find employment to support his planned residency. He thus returned home, a place that had not featured in his plans because of the lack of employment opportunities and poor socio-economic conditions. Osie had in fact decided to return only after securing a contract with an American company doing business in Ghana. This contract did not come to fruition, leading to months of unemployment.

Osie did eventually land a job in Ghana, several in fact, and while he gained a wealth of experience in these positions, the low salary, lack of growth potential, and quality of life standards, affirmed his perspective that Ghana was not the place in which he could develop socio-economically. His response to this affirmation of belief was to leave the country yet again. Osie believed firmly that "The conditions in Ghana did not permit [him] to consider staying in Ghana" (Osie, personal interview, October 20, 2022).

Osie left Ghana for the US after five years from the time he returned from Canada with not only his engineering skills but also the wealth of experience he had gained from his work with Ghanaian companies in the telecommunications industry focused on improving the quality of life of Ghanaians. Choice (his will to better himself) and culture (the conditions of his home country) led him to pursue life in the US. In this prioritization of his personal development, Osie abandoned or put to the side his individual role in the chores of Ghana's nation building.

The decision to prioritize his own development paid off. Osie landed good paying jobs in the US, sent for his wife and child to join him, obtained a Masters degree in Business Administration, bought a car and a house, and maintained the income that would allow him to send money home. Osie managed to persevere even as cultural challenges in his adopted home in the US surfaced, including being passed-over for promotions because of his African identity and the onset of an unprecedented global health pandemic in 2020, which cost him his job. He even managed to establish a fledgling business in men and women's African apparel in the shadows of his job loss during the pandemic. Osie had thus achieved the level of development and had settled in the kind of environment that enabled him to overcome these challenges because of choices that were informed by culture and vice versa.

Ghana did not provide the enabling environment Osie sought for socio-economic development. And while Osie left Ghana for this reason many years earlier, his mind during the course of our interview was now squarely on returning. Osie expressed a desire to return home to Ghana in order to contribute. He shared his desire to take back the engineering, business, and leadership skills he has gained to help move Ghana forward. His reasons for hesitating or delaying this return, however, were the same as those that had led him to leave Ghana many years earlier. Ghana, Osie shared, lacks the socio-economic infrastructure Osie deems necessary for his family. Osie explained his calculations, as he reflected on the tragic deaths of close friends in Ghana due to medical misdiagnosis of basic ailments:

I need to make sure that I have the financial resources to be able to provide for medical care for me and my family outside of Ghana. I need to ensure that I will be able to fly them out of there...This lack of proper medical infrastructure and resources is symptomatic of a broader problem in Ghana. Things that are important for the people are largely neglected (Osie, personal interview, October 20, 2022).

Zahra From Tanzania

Zahra did not take her own life. The presence of her son and her will to live for him, after serious complications during the birth, centered her focus on survival. She battled through depression and what she described as "being in a bad mental space" during the same years that she experienced her fame and fortune decline to levels worse than when she was juggling boyfriends to make ends meet in her early twenties. Single-motherhood took its toll, especially as the father of her child elected to keep both his affection and money from Zahra and their son. Both the government and social custom were no help in enforcing child-support payments. Zahra thus resorted to selling her possessions to make ends meet. The specter of missed opportunities were not lost on her as she described the roller coaster of her social and economic development journey. For one, Zahra admitted to having the chance to become a member of the country's national parliament:

I had an opportunity to take part in politics – to become a member of Parliament for the opposition. This opportunity came because of my fame and public persona. I explored it when I was asked, but my heart was never really into it. The divide between the opposition and ruling Party convinced me to back away...the ruling Party came to my home and talked with my parents about me not getting involved with the opposition. "She is our daughter," they told my parents. "She shouldn't be doing this." The experience turned me off completely. I felt that politics was not for me, even as I saw the opportunity to use my influence to create positive change. My heart was in music and that's where I wanted to be (Zahra, personal interview, January 11, 2023).

Zahra's heart was completely immersed in music, and yet her firsthand experience with and exposure to influential politicians had an equally negative effect concerning political participation. These men, and a few women, showed her the sordid side of politics because they felt a need to exploit her fame. Some wanted her support to increase their standing with the electorate. Some wanted money, and others simply wanted sex. Each desired something different yet they all exposed a motivation that was not anchored to the needs of the people they claimed to serve. Some even confided to her that while they lacked conviction in particular policies and leaders at the forefront of the nation's politics, they were nonetheless inclined to tow the line because doing so ensured their own political survival. Others proved through their lack of education and appreciation for public discourse that they were unfit for the positions they held, demonstrating that patronage and nepotism, not qualification, were the bottomline considerations for work in the public sector.

Zahra thus avoided political participation at the height of her music career because of the nature of politics in Tanzania. She found it abhorrent and the people in it self-centered. The decision at the time did not seem material to her socio-economic development and that of her nation. Music sustained her and she was able to leverage the profession to both make a living and to raise the social-consciousness of her people, much like how one of her early hit-songs gained notoriety. But as life continued to unfold with the interplay of choice and culture causing her music career to fade and rendering her a single-mother with little money and support, Zahra's decision to avoid political participation took on new meaning. The opportunity to positively influence, through a seat in Parliament or another platform years earlier, the social-ills she ultimately experienced – violence against women, gender inequality, and lack of child support enforcement – loomed large. Zahra was now trying to make a come-back with this mindset. She was determined to regain control of her life and to give back to her community and sisterhood of single-mothers through application of the lessons she learned throughout her arduous journey.

Siya From South Africa

His posting in another country in Africa was a lonely place for him during his tour of duty in the country in the mid-2000s, Siya recalled. His family's absence made the experience unbearable. Returning home to South Africa thus became a prime motivation, as did the allure of making money outside of government, which had become increasingly possible due to the redistributive economic policies of the new government. South African companies were mandated by law to open up ownership of their enterprises to the country's indigenous people under the policy of black economic empowerment. Siya left the Foreign Affairs Department upon his return from his posting in another country in Africa to work in a private company that his previous boss at the Department had also left to join months earlier. Siya went on to spend twelve years with the company, leveraging the opportunity in those years to accumulate promotions and to become associated with a statistic he proudly shared: he had become a member of a small elite group, the five percent of South Africans who earned over one million Rands per year.

Siya returned to government service after his twelve year absence. He was recruited into another Department to take over a senior assignment that was crucial to the proper functioning of government. Siya would also eventually leave this assignment after a few years to try his hand at practicing law after obtaining the law degree that had inspired him during his university days. The new government assignment nonetheless paralleled Siya's previous experiences in terms of influence and impact on the life of his nation. As a student leader and member of the ANC Youth League, Siya fought to liberate his people from apartheid, going so far as to orchestrate under-ground activities that undermined the South African government. As a diplomat, Siya helped to shepherd a democratic South Africa's foray onto the international stage, including navigating thorny policy issues, such as the war in Bosnia, conflicts in Africa, nuclear proliferation, and the Israeli/Palestinian conflict, that shaped the young nation's relationships with key allies and multinational institutions. His participation in the nation building of South Africa was undeniable and impactful.

As the seeds of his and others' work started to grow and bear fruit for the country in the mid-2000s, Siya and many like him elected to leave their posts for the private sector. Siya explained his own reasoning for leaving the government the first time: "My decision to leave the Foreign [Ministry] for business interests was a choice I made based on what I felt my family needed at the time. The opportunity was there to go and make money and I felt I had done my time in government" (Siya, personal interview, September 14, 2022). The choice to leave was his to make. His personal situation warranted a transition and focus on money, and his culture (the prevailing political and economic conditions in South Africa) permitted such a transition and focus. Siya admitted, however, that his departure from government and those of many others like him came at an immeasurable cost:

At some point after 1994 – beyond the Mandela years – we assigned our new baby [South Africa] to reckless hands. We stumbled and made huge mistakes as a result. Even as we try to course correct now, there are embedded challenges: corruption, contempt for institutions, state of lawlessness, victimhood when in power, and a lack of citizen activism and participation – all choices that we South Africans continue to make. Many of us were and still are focused on our own development. This created a void, which was filled by people driven by self-interest and a self-enrichment agenda. Others in government simply became state functionaries, which prevented them from focusing on taking actions that could remedy the situation; they were more concerned with service delivery for the people. This left the organization [the ruling African National Congress] in the hands of those who were more concerned with consumption and material gain (Siya, personal interview, September 14, 2022).

South Africa's democratic experiment began to suffer not too long after 1994, Siya reflected. It began to resemble the experience of the other nations on the continent and a contributing factor, Siya explained, was the weakness of citizen participation in the life of the nation.

Amie From Sierra Leone

Amie worked a few years after university, making money and significant contributions as sustainability analyst for an investment firm whose clients were shielded from the brunt of the 2008 global financial crisis as a result of the research and analysis Amie and her colleagues conducted to protect their investments. This impactful work drove Amie toward further self-development in 2011, the pursuit of a Masters in Business Administration that would help her climb the corporate ladder. Her sights were set on the international arena, namely the African continent.

Amie returned to Sierra Leone for the first time since her departure in 1990 during the course of her MBA studies in 2012. The trip was focused on family. What she experienced on the ground there – the state of the nation, development issues, poverty, mismanagement of public resources – changed her perspective. She came away with a sense of obligation, a duty to return and contribute to the betterment of her people. Amie acted on this desire to return in 2014, abandoning her work in South Africa with a private equity firm after just six months for the chance to apply her business knowledge and experience in Sierra Leone's telecommunications sector. Amie recalled that,

There was also a part of me that wanted to relearn my country, to be a part of my homeland once again. Yet, part of the decision to leave was also based on the discrimination I experienced in South Africa, the unfamiliar, communal environment that was hostile to non-South Africans. I did not believe I could endure the experience for much longer. This [tug of emotions] led me to relocate to Freetown...But challenges were yet to come (Amie, personal interview, January 6, 2023).

Amie experienced a honeymoon phase upon her return. She found Sierra Leone peaceful, despite its lack of development and visible issues with systemic corruption. She enjoyed settling in and rediscovering inspirations in the traditions and customs of her country. With time, however, and with the reference point of her previous cultural experience in Sierra Leone, Amie began to appreciate the seismic changes the country and people lived through. She had a visceral reaction to what she witnessed and what she said still prevailed:

Sierra Leone is worse now than it has ever been in its history, with the exception perhaps of the rebel war years. The economy is in ruins, but so too is the social and cultural [fabric of the country]. The value system is worse, morals are down, distorted. Education is not valued. Kids feel entitled, they use drugs, prostitution is rampant, and there is a general decline in the nation's work-ethic. There might be a combination of reasons for this: the rebel war, lack of education in the country, influence of development aid, exposure to western culture…but everyone seems bent on looking for a hand-out, rather than applying themselves to learning and becoming someone (Amie, personal interview, January 6, 2023).

The reality of the social decay in Sierra Leone that Amie described seemed to exacerbate the problems she began to experience in her professional endeavors, problems that stretched far beyond the country's poor business environment. Around 2018, Amie began to participate in the politics of the nation. Her participation coincided with that year's general elections. She was vocal, demonstrated support for the ruling Party, and she opposed the opposition candidate for what she described as his less-than-stellar qualifications. She thought he was a terrible choice for the country because of his background (a former coup leader) and his "limited" vision for the country. Her opposition did not go unnoticed when the ruling Party failed to win and the opposition regained control of the government.

In the ensuing months, Amie transitioned to serving as an independent consultant, a role through which she hoped to develop business (market research and due diligence projects) for clients looking to enter Sierra Leone's private market. Amie soon realized that the success of her new endeavor depended not just on the condition of the country's fragile business infrastructure such as banking, energy, transportation and human capital, but also on political connections. The new government had a controlling influence in private sector development and it leveraged this influence to steer business to those whom it favored and away from those whom it did not. Amie's opposition in 2018 to the new government placed her squarely in the disfavored camp. Business opportunities were thus no longer as robust. Growing professionally became a chore.

With the same government now in its fifth year and seeking yet another five year mandate in the 2023 elections, Amie questioned the viability of what drove her to return to Sierra Leone in the first place: contributing to the work of uplifting the nation. The government had become entrenched in power. Those leading the government did not seem keen on relinquishing power any time soon, Amie reasoned. So, did she regret her decision to return? Amie responded without hesitating: "I do not regret returning to Sierra Leone. The move has stretched my learning and added to my personal growth. But I often wonder what could have been had I stayed in a more developed environment with greater corporate opportunities" (Amie, personal interview, January 6, 2023).

Discussion

How Participants' lived experience informs understanding about achieving social transformation

The Participants' lived experience revealed that participants were largely disengaged from participation in the national life of their nation-states. The disengagement manifested in three ways: (1) participants either elected to or were forced to leave their home country in search of better opportunities in education and employment – some returned home, others did not; (2) participants avoided involvement in or were locked out of participation in the life of their nations due to environmental reasons; or (3) participants actively participated in the life of their nations, but eventually elected to discontinue participation for personal and environmental reasons.

Osie left Ghana to develop himself in Canada, then ultimately immigrated to the United States because of poor educational standards and a lack of social mobility in Ghana. Zahra deliberately avoided involvement in the participatory process of nation building in Tanzania because of firsthand experience with the nature of politics in the country. Siya actively participated in nation building in South Africa, but elected to discontinue participation in order to pursue business interests. Amie left Sierra Leone to develop herself in the United States, then returned home to contribute. Her return was met with a serious challenge to her efforts to participate in the economic life of the country owing to politics.

In each of the participants' lived experiences examined, choice and culture played a role in distancing them from the chores of nation building. It hardened their resolve to prioritize personal development over national advancement. This evidence demonstrated the relevance and validity of the theory of social learning, which posits that human behavior is determined by the "bidirectional influence process" of personal control and environmental sources of control. Each participant made a decision to participate or not participate in the life of their nations based on the prevailing conditions in their nations. Conversely, the prevailing conditions in their nations shaped the decisions each participant made regarding the same consideration.

Evidence of social learning at play in the experience of the participants as it relates to their involvement in the socio-political life of their nations thus highlights the significance of the intersectionality between choice (personal control), culture (environmental sources of control), and socio-economic development (human accomplishments) – the conceptual framework of this study. The framework makes the assumption that if people are empowered to make good choices about our life pursuits, and we are supported, rather than hindered, by our cultural environment, we might be better equipped to navigate the conditions that influence our socio-economic development. Choice and culture interdependently enable individual and societal transformation (Arendt, 1958; Arnold, 1869; Bandura, 1977; Barker, 1997; Gemmill and Oakley, 1992; Soyinka, 2000). This choice and culture empowerment makes change possible through the social process of leadership (Barker, 1997), which encourages people to negotiate, compromise, and sacrifice in the name of nation building – the equivalent of what Barker (1997) prescribed when he identified freedom, education, and social development as goals that require the navigation of complex social and political processes.

Thus, the interplay of choice and culture, as reflected in the examples of the lived experience of the participants, negatively impacted the participants' involvement in the national life of their countries. It hindered the achievement of socio-economic development (human accomplishments) at the national level because participants did not or could not engage in the social process of leadership that would have enabled them to prioritize participation in the national life of their nations. As their narratives demonstrated, Osie and Zahra clearly opted out of direct participation in the national life of their nations. Osie left the country. While he desires a return, he has delayed the decision as a result of the conditions in Ghana. Zahra participated in the life of her country through music, but this was short-lived. She later declined the opportunity for direct engagement in Tanzanian politics when the opportunity was presented.

Siya and Amie elected to participate in the life of their nations but the absence of their engagement in the social process of leadership, which was denied to them by a confluence of choice and culture, influenced the breadth of their participation. They ultimately discontinued their participation because, in Siya's example, self improvement proved more important to him and, in Amie's example, the politics of her country proved more inhibiting for her. Since they were not entirely empowered to make good choices about their life pursuits and they were hindered by their cultural environment, they were not better equipped to navigate the conditions that influenced their decisions to participate in the social development project of their nation-states.

SUMMARY

This chapter presented the data analysis and findings of the study from data collected through a qualitative questionnaire and semi-structured interviews of the participants. The analysis was conducted based on the theoretical and conceptual framework of social learning and the relationship between choice and culture and the social process that yields development. The study leveraged narrative inquiry and case study to explore (1) how everyday Africans describe their lived experience in pursuit of socio-economic development, (2) how choice (decision-making) and culture (environment) influence everyday Africans' ability to develop socio-economically, and (3) how the lived experience of everyday Africans inform understanding about achieving social transformation.

Storytelling was the format the participants used to describe their lived experience. The participants' storytelling demonstrated how each of them made meaning of their lives through stories. They each shared how their lives unfolded through a retelling of stories about events and milestones that shaped the direction of their lives. Choice and culture were instrumental in the socio-economic development process of the participants. Each had experiences in choice and culture operating interdependently to alter – for better or worse – the path of the participants' development. Common among all participants was the fact that (a) choice was often influenced by culture or the environment; (b) culture or the environment often influenced choice; and (c) choice and culture influenced minor and major life decisions such as schooling, residence, career path, relationships, and community/political participation.

Lastly, the Participants' lived experience revealed that participants were largely disengaged from participation in the national life of their nation-states.

This disengagement manifested in one of three ways: (1) the participants elected to or were forced to leave their home country in search of better opportunities in education and employment – some returned home, others did not; (2) the participants avoided involvement in or were locked out of participation in the life of their nations due to environmental reasons; or (3) the participants actively participated in the life of their nations, but eventually elected to discontinue participation for personal and environmental reasons.

These findings demonstrate the power of choice and culture as determinants of human behavior and accomplishments. Both the qualitative questionnaire and semi-structured interview of the participants unearthed dimensions of this truth in ways that are unique to the participants but also universal to the human experience. While the results from these instruments provide answers to the research questions, they are missing the larger environmental context needed to fully grasp and appreciate the power of choice and culture, especially as it relates to the socio-economic development of our study participants. This environmental context – what transpired in the national life of the participants' home countries and its enduring influence on the participants as they embarked on their development journeys – is what we now turn to in Chapters 6 and 7.

REFERENCES

Arendt, H. (1958). *The human condition*. The University of Chicago Press.

Arnold, M. (1869). *Culture and anarchy: An essay in political and social criticism*. Macmillan.

Bandura, A. (1974). Behavior theory and the models of man. *The American Psychologist*, *29*(12), 859–869. doi:10.1037/h0037514

Bandura, A. (1977). *Social learning theory*. Prentice Hall.

Barker, R. A. (1997). How can we train leaders if we do not know what leadership is? *Human Relations*, *50*(4), 343–362. doi:10.1177/001872679705000402

Gemmill, G., & Oakley, J. (1992). Leadership: An alienating social myth? *Human Relations*, *45*(2), 113–129. doi:10.1177/001872679204500201

Soyinka, W. (2000). Culture, democracy and renewal. *Trends in Organized Crime*, *5*(3), 110–117. doi:10.1007/s12117-000-1039-2

Chapter 6
Ghana and Sierra Leone

ABSTRACT

A narrative inquiry and case study of the experience of the participants' home countries within the context of and in parallel with the participants' narratives is the focus of the next two chapters. The chapters further illuminate answers to the research questions posed in this study and help to fully appreciate the power of choice and culture in our lives. The foundation of the chapters are the research documentation and field notes the researcher authored while working as a foreign service officer during the 2004-2017 period. This period overlapped the time-period of the participants' lived experience narratives. The data provided an on-the-ground, contemporary account of relevant developments in Ghana, Tanzania, South Africa, and Sierra Leone, including economic and socio-political events that unfolded around the same period the participants pursued their own socio-economic development. The case study design, conducted instrumentally, enables the learning of broader lessons about Osie, Zahra, Siya, and Amie's lived experiences in their home countries.

INTRODUCTION

The Republics of Ghana and Sierra Leone, roughly 1000 miles apart in the Western region of the African continent, are as alike as they are different in social, economic, and political terms. The two nations have a shared history of struggle against colonialism, religiously devout peoples, experience with major political dramas that routinely cause instability and changes of government, as well as experience with underdevelopment of the national economy owing to blatant mismanagement and corruption that creates massive inequality. And yet the two nations' experiments in political organization and socio-economic

DOI: 10.4018/979-8-3693-2403-5.ch006

development have rendered quietly diametric results, the greatest example of which is the fall-out from the decade-long rebel war with which Sierra Leone continues to contend, juxtaposed with the veneer of political stability that stubbornly prevails in Ghana in view of social problems which frustrate the nation's progress. The depth and significance of these two national narratives on the people who call Ghana and Sierra Leone home are personified by the lived experience of their respective citizens, Osie and Amie.

Republic of Ghana

Osie was born and raised in Accra, Ghana at a time the country was embroiled in a vast political transition, one beckoned by the overthrow, several years earlier in 1966, of the government of independence leader Kwame Nkrumah through a military coup d'état. Corruption, political oppression, and an outsized focus on Pan-Africanism doomed Nkrumah's administration, according to the coup leaders, yet nothing really changed in the lives of the people in the years following Nkruma's demise. Ghanaians, the first peoples of Africa to gain independence from colonial rule in 1957, continued to bear witness to the steady decline of their material conditions, which occasioned additional military takeovers of the government in the ensuing years.

The successive fights over national political power did not result in modern-day Ghana enduring the kind of sustained armed rebellions that are the norm in other countries of the continent and that lead to a massive loss of human life, displacement and the destruction of vital infrastructure. Ghana's fights over political power instead coincided with the degradation of the country's immense wealth in people and resources. The nation of nearly 33.5 million in 2022 has, over the years, ranked among the lowest in the world in standard of living, healthcare, education, and opportunities for social mobility – dismal measures of human development that are readily felt through the experience of the country's physical condition.

At its peak, the weather in the country can be unbearably muggy, making the outside air feel like steam rubbing against the skin. Those who cannot afford air conditioning to escape the heat vastly outnumber those who can. The country's roads are narrow, overly congested with cars and people. Major intersections are often lined with hawkers who sell everything from food to pet animals – creating forced interactions, on-the-go, that pique the curiosity of passing motorists as much as it coaxes them into quiet resentment and scorn.

Impressive structures in the capital city, Accra, like the Holiday Inn hotel and Ghana's Defense Ministry headquarters, curiously named the Pentagon, occasionally surface along the roads, looking out of place among thatched-roof buildings and shipping containers that double as watering holes and salons. The cars on the roads are some of the oldest in the world. Many spew puffs of gray or dark-color smoke from their tailpipes, making the case that they belong to a different era and function just on the sheer force and determination of the people behind the wheel. There seem to be pockets of deserted land or unfinished construction in abundance – places where garbage, human feces, and overgrown vegetation litter the ground and cause visitors to seriously question the moniker, "best in the West," that neighbors who visit are prone to bestow upon the country.

These prevailing conditions were what Osie found when he returned to Ghana in the mid-2000s following his graduation from university in Canada. It was, he reflected during our interview, a far cry from the fond memories of his childhood years when the fortunes of his upbringing were secured by his working-class parents despite the national struggles of the post Nkrumah years. Playing sports with friends and enjoying the general freedom of life in a community setting, with open markets and sandy beaches as anchors for play, was the life Osie knew and thrived in. His retelling of his childhood and adolescent experience was laced with recollections of a nearly hassle-free life, like the many days he spent playing soccer with friends on the beach.

But Ghana had changed, Osie shared, and this change was visible in the very way people fashioned a life for themselves to attain some semblance of economic success and social mobility. All one had to do to get a sense of this reality was to travel at dusk, as Osie sometimes had to do in running errands, along Togo Circle – the long roadway that stretches through parts of Accra and snugs the perimeter of the US Embassy on Fourth Circular Road in the Cantonments neighborhood. There, under the cover of darkness, shapes of young women dressed in mini-skirts begin to appear as one drives past. They are there waiting for customers.

The scene does not seem out of the ordinary for a struggling city in Africa or elsewhere in the world for that matter, until one considers that the women are an eclectic bunch. There are Ghanaians among them, but in equally great numbers are foreigners from as far away as Morocco and as close as Nigeria, Ivory Coast, and Togo. They are there not because prostitution is unique to Accra but because of the easy flow of money available to many of their clients through the drug trade that is so pervasive in the country.

At the time of Osie's return home, the US Embassy's Drug Enforcement Agency (DEA) had a mandate to monitor and counter illegal drug trafficking in Ghana, a country that was fast becoming a hub in the region for drug dealers because of the availability of exploitable infrastructure and people. Much of the DEA's work was done through engagement with private entities and government officials, including those in the security cluster. In this countering effort, none of the aforementioned were able to publicize the full scope of the problem in the way the country's media could or ever did. Newspapers were routinely littered with stories about major interdictions at border crossings or drug deals gone wrong. They detailed the collusion that enabled the trade – private citizens working as drug mules, port authorities clearing inspections, judges dismissing cases on a technicality, and senior government officials looking the other way because of bribes or vested interest in the cargoes on the move.

Within the contours of the stories printed was the ever-present concern over the larger public interest. The choices made by those involved, including figures responsible for leading the country, had a limiting effect on the development of both the nation and her people. Osie witnessed all of this when he returned home. It was a decision, his return, that was rooted in his inability to secure a job in Canada, where he went to school, as well as on the promise of a contract with an American energy company constructing a thermal plant in the country. As almost indicative of his improbable experience finding work in Canada, the said contract fell-through before it ever started, leading to some "lean" years for Osie once he arrived home. It took him some time to find work, but even after finding it as an engineer with local companies, his jobs proved to be gateways for low pay and limited growth, not the path for mobility he had envisioned as a student. The full scope of Osie's experience in those lean years could be observed and felt most precisely in the socio-political dynamics in the country that rendered prostitution and illicit drug trafficking so widespread.

By 2008, the people of Ghana were far removed from the tumultuous coup years of the 1960s, 1970s and 1980s, when successive military men took it upon themselves to try to right the ship of poor governance, only to fail in the same manner or worse than those whom they had overthrown had demonstrated. But the time or years removed from the frequent changes in government did not result in any tangible or lasting material difference for the people. The fragile peace the country enjoyed – for there were deep cleavages within society and amongst the ruling class – was marred by a paucity in socio-economic development because of power struggles over control of the nation's resources.

To be sure, a contested election in December 2008 brought back to power the political party of former military leader Jerry Rawlings: the National Democratic Convention (NDC). This was after an eight-year hiatus resulting from an election defeat by the National Patriotic Party (NPP) in 1999, at which point Rawlings finally stepped down as President after some eighteen years of leadership that had originated in a military coup. Ghana was hailed as a model of stability after the NPP's victory in 1999, and when the same NPP willingly conceded power to the NDC after losing in 2008 by a razor-thin margin, most of the world concluded democracy had become entrenched and that Ghana was better off by all indicators than its conflict-prone neighbors.

The fact remained that the gap between the rich and poor in the country continued to widen well after the 2008 elections, which further deepened political divisions. Upon assuming power, the NDC focused less on governing and more on creating favorable conditions for its re-election. The Party systematically removed senior and mid-level officers within the civil service allegedly aligned with the NPP, prosecuted NPP officials for alleged corruption and rescinded government contracts awarded to private companies by the NPP. These actions led to nothing but bickering and the halting of much needed services, as in the example of the public tender for biometric passports that the NDC short-circuited because the company awarded the contract was alleged to have been supportive of the former regime.

Similar squabbles over existing public tenders were indicative of the priorities of Ghana's new leaders, but their calculating decisions in 2010 about oil discovered off the country's shores removed any lingering doubts. Deals were cut with foreign companies well before a single drop of oil was pumped. Those deals were said to have been made on ideological and economic grounds. Yet, through the US Embassy's direct involvement with the negotiations on behalf of American firms for exploration and production, it became apparent that influential NDC officials advocated the sale of production rights to companies from the East, like Iran and China, because these companies were willing to offer bribes and structure contracts to ensure kickbacks. It mattered less that these companies lacked substantive expertise or had the wherewithal to make environmental safety and human rights issues a centerpiece of their contractual obligations.

As Ghanaian officials held on to such beliefs and continued to make decisions that had minimal benefit for the public, many of their people expressed concern about their future. They did not see democracy as being entrenched, like the rest of the world saw it; rather, they saw resentment among those locked out of power toward those in positions to exercise power. For this reason, many considered it only a matter of time before another contested election brought about the same political conflicts of which Ghana's neighbors were routine victims.

Osie did not wait to find out which way the political winds might blow. He looked outside of Ghana for relief by way of immigration to the United States, where his brother had been born and was a citizen. "I knew that I wanted to immigrate to the United States, even as I worked in Ghana," Osie explained. Professional development was important to him and, he shared, "I wanted a better quality of life. The [socio-economic] conditions in Ghana did not permit me to consider staying in Ghana."

A better life is precisely what Osie secured in leaving for the US in 2011. Gainful employment with better pay enabled him to resettle his wife and child in the US a few short years later. He purchased a home and, years on, obtained an MBA, which further increased his earning potential. By 2017, Osie and family were living the American Dream as middle-class homeowners in a suburb in the American South. Yet, even as his fortunes changed for the better, Osie could not completely shield himself from the darker aspects of his new cultural environment in the US. He experienced discrimination at work, which prevented him from advancing in his career as he had envisioned. "I couldn't be my real self with people above me," Osie recalled. "I always had to be who others wanted me to be, and then even making this transformation was not enough. I was passed over for promotions because of my skin color and identity as an African."

This experience cut deeply. Osie had a hard time reconciling what he was going through with what he knew to be true. Discrimination exists in Ghana, largely with tribes fighting over resources, Osie admitted, but not on the personal level he was now being forced to deal with in America. "The skin color dynamic" and the questioning of one's very humanity extended far beyond simple economics. The situation only worsened for Osie. The onset of the 2020 health pandemic set in motion an economic downtown that further rendered him expendable in the company. Osie got laid off during the height of the pandemic.

Environmental factors–racism and a pandemic–were at play, Osie reflected on the experience. But, he continued, "I likely could have prepared for the job loss by hedging toward something else. I could have made better decisions, anticipated the likely changes in my industry and the job market. But I did not. I did not seek out new job opportunities in a proactive fashion," even as he confronted an underlying truth about racial politics in corporate America and a pandemic no one could truly foresee.

Osie understood from losing his job that he had to constantly prepare for what might be next and this preparation required deliberate decision-making to anticipate change in uncertain environments. His previous life experiences had demonstrated this much. Choice (his will to better himself) and culture (the conditions of his home country) led him to pursue life in the US. Discrimination and a health pandemic, conditions of his new environment, erected roadblocks in the US, not unlike (in a figurative sense) the barriers to socio-economic development that he encountered in Ghana.

But unlike in Ghana, Osie was able to lean on his education in the US, the work experience and skills he had developed, and a professional network he had built to take advantage of the opportunities that availed themselves in his environment. Osie confidently secured work with a major US company looking for engineering expertise for its southern US locations only months after he was laid off. Not satisfied, however, and learning from his immediate experience, Osie leaned further into creating what he called "a side hustle" – a fledgling business in men and women's African apparel that combined fashion talent in Ghana with the vast infrastructure of the internet to make and sell the apparel to customers across the globe. Osie was once more on the path to securing the social mobility he had long sought. It was all made possible because he prioritized his personal development, and central to this prioritization was the decision he made to leave Ghana when Ghana proved incapable of helping him.

Over a decade removed from that fateful choice and as financially secure as he ever had been, Osie now contemplated another transition: his desire to return home to take back the engineering, business, and leadership skills he had gained to help move Ghana forward. But, he clarified, he was not quite ready to make the journey home. The source of his angst and hesitation was Ghana itself. Osie had recently, in the weeks of our interview in 2022, lost a friend to what Osie described as an avoidable misdiagnosis. His friend lost his life despite having the financial resources, as a practicing Dentist, to pay for the medical care he needed and yet could not receive because of the quality of care available in Ghana. The friend's death was eerily similar to another Osie experienced just as he was preparing to leave Ghana for the United States in the late 2000s.

In those years, 2008 and 2009 more precisely, Osie spent a lot of his free time playing basketball, a game he loves because of his passion for sports and the growing popularity of NBA stars in Ghana. Kobe Bryant and Lebron James were idolized by Ghanaian fans and this idolatry pushed many of them, Osie and a group of friends included, to try to imitate the NBA stars' play on basketball courts across Accra. Evans was among those friends who regularly played pick-up games with Osie. Evans, a slightly pudgy 25-year-old, standing about 5 feet 11 inches, 200 pounds, with short bushy hair and a dark complexion, had a killer jump shot and an infectious smile. His pearly whites never shone more brightly than when he put the ball through the net to win a game for his team. He was competitive, Osie recalled, and serious about his craft.

Around 2006, Evans had completed his studies in the US and returned to Ghana to help his family business. His mother sold textiles, a profitable trade which required honest hands to run the day-to-day operations to prevent theft and revenue loss. Evans never voiced concerns about returning home during conversations on the margins of their pick-up games. He was rather practical about it. "It was a family decision," he told friends, as he highlighted the difficulty the family had finding someone trustworthy to run the shop. Evans seldom missed a pick-up game, Osie remembered, until sometime in the early months of 2008 when he did not show up for two consecutive sessions. He had caught malaria, friends in the know shared with others, and had sought treatment at a nearby hospital.

No one believed Evans was in any real danger given how common malaria was in the country. In fact, as they considered Evans' situation on the margins of their pick-up games, some shared stories of their own experiences with malaria and the more unorthodox measures people took as a remedy. But when they gathered once more for pick-up games in the ensuing days, they were seized with much more than news about Evan's repeated no-shows: the lights to the outdoor court they regularly played on would not come on. The friends milled about for some time, waiting, until it became obvious that there would be no games on that night. Many attributed the affair to the routine black-outs that plagued the city from time to time. But then came the news of Evans' death following the night of that power outage a few days later.

It was gut-wrenching, Osie admitted. It came without warning or any signs of possible trouble ahead for the 25 year-old. What was thought to be ailing him, a cold flu, was diagnosed as malaria, then pneumonia, then typhoid. Each diagnosis brought with it a day or two of the wrong treatment, which allowed the sickness to spread into the body until it was too late. Evans lost his life because what was making him sick could not be detected in time. It was a catastrophic failure, yet all of his friends, including Osie, knew that it was not an uncommon occurrence. People in Ghana got sick, much like everywhere else in the world. But their chance of survival was greatly diminished by the level of medical care that was available. While there were decent hospitals and competent medical professionals in the country, they were limited in number and accessible only by the super wealthy. The vast majority relied on mediocre service, or painfully, went without any service at all.

Osie and his friends grieved Evans' passing by abandoning their pick-up games for some time. It was too difficult to carry-on without him. Even after they resumed play, a few elected not to return at all. Perhaps the experience was an unwelcome reminder of their own mortality. Each was mindful of the fact it could have happened to any one of them. In their occasional meetings after Evans' passing, the friends would talk about the strange night that the lights to the outdoor court would not work. Even those who never showed interest in religion or expressed a belief in spirits were moved to wonder whether it was not Evans himself that night bidding them a final goodbye in a way he knew his friends would come to understand.

Evans' choice to return home, the connection between that decision and his eventual death, and whether things might have turned out differently had he stayed and lived his life in the US, was foremost in Osie's mind as he contemplated immigrating to the US a year or so later. The conditions in Ghana, the neglect of its healthcare system, which let Evans and his family down when they needed it most, were inescapable realities.

Over a decade later in 2022, as Osie basked in the glow of his socio-economic development in the US, Evans's own lived experience forced Osie to think carefully about returning to Ghana so that he might serve his community. Osie was not ambivalent about the calculations that he needed to make.

I need to make sure that I have the financial resources to be able to provide for medical care for me and my family outside of Ghana. I need to ensure that I will be able to fly them out of there [should the situation call for me]... This [need] is symptomatic of a broader problem in Ghana. Things that are important for the people are largely neglected.

And so, Osie waits – ready to return home permanently but unwilling to do so right-away because of the risks and lack of socio-economic opportunities that compelled him to leave in the first place so many years earlier.

Republic of Sierra Leone

Amie was born in a small village in Northern Sierra Leone in the 1980s, a decade in which the country experienced an outstanding meltdown in its body politic and socio-economic development. The deterioration had been gradually in the making, in retrospect, going as far back as the time of the country's colonial experience. To be sure the territory was invaded in the late fourteenth century by the Portuguese – who branded it Sierra Leone ("Lion Mountain" in Portuguese) because of the shape of the mountains behind the eventual Capital City of Freetown – to make it a departure point for the transatlantic slave trade. It was later invaded by the Dutch, then the French, and finally the British, for the same expressed purpose of forcing the indigenous people of the land and those nearby into slavery.

In what would be one of many ironies, the territory was later appropriated by the British and made a permanent home for displaced slaves following the trade's abolishment. The British eventually colonized Sierra Leone by the end of the 1700s, compelling the indigenous population to submit to colonial rule. It was an uneasy exercise of political control. The people of the land spoke twenty-five different languages. Family and tribe were immediate concerns for them, and Britain's proclivity to tax even the most basic elements of their needs naturally provoked a constant backlash. A hut tax, for example, proved to be a bridge too far for many, and in 1898, the Temme and Mende tribes steered a rebellion known as the Hut Tax War that killed several hundred British soldiers. And yet the British would still prevail, succeeding over the years to generate wealth for the Crown—not only through taxation, but also through free labor and uninhibited extraction and plunder of raw minerals like diamonds from the country's soil.

That the people were fundamentally opposed to Britain's occupation would be an understatement. Their concerns ran as deep as a proven water well, even if, in its process of exerting control over the land and people, Britain laid some important foundations in a style of government, infrastructure, and education system the revolting populace would later inherit. Sierra Leone, for instance, maintained the only higher learning institute in the whole of West Africa, dating as far back as the early 1800s. The school produced professionals, educators, and administrators for the entire region for over 120 years.

Yet the advancements that the British introduced did not reach everyone, nor did they create the kind of environment that could spur on a middle class. Many continued with the laborious but highly profitable task of extracting gold, bauxite, titanium dioxide, and diamond for Britain's economic benefit, while others relied on subsistence fishing and agriculture to eke out a living. The people would remain hopeful about their lives nevertheless and nothing reassured them about the future than the steady decline of Britain's hold on the country's political life. By the late 1950s, Sierra Leoneans seemed poised to gain their independence. A handful of nationalist leaders would help make the dream of political independence possible in 1961. But even in this unifying effort, there were cleavages among the nationalist leaders about how much control or influence Britain ought to retain in an independent Sierra Leone. The divisions seemed manageable, until competition for political power through elections and, by extension, control of the nation's resources, became a five year ritual.

The nationalist movement soon broke apart, with the leading faction, the Sierra Leone People's Party (SLPP), ascending to power. Their hold on power would not last. Coups and counter-coups resulted in the opposition

All People's Congress (APC) gaining control of the government. In so doing, the APC demonstrated that it had learned from the mistakes of the previous regime and the military coups that came in their wake. The leader, Prime Minister Siaka Stevens, a co-founder of the very opposition party, SLPP, he was fighting to keep at bay, used draconian measures to suppress dissent and maintain his authority. His actions were rooted in the personal experience of having won the 1967 elections only to then be detained mere minutes after taking office during a military coup.

Stevens regained his post in 1968 but would learn the wrong lessons along the way about nation-building. His first order of business, once he resumed office, was to orchestrate the introduction of a republican constitution that gave him vast executive and legislative powers. Next, he turned to repression and violence as tactics of deterrence. Those who opposed his rule and others whom he viewed as potential rivals were either jailed or assassinated, with most of the heavy lifting in these operations being carried out by Stevens' personal death squad, infamously known as the "Internal Security Unit."

To cement his grip, Stevens forced through a referendum on a new constitution in 1978, officially ushering in a one-party state. As awful as his actions were, they might have stung just a little less had the country's economy stayed afloat following the boom years of independence. But in a true autocratic fashion, Stevens managed to ruin this too with corruption and fiscal mismanagement. His handling of the economy, as the country surpassed the midway point of the 1980s, was so bad that the government ran out of money to provide even basic social services. The country's education system, once the envy of the region, was rendered defunct.

Sierra Leone was in full melt-down mode by the late 1980s when tragedy struck Amie's family. Her father died unexpectedly, forcing Amie, then age 10, and her older sister to relocate to Freetown, the capital city, where their mother ran her trading business. It was a shocking transition from Amie's perspective. The communal life and safe environment she knew in her village gave way to what she described as a filthy urban setting, where people barely tolerated each other as they pursued their interests. The living conditions in Freetown were such that anyone who could find a way out of the country did just that. And so it was for Amie after what seemed like three long years living in a place that was so foreign to her sensibilities. The eldest sister of the family had earlier immigrated to the United States. Amie and her older sister joined their eldest sister in Northern Virginia in 1990.

The transition was life altering not only because of the opportunities that lay ahead for Amie. The reason is that a rebel war had broken-out in the country just months after Amie's departure for the very reason Amie and her family had decided to leave. By the opening of the new decade in 1990, Sierra Leoneans had clearly grown tired of the one dominant political party of the ruling APC, with its abuse of power, targeted killing of political opponents, and mishandling of the nation's economy. As a result, some citizens rose up in the only way that they knew would get the government's attention. But what finally lit the fire for the ensuing conflict was something people gave little attention to at the onset.

Several months before, the leader of the National Patriotic Front of Liberia (NPFL), Charles Taylor, visited Sierra Leone to ask for help from Sierra Leone's ruling APC. Taylor wanted to use Sierra Leone as a base to mount raids into Liberia to oust that country's leader, Samuel K. Doe. President Doe had by that time abused his power and triggered his country's decline to such a staggering degree that his abuses rivaled the worst of the lot on the continent. Taylor offered money to senior APC officials to secure their agreement, but while money may have exchanged hands, Taylor was never granted the approval he sought. In fact, he ended up getting arrested and imprisoned in a Freetown jail for a time before being deported. The APC later allowed Sierra Leone to take part in regional military efforts to prevent Taylor's NPFL from overrunning Doe's government in Monrovia.

People who are determined to get what they want seldom forget when they are denied. Taylor went on to wage his war in Liberia, but he never let go of how he was mistreated in Sierra Leone. As he took to battle for control of Liberia in March 1991, he saw an opening to avenge the humiliation he had suffered. Taylor unleashed about one hundred of his fighters, led by Sierra Leoneans who had grievances of their own, against two border towns in Sierra Leone's eastern district of Kailahun. Armed conflict on a national scale thus breached Sierra Leone's borders.

The government struggled to contain the conflict because of major weaknesses of the Sierra Leone army and corruption, notably senior military officials embezzling funds meant for the war, thus creating massive supply shortages for soldiers on the front lines. While those who controlled the money for the war stole it, others who commanded the soldiers colluded with the rebels, not only by providing information on troop movements, but in several cases engineering fake ambushes to hand over soldiers to rebels as reinforcements. Inevitably, the rank-and-file soldiers reacted to the lack of adequate supplies and pervasive misconduct on the part of their superiors. For one thing, as the fighting intensified, so did the rate of desertion. Such developments should not have come as a complete surprise to the country's leaders, yet their response to legitimate grievances made a bad situation even worse.

In April 1992, a group of young soldiers left the front lines of the war and drove the two hundred kilometers to the State House, where they demanded an audience with President Momoh and his military advisors. Instead of handling them with any degree of tact, the President and his advisors announced that a few "dissident soldiers" at the State House were to be arrested. The effect of their action was felt immediately. Led by a mere captain, the soldiers forced the President to take refuge at the Nigerian High Commission and later to flee to neighboring Guinea the next day. Within twenty-four hours of their attempt to confer with their civilian superiors, the soldiers announced that they were taking over the government, thus putting a quiet end to a regime that had held power in the country for twenty-four years. The rebel war, meanwhile, continued for the next decade, with more military coups, conflict diamonds, and atrocities against innocent civilians serving as headlines during arguably the most appalling chapter of the nation's short history.

Amie was among the lucky Sierra Leoneans who escaped the country's rebel war years. The memory of lost family and friends to the war and her desire for a changed life kept her motivated amidst challenges of integrating into the cultural fabric of the US. Settling in, Amie recalled, was not easy in the US, where the idea of community was different and children poked fun at her for being African and for speaking English with an accent. She needed a really thick skin and the backing of her assertive nature. Amie held her own, despite the numerous times she found herself wondering whether she might ever pull through or be accepted.

Propelled by a good education and professional experiences in the US in the years following her immigration, Amie returned to Sierra Leone for the first time since her departure in 1990. She made the trip back during the course of her MBA studies in 2012. Her homecoming was focused on family. What she experienced on the ground there – the state of the nation–changed her perspective. The rebel war had shattered lives and communities and, even as people tried to piece themselves back together, the after-effects of the prolonged conflict lingered literally and figuratively. Men, women, and children walked around with limbs–an arm or a leg cut off by rebels in the heat of battles for complete capitulation of their victims. Bombed-out buildings stood neglected, while infrastructure for such basic needs as clean water, sanitation, and safe roads for travel remained wanting because of more pressing needs like food and medical care.

Sierra Leone was still in the midst of reconstruction when Amie returned home for a visit but the only aspect of this national rebuilding effort that seemed durable was the peace and stability that had forsaken the country for over a decade in the aftermath of the 1991 rebellion. Following the rule of the SLPP after the war, the APC, under President Ernest Bai Koroma, won two consecutive elections in 2007 and 2012. Democratic governance reigned once more, yet everything else was at a standstill or degrading, especially the national development prospects of the recovering nation. One reason for this was the depth of the destruction the country endured and the scale of resources, both human and material, needed to mount a recovery. Another reason was the priorities of the ruling government. Koroma's Administration was infamous for tying kickbacks to contracts for national projects, including the sale of land to foreign governments like the Chinese, whose under-the-table payments, made it easier for them to escape fiduciary responsibilities, including helping to develop area communities and ensuring that Sierra Leone retained rights to whatever the Chinese might find on the land and in the waters they contracted to exploit.

The experience of witnessing the conditions in Sierra Leone in 2012 stirred within Amie a sense of obligation, a duty to return permanently and contribute to the betterment of her people. Amie acted on this moral imperative to return in 2014, abandoning her work in South Africa with a private equity firm after just six months for the chance to apply her business knowledge and experience in Sierra Leone's telecommunications sector. Amie experienced a honeymoon phase upon her return. She found Sierra Leone peaceful, despite its lack of development and visible issues with systemic corruption. She enjoyed settling in and rediscovering inspirations in the traditions and customs of her country. With time, however, and with the reference point of her previous cultural experience in Sierra Leone, Amie began to appreciate the seismic changes the country and people lived through. She had a visceral reaction to what she witnessed and what she said, during our interview, still prevailed:

Sierra Leone is worse now than it has ever been in its history, with the exception perhaps of the rebel war years. The economy is in ruins, but so too is the social and cultural [fabric of the country]. The value system is worse, morals are down, distorted. Education is not valued. Kids feel entitled, they use drugs, prostitution is rampant, and there is a general decline in the nation's work-ethic. There might be a combination of reasons for this: the rebel war, lack of education in the country, influence of development aid, exposure to western culture…but everyone seems bent on looking for a hand-out, rather than applying themselves to learning and becoming someone (Amie, personal interview, January 6, 2023).

The reality of the social decay in Sierra Leone that Amie described seemed to exacerbate the problems she began to experience in her professional endeavors, problems that stretched far beyond the country's poor business environment. Amie's support of the ruling APC and vocal dislike of the opposition candidate during the 2018 national elections severely handicapped her professional pursuits as an independent consultant when the same opposition candidate was declared the winner of the run-off elections by a mere three percent of the vote. The new SLPP government exercised a controlling influence in private sector development and it leveraged this influence to steer business to those whom it favored and away from those whom it did not. Amie's opposition during the election placed her squarely in the disfavored camp. Business opportunities were thus no longer as robust. Growing professionally became impossible. But the new Administration, led by one of the coup leaders in the shadows of the 1991 rebellion, was far from putting its print on the nation to solidify control.

The partisanship that prevailed during the election cycle was made a centerpiece of the new Administration. Those who offered their money and vote were rewarded with government jobs and public tenders, creating in the process a system of patronage that valued political connection over merit and qualification. In addition to the unhealthy competition for jobs this practice bred, it swelled the civil service ranks with employees who were ill-prepared to meet the serious challenges of the people. The practice also made it possible for those constituents and areas of the country that did not support the Administration to be denied critical services and community development. Further still, the practice had an even deeper impact on the conscience of Sierra Leoneans given the country's political divide – with people in the Southeast supporting the SLPP and those in the North supporting the APC.

Upon assuming office, the Administration made the decision to fill the government positions, including the Cabinet, with Roman Catholic Southeasterners of the Sherbro and Mende tribes. The most calculating of these decisions concerned the military and security services, including the appointment of the country's Chief and Deputy Chief of Police in March 2020. As an editorial in one of the country's news outlets highlighted when the announcement was made, the Administration appointed individuals from the President's own Sherbro/Mende tribe to "such a strategic institution like the Police, only further [reinforcing] the widely held notion that the Sierra Leone President is blind to tribal and regional balance at a time when Sierra Leoneans are craving for a unifier to mend a deeply divided country" (Shaw, 2020).

The editorial, in light of the sheer number of appointments of ethnic and tribal loyalists made by the Administration, was rightly focused on the one element Sierra Leone could ill-afford to get wrong: the need for a balanced representation of the country in government. A vast majority understood that merit-based employment and a balanced representation of the people within the corridors of national power are vital considerations; that they are foundations for nation-building and, perhaps even more significantly given Sierra Leone's history, for establishing the kind of participatory political culture that can serve as a check against potential ethnic-based conflict, as well as cultivate national cohesion and unity, which Amie declared, remained the most daunting national project facing the nation as it barreled toward another presidential election.

With the same Administration, now in its fifth year, seeking yet another five year mandate in the 2023 elections, Amie questioned the viability of what drove her to return to Sierra Leone in the first place: seeking to contribute to the work of uplifting the nation. The SLPP government had become entrenched in power. Those leading it did not seem keen on relinquishing that power any time soon, Amie reasoned. When asked, she thought carefully about her decision to return home before admitting that while the move challenged her to grow as a person, the conditions in the country have not made it possible for her to reach the heights she envisioned for herself, namely establishing a thriving business and finding a life partner. Sierra Leone was too far removed from the potential it presented its people on the heels of independence six decades earlier.

CONCLUSION

A closer look at the conditions in Ghana and Sierra Leone within the space and time of Osie and Amie's development years demonstrates a strong correlation between the nations' political and development trajectory with that of their citizens' socio-economic achievements. What Osie and Amie were able to achieve and not achieve was conditioned by the prevailing environment in their home countries. Both ultimately departed home to pursue education and employment elsewhere. The enabling environments in which they landed, coupled with their commitment to self-develop, proved to be the catalyst for their transforming adult lives. The irony in their departures from home (and Amie's subsequent return) is that the same conditions from which they earlier escaped prevailed on their decisions to abandon participation in the national purpose of their home countries. It is the same experience we will see unfold in the lives of Zahra in Tanzania and Siya in South Africa in the next chapter.

REFERENCES

Allen, P. J., Lahai, S. B. S., & O'Connell, J. (2003). *Sierra Leone's Truth & Reconciliation Commission and Special Court: A Citizen's Handbook.* International Center for Transitional Justice & Freetown, Sierra Leone.

Dowden, R. (2009). *Africa: Altered States, Ordinary Miracles*. Public Affairs.

Harris, D. (David J. (2014). Sierra Leone : a political history. Oxford University Press.

Kabbah, A. T. (2010). *Coming Back from the Brink in Sierra Leone*. EPP Book Services.

Meredith, M. (2005). *The fate of Africa: from the hopes of freedom to the heart of despair: a history of fifty years of independence*. Public Affairs.

Shaw, A. (2020, March 15). *President Bio Appoints Sierra Leone Police Chief & Female Deputy from his Mende Tribe*. The Organiser.net. https:// theorganiser.net/sierra-leone/1143-president-bio appoints-sierra-leone-police-chief-female-deputy-from-his-mende-tribe.

Sierra Leone State House. (2022). *The Republic of Sierra Leone State House*. Sierra Leone State House. https:// statehouse.gov.sl/

The Sierra Leone Web. (2003). *A Statement by President Ahmad Tejan Kabbah Made Before the Truth and Reconciliation Commission on Tuesday 5th August 2003*. Sierra Leone State House. http://www.sierra-leone.org/ Speeches/kabbah-080503.html

Williams, A. S. (2021). *White malice : the CIA and the covert recolonization of Africa* (1st ed.). PublicAffairs.

Ziorklui, E. Doe. (1989). Ghana : Nkrumah to Rawlings (Revised edition.). Em-zed Books Centre.

Chapter 7
Tanzania and South Africa

ABSTRACT

Tanzania and South Africa, the homes of study participants Zahra and Siya, are the focus of this chapter, which offers a narrative inquiry and case study of Tanzania and South Africa within the context of and in parallel with the lived experiences of Zahra and Siya. As demonstrated in the previous chapter with a deeper dive into the socio-political and economic dynamics of Ghana and Sierra within the space and time as Osie and Amie attempted to piece their lives together, a closer examination of Tanzania and South Africa in the same vein yields a correlation between the nations' political and development trajectory with that of their citizens' socio-economic achievements. Zahra and Siya in particular chart the course of their lives according to the dictates of their environments, which were overwhelmingly influenced by the condition of their nation-states. But Zahra and Siya remained, for the most part, in their home countries, notwithstanding the conditions therein.

INTRODUCTION

Tanzania and South Africa are polar opposites despite their relative proximity in population and geography, as well as the reality of the political dominance of the nationalist organizations that helped each nation secure its independence. The former is united by a lingua franca, Kiswahili, that has held the nation together since the end of the colonial experience and is home to the seventh largest economy among the nations of Eastern, Western, Central, and Southern Africa. The latter is a country with 11 official languages united by a contemporary history of struggle against government sanctioned discrimination and is home to the second largest economy in all of Africa.

DOI: 10.4018/979-8-3693-2403-5.ch007

These opposing realities deeply inform the two nation's experiences in political organization and socio-economic development, as manifested in the lives of their respective citizens, Zahra and Siya.

United Republic of Tanzania

Tanzania is a unification made in 1964 of the separate states of Tanganyika and Zanzibar Island. The East African nation of over 63 million people sits along the Indian ocean and borders several neighbors, including Uganda and Kenya to the north and Malawi and Zambia to the south. While Dar es Salaam and Zanzibar are the country's more well known locations due to the commercial activity and tourism in these places, a number of other cities and towns in the country reflect the spirit of a domestically stable nation, whose people are united by language but also share a troubled history of political and socio-economic development that has caused nearly half of them to live below the poverty line (World Bank, 2022).

Thirty-nine year old Zahra was born in one of those locales, Arusha, Tanzania, that embodies the country's peaceful yet uneasy character on account of its development experience. Arusha is a relatively small town that leverages tourism as its primary source of income, which is the reason the town is known in most parts as the gateway to safari destinations and Africa's highest peak at Mount Kilimanjaro. As small towns go in Tanzania, Arusha seemed an ideal place to raise a family in the 1980s, and yet Zahra spent a considerable part of her early years in neighboring Nairobi, Kenya because of her parents' involvement in the Tanzanite trade. The rare stone, the blue and violet variety of the mineral zoisite, was sourced in the Manyara region of Tanzania but the market for it in the 1980s and 1990s was far more robust in Kenya. The family lived in a housing project reminiscent of those concentrated in the heart of urban cities all over the US. Multiple units were sandwiched together, forcing a living situation in which neighbors knew more about each other than they might have ever cared to know.

Both Tanzania and Kenya in the early 1980s were dominated by the actions of political giants, men who helped to shephard their nations through the thorny business of political independence from colonial rule and, as a consequence, were rewarded for their efforts with the mantle of national leadership. Julius Nyerere in Tanzania and, in Kenya, Daniel arap Moi, the former vice president of independence leader and first President of Kenya, Jomo Kenyatta. Nyerere and Moi were larger than life on account of their persona and politics. Zahra recalled Nyerere's policies of African socialism, namely Ujamaa, and Moi's use of his Kalenji tribesmen to fashion a government that ensured his rule. Each of them left an indelible mark on their nation.

In Zahra's words, the socio-political situation in Tanzania was in flux during the years of her upbringing. Some worked in the mining, farming, or tourism sector, but there was a lack of independence to make money, to live in luxury or to have greater access to consumer goods. Nyerere was fixated on people living in ujamaa communities, where they were expected to live on quotas. No one could have more than what the authorities decided was his or her "fair share, nor could anyone produce or provide a service that was not authorized by those in power. So, the people resorted to hiding both what they produced and what they consumed to the detriment of the larger Tanzanian community.

The situation was far less friendly or communal in Kenya. Zahra recalled that Mio's regime also prioritized social cohesion but for far different reasons. She explained that,

The socio-political situation in Kenya in the 1980s and 1990s was best characterized as tense. I felt like I was living in a police state. President Moi was running an autocratic regime, with his Kalenji Tribesmen in total control of every state apparatus. People were killed, jailed, or made to disappear in exile if they opposed the regime. A lot of people wanted to leave the country, to go to the States, because of lack of social mobility and crime. The political environment was not stable. My parents' business was not impacted, but people in the country were looking for better opportunities.

Kenya's political environment did not have quite the same effect on Zahra at that time. She was young. Her concerns were naturally centered on home and school, the pillars of the life she was beginning to put together. She found subtle differences between her childhood experience in Tanzania and Kenya, where she was fast growing into a young adult. The greatest difference she found was in the way children were encouraged to develop. In Tanzania, she and her siblings were compelled to focus on conventional disciplines (law, science, math or engineering). The arts were not encouraged or supported.

Kenyans were also advocates of conventional subjects, she affirmed. But their advocacy did not come at the expense of other areas. The Kenyan society in fact supported and provided infrastructure for childrens' involvement in extracurricular activities, including music and the arts. It was the former that piqued Zahra's interest at an early age. She doggedly pursued music as a profession, navigating serious opposition from her father and her community along the way to embark on a transformational career that changed everything for the better…and for the worst.

As Zahra grew up and music enveloped her life, Tanzania experienced a transformation of its own that would come to manifest in the environments in which citizens like Zahra attempted to piece their lives together. The transformation was informed by the country's failed experiment with African socialism, but it was propelled by national efforts years on to move beyond this system, to modernize while entrenching the country's political dispensation under the ruling party's banner. The little-known town of Dodoma and what authorities attempted to fashion there heralds the root of the transformation that began to take shape and grow in Tanzania.

Dodoma. In 2004, the landlocked town of Dodoma and the surrounding central Tanzania region made up for what it lacked in marine resources with fertile land for farming. From major food crops such as maize, rice, and sorghum to tropical fruits and vegetables such as grapes, groundnuts, sunflower, oranges, mangoes, and guava, the entire region was a serene homestead for agribusiness. Yet, the town of Dodomo and its approximately 400,000 citizens during that period were largely tethered to subsistence farming. They lived in relative peace but were troubled by material poverty and political irrelevance, not unlike many other small towns in Africa that had the misfortune of being geographically dislocated from important decisions on national development in their capitals.

Modest brick constructions lined Dodoma's main road just about every mile or so, while mud huts housing the core of the towns' people dotted the interior and outlying areas. As small towns went, Dodoma's hub for activity was always the central market. It was where trade and social calls were commonplace. But so too were private and public spaces that offered food and entertainment, much like the unassuming Dodoma Hotel. German colonists built this garden-style lodge in 1904 to commemorate the inauguration of the National Railway Line, which was intended to expand trade in the German East Africa enclave and beyond (Siebolds and Steinberg, 1980).

It was here in 1973, in nearly the exact geographic center of the country, that Tanzanians clamored to have their nation's capital transplanted from Dar es Salaam after securing Independence. Their decision in a referendum that year was reminiscent of a trend that would take hold in Africa: governments electing to center their capitals within the country not only for political reasons but also to spur economic development in the surrounding areas suffering from years of neglect. In establishing Dodoma as its capital, the government of Tanzania sought "to create significant social and economic improvements for the central region and to centralize the capital within the country" (Britannica, 2019).

But little changed in the decades after Tanzanians made the decision to move their capital. The ambitious plans to remake Dodoma hardly materialized, notwithstanding the political will demonstrated for the cause. The well-to-do resisted the calls to move, as did diplomats, market makers and other professionals. For many, Dodoma was a bridge too far from all they were accustomed to in Dar es Salaam. Years more of efforts to compel action and the construction of the national parliament building in the heart of Dodoma in 2006 made only a slight difference. People of influence eventually began to travel to Dodoma, but only to cover legislative matters that concerned their interests, not to establish any lasting roots. The government of Tanzania signaled its own priorities by retaining the lion-share of its presence, including State House, where the President works and resides, in Dar es Salaam.

So, Dodoma remained as it had always been, a place with untapped potential for development because of favorable climate, rich soil, and central location and yet an after-thought to the more "desirable" industrial center that was Dar es Salaam. But the "Abode of Peace" (as Dar es Salaam is translated in English) was itself suffering from the same problems that had compelled the authorities to earlier consider Dodoma as an alternative capital (Siebolds and Steinberg, 1980). The seemingly coastal oasis was bursting at the seams from problems of overpopulation, poor infrastructure, and a scarcity of resources. Concerns about the air quality from pollution and massive traffic jams paled in comparison to the daily burden people confronted in accessing clean water. Those with the means had water trucked weekly to their residence. The rest used what they could access – namely, polluted surface and groundwater sources that were a cause of avoidable waterborne illnesses.

By nightfall, Dar es Salaam sat in shadows, almost completely dark. Street lights either did not function or were nonexistent. Worse were the power outages, a source of constant angst for residents and businesses alike. It became commonplace to see people sit in the dark in bars and restaurants, drinking beer and eating nyama choma (roasted meat). People were blinded even to each other as if talking to the open air. This physical deprivation, induced by a neglect of energy resources in much the same way Dodoma was not prioritized, could have been a metaphor for how indifference to man was common in the streets of the country. People were preyed upon or left to fend for themselves – a huge departure from the Tanzanian society that had once embraced the ideals of collectivism. Far too many more were ostracized for their personal choices that did not match the going-social convention. And far too many more were made irrelevant because of simple economics, including drivers being so desperate to pick-up passengers at taxi ranks in Kariakoo market that in their haste to do so they ran-over pedestrians and failed to stop to attend to them.

Palpable was the cultural shift in how people treated one another and in what was deemed acceptable in society. Zahra experienced the shift upon her return to Tanzania in the early 2000s after both of her parents' were diagnosed with HIV. For one, the Tanzanian community, she recalled, did not promote the arts as a professional calling. People "demonized" music in particular and families went to great lengths to prevent their children from getting involved because music and the arts in general were deemed "worthless" endeavors. They were, it was said, idle pursuits that encouraged hedonistic behavior, namely the pursuit of pleasure at the expense of more worthy human endeavors like making more from a good (more conventional) paying job.

This same outlook was what informed Zahra's uncle, when he told her to stop singing and threatened to tell her father after Zahra had latched onto a local group in Dar es Salam as a background singer in 2005. Zahra did what she was told. She had to if she wanted to keep living under her uncle's roof with her siblings while their parents' remained in Arusha to nurse themselves back to health.

Zahra focused attention on taking care of her siblings in Dar es Salaam. She needed a lot more help than a roof over their heads, however. So, she began to lean on boyfriends, including an older, married man to help meet her needs. It was an experience – having romantic relationships based on need – that she connected to both circumstance and childhood memories of her parents' relationship. There always seemed to be something or someone standing in the way of what she wanted and it always resulted in her having to make accommodations. The situation reminded her of the reason music had somehow become secondary in her life, how the lack of support for it from her family and community led her to study political science and communication, the "anything but music" option that her Dad forced upon her during Zahra's university years.

Music remained a passion still. Zahra rebelled by skipping classes and instead going to Nairobi's national theater to look for roles in music and acting projects. Zahra was deliberate and persistent in becoming a singer, yet opposition from her community and obligations to family had erected roadblocks she had been unable to fully surmount, especially upon her return home to Tanzania. There was more. Zahra experienced resistance even as she tried to contort herself into becoming what her family and community wanted.

Returning home, Zahra attended a small college in Dar es Salaam and secured a diploma in Animals and Wildlife, an area she said she could see herself thriving in because of her love of nature. She could not get a job after graduating, however, because the authorities would not hire women in the Park Service. The work was too demanding, they told her, too physical and tough for someone so feminine. Zahra thus abandoned this potential career path to focus on giving literal care to her siblings with the help of people willing to take an interest in her, in exchange for her affection, over the course of the next three years.

The indifference Zahra experienced within her community was far from an aberration, and nor was it born out of experiences unique to her and the common man. It was embedded in and made all the more tolerable in society by the national life of the country, which Zahra experienced firsthand during the peak of her music career in the late 2000s. She explained that she,

Had an opportunity to take part in politics – to become a member of Parliament for the opposition. This opportunity came because of my fame and public persona. I explored it when I was asked, but my heart was never really into it. The divide between the opposition and ruling Party convinced me to back away…the ruling Party came to my home and talked with my parents about me not getting involved with the opposition. "She is our daughter," they told my parents. "She shouldn't be doing this." The experience turned me off completely. I felt that politics was not for me, even as I saw the opportunity to use my influence to create positive change. My heart was in music and that's where I wanted to be (Zahra, personal interview, January 11, 2023).

Zahra's heart was completely immersed in music, and yet her firsthand experience with and exposure to influential politicians had an equally negative effect concerning political participation. These men, and a few women, showed her the sordid side of politics because they felt a need to exploit her fame. Some wanted her support to increase their standing with the electorate. Some wanted money, and others simply wanted sex. Each desired something different yet they all exposed a motivation that was not anchored to the needs of the people they claimed to serve. Some even confided to her that while they lacked conviction in particular policies and leaders at the forefront of the nation's politics, they were nonetheless inclined to tow the line because doing so ensured their own political survival. Others proved through their lack of education and appreciation for public discourse that they were unfit for the positions they held, demonstrating that patronage and nepotism, not qualification and merit, were the bottomline considerations for work in the public sector.

The kind of politics Zahra experienced privately had already played out publicly. Around the time Zahra transitioned to Dar es Salaam to care for her school-aged siblings in the early-to-mid 2000s, the country was preparing for a national election. Jakaya Kikwete had vied for the presidency ten years earlier. The rank-and-file of the ruling Chima Cha Mapunduzi (CCM) supported him overwhelmingly in the lead-up to the 1995 elections not only because of his performance as Finance Minister but also because he displayed the kind of charisma that seems to come naturally to men with national leadership aspirations. Yet his timing was off. Kikwete tried to succeed a fellow Muslim while Kikwete was still in his forties. Kikwete never gave up on his presidential aspirations, however, even as he accepted the role of Foreign Minister under the more senior and Christian observer, Benjamin Mkapa, through a deal brokered by the country's independence leader Julius Nyerere for the sake of party unity.

Kikwete spent the next ten years building his name and working the CCM Party to solidify his position for the 2005 elections, including making promises to placate supporters and potential rivals. The CCM's dominion over politics in the country made the selection of its presidential candidate the only race that really mattered. Kikwete thus coasted to victory in the December 2005 elections, just in time for Tanzania to experience one of the most severe power cuts in the country's history.

The power outages were caused by drought-induced low water levels in dams the country relied on to generate electricity during the warmest weather period of the year. The outages created havoc for citizens at home and work for upwards of twelve hours a day. Even those who could afford generators suffered heat deprivation, food spoilage, and work stoppages. The new government responded by contracting US-based electricity company Richmond Development to restore power. The company failed to deliver on the contract, nonetheless, even though it was paid $100,000 a day to perform the work.

An ensuing investigation by the country's National Assembly in November 2006 led to the uncovering of serious wrongdoing. The most significant charge was against Kikwete's Prime Minister, Edward Lowassa. Parliamentary investigators found that Richmond Development failed to deliver the generators on time, and when they did deliver them – long after the power crisis had come and gone – they were found to be inoperable. Parliament concluded that "Mr. Lowassa's office later influenced the government's decision to extend Richmond's contract, even after advice to the contrary from the state-run energy company Tanesco" (BBC News, 2008).

Despite Lowassa's denials, parliament made it clear Lowassa had a "personal interest" in the contract the government awarded to Richmond. Thus, Lowassa was forced to resign from his post, triggering parliament's dissolution and the naming of a new Cabinet. Until that moment, no Prime Minister in Tanzania's history had ever been forced to step down from office. Lowassa had previously served as a Minister under former President Ali Mwinyi. He had likewise not fared well in that government. In fact, he was "relieved of his duties as a Land Minister because of allegations of corruption."

Lowassa retained influence inside the Party even after his removal as Land Minister, to a point he was also considered a presidential hopeful in 2005. His challenge of Kikwete for the presidency was thus viewed by some as disruptive to Party unity. Echoing the 1995 deal made by the father of the nation, Julius Nyerere, who died four years later, Lowassa was asked by the Party brass to step aside in return for a plume post, which turned out to be Prime Minister under Kikweter.

As Kikwete's administration carried through 2015, ensuring similar decisions about state resources remained decidedly in the hands of the favored within the ruling CCM, social mobility and living standards for the people of Tanzania continued to decline, measured by the 49 percent of Tanzanians who lived below the international extreme poverty line of $1.90 per day (World Bank, 2011) and the poor condition of social services that Tanzanians such as Zahra could hardly count on as they attempted to put their lives together.

Zahra wanted no part of Tanzania's torrent political world, not at the apex of her music career. She found the field abhorrent and the people in it self-serving. The decision at the time did not seem all that material. Music sustained her and she was able to leverage the profession to both make a living and to raise the social-consciousness of her people, much like how one of her early hit-songs gained notoriety. Her success came about in 2008 with her participation in a television series, which offered the visibility and networking she needed to break into the Tanzania music scene. Zahra recorded her first album and filmed a video for a hit single with the financial backing of a new lover to help launch her career. She went on to leverage her fame and stardome for acceptance into Tanzanian high society. She traveled the world; rubbed shoulders with famous people, influence makers, and even politicians.

People everywhere embraced Zahra. The voice she gave to issues of the day resonated because Zahra sang from experience. Her life, colored by struggle, was the source of the lyrics that drew people to the music she produced. Audiences were captivated by her authenticity, the fact that she had lived the life that they led but that she had somehow managed to overcome the odds of their broken experiences to help make meaning out of it all. This social contribution was as gratifying for Zahra as the fame, money and success that her career in music had rendered possible in just a few short years. It would all be short-lived, however. The choices she made for love and her environment – the pressure of community and absence of social security – had a lot to do with it.

When the love of her life had an affair in 2009-2010, Zahra retaliated with an affair of her own, a choice that rendered their once promising relationship irreconcilable. Zahra tried to move on by physically relocating to another city and embracing the arms of another man. The relationship "was supposed to be a rebound, and while many of my friends told me to ditch the relationship for reasons obvious to them, I insisted on continuing it. The sex was great, I admit, and the romance quickly developed into a deeply intimate relationship. What I didn't count on was the relationship being toxic. The man abused me," Zahra shared with lament. Beatings and emotionally abusive exchanges were commonplace. Zahra elected to stay in the relationship through it all. In fact, she doubled-down on this decision by conceiving a child with the man. She felt "the weight" of her community and culture bearing down on her at the age of 30, many years beyond the age women in her society were expected to marry and have children. Zahra explained:

He was more like my father, very domineering. He slapped me for talking back, talking to other men, for not coming home at a certain time. I tried to rationalize the behavior. I needed him. I needed to be loved, to belong to someone, to be validated, to have someone to show-off and be seen as having someone…my parents' [relationship] likely contributed to me rationalizing the behavior (Zahra, personal interview, January 11, 2023).

Zahra was also fearful that the fame she had garnered from music would render her vulnerable to being blamed. So, she kept quiet and endured the pain. Depression set in, as she looked around and realized that she had lost the father of her child to another woman with whom he had also fathered a child. Depression deepened, as she realized that she was far removed from the music career she had in Dar es Salaam. Depression overwhelmed, as she realized that her savings had run-out. Zahra had reached a breaking point. She was literally and figuratively flat broke. So, she did and thought of little else but to end her own life.

In the end, Zahra would not take her own life. The presence of her son and her will to live for him, after serious complications during the birth, centered her focus on survival. She battled through depression and what she described as "being in a bad mental space" during the same years that she experienced her fame and fortune decline to levels worse than when she was juggling boyfriends to make ends meet in her early twenties. Single-motherhood took its toll, especially as the father of her child elected to keep both his affection and money from Zahra and their son. Both the government and social custom were no help in enforcing child-support payments. Zahra thus resorted to selling her possessions to make ends meet.

The specter of missed opportunities were not lost on Zahra as she described the roller coaster of her journey. Life unfolded in a way she did not anticipate. Her music career fading, when it had barely started, was hard to fathom. Having little money to care for her son as a single-mother was troubling. The conditions in Tanzania that made it difficult for her to get the support she needed was baffling. How could everything that meant so much to her life succumb or fall to such appalling levels? The thought, especially about the conditions of her country, placed Zahra's decision to avoid political participation at the peak of her music career in perspective. It was a decision that now took on new meaning. Looming large was the lost opportunity for her to perhaps more directly influence, as a member of Parliament, the social-ills she experienced: violence against women, gender inequality, and the lack of enforcement for child support on behalf of the mounting number of single-mothers in the country.

While those years were now long gone, Zahra was committed to making a come-back through music and an events management company she established years earlier. She was determined to regain control of her life by applying the lessons she learned from the pain of loss, including the value of community. Above all, Zahra, planned to give back – a service to others orientation that was in sharp relief of the prevailing national practice she witnessed on a daily basis in Tanzania.

Republic of South Africa

South Africa is the southernmost nation on the African continent. The country of 60 million people is where modern history shows an indelible example of human resilience in the face of out-right oppression that saw the majority indigenous population of a country forcefully segregated into impoverished townships. Siya, a 60 year old introvert who is adept at moonlighting as an extravert when the situation calls for it, was born in the 1960s to illiterate parents in one of those impoverished townships near Pretoria, the country's capital city. His small shack of a home that housed his parents and multiple siblings, many of whom did not survive, epitomized the family's poor material condition.

Everything about living life was a dogged struggle and this reality was rooted in what apartheid did to the country. Siya recognized the forced depravity of apartheid for what it was at an early age and he quickly embraced the responsibility to "extricate" his family from it. His will to do so, along with his excitable temperament at the time, was at odds with the environment he had to navigate. Siya was troublesome, to put it mildly. He behaved poorly in school and displayed an exasperating knack for indiscipline. These traits, especially during his adolescent years, put in serious jeopardy his goal to pull his family out of poverty. Siya was eventually arrested and sent to prison at the age of 16. The reason? "I would describe the experience as being in the wrong place at the wrong time – a common refrain for many young people in my day," Siya recalled without going into greater detail. "Going to prison fundamentally changed my perspective. It was a wake-up call. I realized that I had to change my ways if I wanted to survive, let alone make good on my promise to extricate my family from poverty."

Prison more closely oriented Siya to the reasons behind the abject living conditions of his people: apartheid. Their material poverty was made worse by a lack of freedom and the rampant extrajudicial killing and dislocation of family, friends, and neighbors. Siya grew convinced that his own survival depended on what happened to his people. He turned his focus to personal development through education with a fervor that could not be diminished. In doing so, he found a way to fight as an activist student leader during what he described as the height of the liberation struggle in the late 1980s at the University of the North, an institution that would become the hotbed of the liberation movement. The school was under a state of emergency law when Siya attended, rendering it vulnerable to years of occupation by soldiers and policemen.

Siya assumed leadership of the movement on campus by way of his oratory skills and his ability to organize. "On a memorable occasion," he shared, "I led student protests with a speech in which I conveyed to the authorities that we are not going to class until our leaders were released. Nearly 3,000 students heard me speak that day. The scene was unreal. We had the police and the military all around us, threatening to strike us down. We were ready to die in pursuit of what we believed was just."

The right to self-determination, the freedom to decide for themselves how to shape the course of their social, political, and economic lives, was what Siya and his fellow student activists believed in. It was a fight for independence that the African National Congress (ANC), the organization Siya represented on campus, largely spearheaded long before Siya was even born. In 1912, the organization was established under the name of the South African Native

National Congress to agitate for the voting rights of the marginalized mixed race (colored people) and the indigenous population in the Cape Province. By the 1940s, the focus shifted to fighting racial segregation, which the National Party codified as national policy after seizing power.

Success for the organization came at a price. The National Party banned it in 1960. The move forced ANC members to work underground and, with the help of neighboring states and international allies, to mount activist and military campaigns to make South Africa ungovernable until the government saw the error of its ways. The ANC was finally unbanned in 1990 and, four years later, it led the country to majority rule with Nelson Mandela as President.

Siya's education in social sciences and his direct activism as an ANC youth league member ultimately paved the way for his entry into public service once the ANC was in power. The organization assumed the task of transforming the country's institutions after the 1994 elections and this work required the education and talents of people like Siya. He was in the right place at the right time when candidates were needed to fill openings in South Africa's foreign affairs department and he parlayed the invitation into a prosperous diplomatic career, including serving as a senior advisor to important principals. Siya not only traveled the world and gained a wealth of experience during those years, but he also played an instrumental role in shaping South Africa's foreign policy and relationship with key allies.

The life of a diplomat is not without change and transition. In the mid-2000s, Siya leveraged his experience and networking to gain a senior posting in a southern African country. His career was on an incredible trajectory, one bound to land him in a principal position within the very circles in which he once sat and advised others. He just needed a bit more field experience as an executive outside of South Africa and this posting promised to provide all that he needed, plus the benefit of experience with a regional rivalry. The posting turned out to be a lonely experience for Siya. His family's absence made the place unbearable. Returning home to South Africa thus became a prime motivation, as did the allure of making money outside of government, which had become increasingly possible due to the redistributive economic policies of the new government that were intended to fight the country's history of social injustice.

One policy in particular, Black Economic Empowerment (BEE), was aimed at creating an even economic playing field for the country's African majority. At its core, BEE was supposed to redistribute wealth, provide employment opportunities for Africans by mandating that South African companies take proactive steps to hire Africans, develop their professional skills, prepare them for executive leadership, and enable them to own shares of the companies for which they also worked. The companies that complied with the BEE policy were favored when the time came for the government to issue public tenders.

South African civil servants began to see one boss after another flee government for the private sector in the years that followed BEE's introduction. A former boss of Siya's was among the many who jumped ship. Siya watched these events unfold from his perch outside the country and he concluded, with home and family beckoning his permanent return, that he too had to make a career change. Siya left the Foreign Affairs Department upon his return from his posting in the mid 2000s for a mid-level management position with a private company that his former boss at the Department had also left to join months earlier.

The career change was massively fruitful for Siya. He spent twelve years with the said private company, leveraging the opportunity in those years to accumulate promotions and to be associated with a statistic Siya had become a part of: a member of a small elite group – the five percent of South Africans who earned over one million Rands per year.

Siya's success as a millionaire South African was everything his government intended. But as sweet as life had turned out for him, it proved just as bitter for the vast majority of his fellow countrymen. BEE gave rise to a small group of indigenous elites but it did not redistribute wealth in the country in the way it was intended. South Africa's minority retained control of the lion's share of the economy and the gap between the rich and the poor widened even further.

The failings of BEE to redistribute wealth and jobs and to create economic equality were undeniable. Even the country's senior leaders acknowledged that the policy had benefited only a few, though they did not articulate precisely who those few were, as they called for a comprehensive review to try to determine how to make the policy more broad-based. Yet Siya's experience and those of others who followed in a similar footstep offered lessons about some of the circumstances that plagued South Africa's advancement and the development of its people. The immediate impact of Siya's departure from government, as he himself admitted, was the vacuum of experience he left in his ministry. The expertise he gained from his decade-long work on issues germane to the creation and implementation of foreign policy was difficult to replace, and this invariably affected the pace and effectiveness of his ministry's work.

This was also true for others who left government, especially those at the senior level. The ministries each of these individuals left in favor of BEE opportunities were disadvantaged. And yet still BEE would help bring about even worse unintended consequences for the nation. The trappings of power and wealth, particularly among the small group of black capitalists who benefited from BEE, resulted in a sudden case of amnesia. Many who once suffered under apartheid and understood the root cause of their suffering proved incapable of relating to or empathizing with the poor economic circumstances of their fellow citizens. The more they became invested in the companies and industries that made them wealthy, and once this wealth changed their material condition, the more it seemed that they forgot about the origins of their own humble beginnings and the reasons they struggled to liberate the country in the first place. Years of this kind of imbalance naturally provoked a black-lash, and there proved no greater example than the xenophobic attacks of May 2008 against African immigrants.

Just over a matter of days, mere quarrels between neighbors in the country's townships that had taken place before without problems quickly flared up to bitter and violent disputes. The violence enveloped many parts of the country, beginning in Alexandra Township and spreading to townships in KwaZulu-Natal, Mpumalanga and Western Cape provinces. In all, 62 black Africans were brutally murdered; over 600 were injured and tens of thousands were displaced from their homes. The one lasting image that captured the cruelty netted-out was the picture of a burning Mozambican national by a mob.

A lot was offered in the public domain to explain the violent outbreak, including blame on the country's poor immigration policy. But inescapable was the reality that the attacks were a citizenry's reaction to the neglect of their poor conditions by those responsible for ensuring their welfare and development. It just so happened that the citizenry directed their anger at the wrong group of people.

South Africans' reliance on social welfare programs funded by the State had the negative effect of discouraging entrepreneurship. In comparison, the historical hardships others on the continent had to deal with in their homelands triggered different results. Africans on the continent by-and-large had grown adept at creating and growing small businesses because their governments had failed them. Well before the onset of the attacks, for example, Nigerians fared well economically in Johannesburg and Durban, while Somalis had an equally firm economic foot-hold in Cape Town.

But there was also a bit of cheating on the part of the African immigrants. Enabled by corrupt South African officials, especially those within the Immigration Services, the Africans managed to build and sustain their small business empires. Over time and through bribes, they secured work and residence permits and, ultimately, government-provided allowances meant for South African citizens, such as RDP houses, the acronym for Reconstruction and Development Program. RDP was a socio-economic policy framework introduced under Nelson Mandela and designed to help South Africa's poor black majority, specifically with the alleviation of poverty and addressing the shortfalls in social services.

South Africans had for years put up with losing out on jobs to their African neighbors and even their African neighbors bribing local officials for permits to live and work in the country. But as time passed, they grew tired of the repeated encroachment on more bread-and-butter issues like housing. The African immigrants' ability to gain access to RDP houses was, it turned out, adding insult to injury. So, South Africans reacted violently against those whom they felt were taking away what was rightfully theirs. There was no denying the poor conditions in which they lived. Some 14 years after their liberation, the indigenous majority and an increasing number of the poor African-born Dutch population were still living in slums or squatter settlements without proper sanitation, electricity and other basic human services. And with a bulging population further exacerbating their already improvised conditions, it all proved a perfect storm for mass action.

Reasonable people understood the basis of the frustration and anger. Yet for South Africans to act on it in the way they did was a frightening experience for those inside the country and close to the action. Everyone was concerned, whether for their own safety or for the safety of their colleagues, friends or relatives. The memory of those days lived on for months. For many, the reality set in that South Africans were fighting literally to protect the little they had from "outsiders" because they felt their national wealth was not reaching them. They had a legitimate gripe considering what else was going on in the country.

For one, money was being wasted on some troubling initiatives, such as the country's first major post-apartheid arms deal, at the expense of more needed development projects. At the time, many observed the paradox in the country's decision to spend so many billions to acquire machines for warfare when South Africa faced no immediate or discernible national security threat. The reason for the large expenditure – to facilitate hefty kickbacks for politicians and their Party from foreign contractors awarded the tenders – became apparent over time, as detailed in Andrew Feinstein's seminal work *After the Party*. Feinstein was a particularly credible voice on the subject because he was the ANC's ranking Member on Parliament's Public Accounts Committee, which was charged with investigating the arms deal.

Inevitably, the arms deal revelations, government's inability to meet the needs of the poor majority in delivering basic service and the severe crime problem this neglect brought on created real public anxiety in the country over the ANC's governance. But comforted by the reality of the organization's nearly two-thirds electoral majority, the ANC pressed on as if nothing was wrong. Their presiding leader at the time, President Jacob Zuma, even voiced with confidence once he took over the reins of the ANC that the organization would continue to rule the country until the second coming of Jesus. Zuma's words would prove prophetic because of events that subsequently unfolded.

In 2005, then President Thabo Mbeki took the decision to remove his Deputy President, Jacob Zuma, from office. He made the decision because Zuma was implicated by a court to have had a corrupt relationship with an associate involved in the aforementioned arms procurement deal. Mbeki's decision would have a far reaching impact inside the organization. Many ANC members seethed with anger over his decision, and they let their feelings show by blocking Mbeki's efforts to also strip Zuma of his position as the ANC's Deputy President. This defiance of Mbeki's leadership, encouraged by the popular belief that Zuma was no more guilty of wrongdoing in the arms deal than others who had been implicated, set off what became the slow drumbeat of calls inside the organization for re-evaluation of the ANC's leadership. Mbeki at the time had a few more years in his position as Head of State before being term-limited. The general assumption was that he would seek another term as President of the ANC during the Party's elective leadership conference in 2007, and thus continue to influence the direction of the organization, including the selection of his replacement in Government.

But while the decisions Mbeki made regarding Zuma were the catalyst for calls for a re-evaluation of leadership, it turned out that some in the Party had a much deeper rooted problem with Mbeki. Zuma's supporters in the ANC pounced when a Judge assessed in a separate court ruling in the case against Zuma that the charges against Zuma were politically motivated and emanated from within Mbeki's office. His supporters rallied against Mbeki to remove the latter from the presidency. The person who would eventually replace Mbeki was none other than the man Mbeki tried to get rid of in the first place. But by electing Jacob Zuma President of the ANC in 2007, the Party seemed to be willing to look past the problems that caused Mbeki to fire Zuma years earlier: charges of corruption through abuse of public office. The mindset that this episode revealed proved to be a telling sign of things to come.

To be sure, as the country's Mail & Guardian newspaper reported, by 2008 "27 ministers and deputies in [the President's] executive were registered as active directors or members of 184 companies and close corporations…Many resigned as directors soon after their government appointments but remained shareholders. [In 2007 for example], the Auditor General's report revealed that more than 2,000 government officials were doing business directly with the government and had directly or indirectly benefited from government tenders worth more than R600-million" (Mail & Guardian, 2009). With significant opportunities for personal enrichment at stake, the premium on attaining positions in government greatly increased.

Zuma's ascendency to the top job thus came with fights for positions within the ANC like never before in the organization's history. Right through and after the ANC's elective conference in 2007 and the country's general elections two years later, ANC members resorted to violence against each other on a scale that frightened many in the country. For one thing, reports of political assassinations, especially in far-flung corners of the country's nine provinces, gradually became a new normal. The problem became so severe that by 2009 the Congress of South African Trade Unions (COSATU), an alliance partner of the ANC, declared in a political report to its 10th National Congress:

If political positions are the means to enrich oneself [it is] little surprise that comrades murder each other to win positions since these positions have become a stepping stone to resources. The politics of patronage have destroyed the self-sacrificing and service ethic that characterized the movement for decades. It is cancer eating slowly at all components of the mass democratic movement from branch to national level...All of this combines to spell five words: our revolution is in danger! As more and more join this, the more the needs of workers and the poor take a back seat. Individualism takes root, then soon we will be en-route to Zimbabwe and other failed revolutions elsewhere in the world (COSATU, 2009).

Equating South Africa with Zimbabwe was an astonishing admission of just how much the situation had deteriorated given the unbelievable turmoil that country was going through in the lead-up to and in the aftermath of its own general elections in 2008. The comparison was not lost on Siya, as he returned to government service after his twelve year absence around the time of the seismic political events taking place in South Africa. His comeback was in recognition of a pressing need for his kind of talent and experience to help address some of the government's self-inflicted wounds. Notably, Siya was recruited into a separate ministry to take over a top-level position that was crucial to the proper functioning of government departments. The work centered his focus once more on the task of leveraging the powers of government to erase the wrongs of the past. But the prevailing politics in the country rendered this focus of the government a seemingly secondary consideration.

South Africa had long before experienced its own share of ethnic tension and violence, not unlike many other countries on the continent trying to settle into democratic governance which demanded citizen participation and inclusion. The root of the conflict in Africa's southernmost nation was, again not unlike the other countries on the continent, a struggle for power. South Africa's version of the dispute pitted the Xhosa dominated leadership of the ANC against the Zulu dominant Inkatha Freedom Party (IFP) during South Africa's struggle for freedom from apartheid. As a risk assessment by the Minorities at Risk Project observed,

During the late 1980s, South Africa began the transition from [minority]-rule to democracy with equal participation by all ethnicities in the running of the country. The ANC became the major actor in this process, and the IFP resorted to a violent campaign in KwaZulu-Natal and the townships in an attempt to bring its agenda more firmly to the negotiating process (Minorities at Risk Project, 2003).

What resulted from this violent campaign in the span of five years from 1990 was the death of tens of thousands of South Africans. The ANC, equally culpable in the violence, won the power struggle, but it did not allow victory over its rival IFP to undermine the ANC's governing responsibilities. The latter helped South Africa turn the page on this lesser-known history of the country by conceding some regional autonomy to the KwaZulu-Natal province and by ensuring inclusion of the province and the Zulu people in the country's redistributive economic policies. Tipping the scale even further toward national cohesion, the ANC permitted the ascension within its leadership ranks of Zulu politicians who played instrumental roles in the struggle against apartheid. One of the more prominent members among these politicians was the former leader of the organization's military wing, Jacob Zuma. The affable Zuma would rise all the way to the number two spot in government and in the ANC, making him the next-in-line to replace Mbeki in keeping with Party tradition.

Zuma's tribal affiliation was not lost on anyone inside the ANC, not especially the Zulus and non-Xhosa members. So, when President Mbeki fired Zuma from the government, Mbeki's decision, with the control of national resources at stake, proved decisive. It was true that the rank-and-file of the ANC were fatigued by Mbeki's leadership. A lot of the angst had to do with their perception of him as an "arrogant micro-manager." Everything had to go through Mbeki, according to members of the former President's inner circle. But at the core of the movement against Mbeki in favor of Zuma was the desire by many who also felt left out to finally be able to take over the reins of the government. They wanted control of the public tender process in their own provinces, in the way others under Mbeki had control, so they too could get rich. This desire was not aired in public and, because of the corners of the ANC from which it germinated, support for Zuma took on meaning that echoed the years past when the Zulus, under the banner of the IFP, fought the ANC for autonomy – the right to independently exercise political and socio-economic decision-making.

From the Zulus' perspective, Mbeki and the Xhosa leadership of the ANC were attempting to lock them out of power and, in so doing, deny the Zulus access to the sources that would guarantee their economic security. The drumbeat about the negative effects of Mbeki's leadership style that aired in public was smokescreen. There was real exasperation and anxiety over the Xhosa's seeming blockade of a Zulu presidency. This reality gave rise to an ethnic divide within the ANC that made a lot of people in the organization, including Siya, uneasy about the future, to say nothing about their focus on the jobs they committed to perform within government. And just as the organization was wrestling with these concerns, the surest sign of the divide that could legitimately threaten the ANC's hegemony spilled out in the open.

South Africans were offered an alternative with the formation of the Congress of the People (COPE) right on the heels of Mbeki's outster in 2007 in retaliation for his firing of Zuma from government just several months earlier. Outraged ANC supporters of Mbeki, those who held prominent positions under him in all levels of government, challenged the ANC Executive Committee's decision to remove him on the grounds that it was unfair and politically motivated. The Party held firm to its decision, asserting that after having lost the ANC Presidency to Zuma, Mbeki was now undermining the new ANC leadership from his seat as President of South Africa. There could not be "two centers of power" was the common refrain. Some aligned with Mbeki were not convinced.

Mbeki's Defense Minister, Mosiuoa Lekota, and Gauteng Premier, Mbhazima Shilowa, famously declared in September 2008 that they were serving divorce papers to the ANC. They were leaving the party for good to form what they described as a credible alternative for South Africans tired of the ANC's monopoly. Public reaction seemed welcoming. Lekota (Party President) and Shilowa (Deputy President) steered COPE to a respectable showing in the general elections, hauling in 1.3 million votes and a sizable representation in Parliament. The early commentary, based on COPE's showing, was that the ANC could expect to be in the minority by the next election cycle. Those expectations receded, however, as COPE embarked on the work it needed to do to remain politically viable.

The drive to establish itself and to build a national platform from which to challenge the ANC somehow led to internal squabbles that confirmed what many suspected from the moment there was talk of a breakaway faction of the ANC: that the breakaway would be void of a national agenda different from the ANC and that its central appeal would be that party members could claim ANC affiliation while also denouncing it as having failed to provide the right political leadership for the nation in the wake of Mbeki's recall. COPE became a national punch line as supporters and detractors alike watched Lekota and Shilowa feverishly battle for control of the Party Presidency. The matter moved from within COPE structures – where for example an elective-conference in 2009 ended in a deadlock and no decision taken on the position of Party President – to inside South Africa's court rooms.

The litigation, aside from drawing the wrong kind of attention to the Party, resulted in the embarrassing spectacle of Shilowa's property being seized to repay court fees incurred by Lekota in defense of his position as the Party leader. The court ruling did little to mend fences. Factions hardened and each poured significant resources in the fight for leadership at the expense of COPE establishing solid organizing structures in local communities to contest elections. The Party saw its fortunes further deteriorate once its former Presidential candidate and leader in Parliament resigned and the infighting continued unabated. COPE lost ground and succumbed to labels and public perceptions that suggested it would likely never recover the political space it once enjoyed to offer the South African public a serious alternative to the ANC.

The combined force of all these events proved to be a shock to the system. It caused the country's currency to nosedive against the US dollar and people to lose confidence in South Africa as a source of stability in an otherwise volatile part of the world. But far more important than all of that was the fact that the needs of ordinary South Africans – bread and butter issues, along with critical social services – were severely strained, if not unmet, as a result of the circumstances. Siya swam against this current in the work he was hired to perform. He did it admirably for a few years until he was again bitten by the bug of striking out on his own in the private sector. He left government this time around to try his hand at practicing law after obtaining a degree in the field that had inspired him during his university days.

Between the time he first left government in the middle of the decade and the start of his law practice some 15 years later, Siya experienced a South Africa that weighed on his conscience. The legacy of apartheid – sanctioned discrimination that led to the juxtaposition of vibrant and wealthy communities along-side depressed and impoverished ones – was inescapable in the country even decades after the policy came to an end in 1994. Siya could see glaring examples near his home in Pretoria. He could see the same where he worked in Johannesburg. But it was Cape Town, where he worked for years as a foreign affairs advisor and where he now routinely traveled to, that offered arguably the most jarring example of a country that basked in the glow of political freedom and material wealth while the vast majority of its people struggled mightily to achieve economic security.

Cape Town's affluence was readily apparent in its posh residential communities, rich commercial centers, spectacular beachfront properties, world-renowned tourist destinations, and acres of fertile land in places like Stellenbosch that are central to some of the world's finest wine estates and berry farms. These riches, largely the preserve of the minority African-born Dutch population and a small number of upper and middle income class Africans, were inconveniently situated next to or in close proximity to locales of staggering poverty that consumed the life of the ordinary man. Many of these places, the townships in particular, suffered from poor conditions that impinged on the peoples' very existence.

One glaring example was the Cape Flats, the sandy plains located southeast of Cape Town's central business district and historically known as the "dumping ground of apartheid." The residential community could not shake this unfortunate name because thousands of non-Europeans were forced to relocate there beginning in 1948 after the National Party took control of the government and mandated racial segregation. Cape Flats developed over the years into a homestead for over a million people who struggled with gang violence, robberies, kidnappings, and drug abuse – social ills rooted in the historical neglect of the community by way of a lack of resources and misplaced priorities of the state.

Another glaring example of the city's deep socio-economic divide was Crossroads, the informal settlement at the mouth of Cape Town International Airport. There, scores of box-shaped aluminum shacks illuminated the desolate conditions that a lack of security, running water, sanitation, and paved roads brings to bear on a community. The shanty town wore on the eyes, suggesting an unforgiving betrayal of the ordinary man in perhaps the finest city Africa has to offer to the world.

The gaping divide between the rich and poor that Cape Town showed and the social tension it created amplified for Siya, and many like him, the depths of South Africa's woes. In an ironic twist, the same dichotomous conditions imbued in Siya (and those fortunate to visit the city) the inspiration to imagine just what might be possible for a social transformation in South Africa that took into account the welfare of the ordinary man – an inspiration beckoned by the city's majestic winds, oceanside living, and the strength of Capetonians to push through their struggles no matter the odds. Siya firmly believed that the answer for such a transformation lay in the performance of the very government he worked for but ultimately left for the private sector. In making his case, however, Siya conceded that his departure from government and those of many others like him came at an immeasurable cost. He observed that,

At some point after 1994 – beyond the Mandela years – we assigned our new baby [South Africa] to reckless hands. We stumbled and made huge mistakes as a result. Even as we try to course correct now, there are embedded challenges: corruption, contempt for institutions, state of lawlessness, victimhood when in power, and a lack of citizen activism and participation – all choices that we South Africans continue to make. Many of us were and still are focused on our own development. This created a void, which was filled by people driven by self-interest and a self-enrichment agenda. Others in government simply became state functionaries, which prevented them from focusing on taking actions that could remedy the situation; they were more concerned with service delivery for the people. This left the organization [the ruling ANC] in the hands of those who were more concerned with consumption and material gain (Siya, personal interview, September 14, 2022).

South Africa's democratic experiment began to suffer not too long after 1994, Siya reflected. It began to resemble the experience of the other nations on the continent and a contributing factor, Siya explained, was the weakness of citizen participation in the life of the nation. While not quite ready to make another return to government because of his law practice, Siya understood that the course correction his country now needs requires the kind of involvement and contribution he and many others so readily offered to overcome apartheid.

CONCLUSION

The country narrative and case study of Ghana, Sierra Leone, Tanzania, and South Africa help to crystallize the dynamic of personal control (choice) and environmental sources of control (culture) in the lives of the study participants. These constructs are powerful determinants of human behavior and accomplishments, as social learning teaches, and as we see illustrated in the lived experience of Osie, Zahra, Siya, and Amie inside and outside of their home countries. How choice and culture prevails over the participants' lives is a revelation that permeates the findings of this study, which is the focus of Chapter 8.

REFERENCES

BBC News. (2008). *Tanzanian PM to resign over graft.* BBC News. http://news.bbc.co.uk/2/hi/africa/7232141.stm

Britannica. (2023). *Tanzania.* https://www.britannica.com/place/Dodoma

Butler, A. (2010). *Paying for politics : party funding and political change in South Africa and the global South.* Jacana.

Callaci, E. (2016). Chief Village in a Nation of Villages: History, Race and Authority in Tanzania's Dodoma Plan. *Urban History, 43*(1), 96–116. doi:10.1017/S0963926814000753

Dowden, R. (2009). *Africa: Altered States, Ordinary Miracles.* Public Affairs.

Feinstein, A. (2009). *After the party: Corruption, the ANC and South Africa's uncertain future.* Verso.

Manby, B. (1995). *South Africa: threats to a new democracy: continuing violence in KwaZulu-Natal.* Human Rights Watch/Africa.

Meredith, M. (2005). *The fate of Africa: from the hopes of freedom to the heart of despair: a history of fifty years of independence.* Public Affairs.

Meredith, M. (2011). *Born in Africa the quest for the origins of human life* (1st ed.). PublicAffairs.

Minorities at Risk Project. (2003, December 31). *Assessment for Zulus in South Africa.* RefWorld. https://www.refworld.org/docid/469f3ad2c.html

Russell, A. (2009). *Bring me my machine gun: The battle for the soul of South Africa from Mandela to Zuma* (1st ed.). PublicAffairs.

Saul, J. S. (2012). Tanzania fifty years on (1961-2011): Rethinking ujamaa, Nyerere and socialism in Africa. *Review of African Political Economy, 39*(131), 117–125. doi:10.1080/03056244.2012.662386

Siebolds, P., & Steinberg, F. (1980). Dodoma: A future African Brasilia? *Habitat International, 5*(5-6), 681–690. doi:10.1016/0197-3975(80)90008-9

BBC. (2009). South Africa's Congress of the People party facing "leadership" crisis. *BBC Monitoring Africa*. BBC Worldwide Limited.

South African History Online. (2023). *Athlone or Cape Flats, Cape Town*. https://www.sahistory.org.za/place/athlone-or-cape-flats-cape-town

The Mail & Guardian. (2009, May 15). Zuma's Cabinet Inc. *The Mail and Guardian*. https://mg.co.za/article/2009-05-15-zumas-cabinet-inc/

Williams, A. S. (2021). *White malice: The CIA and the covert recolonization of Africa* (1st ed.). PublicAffairs.

World Bank. (2022). *Understanding Poverty*. World Bank. https://www.worldbank.org/en/news/factsheet/2022/05/02/fact-sheet-an-adjustment-to-global-poverty-lines

Section 3

The Conclusion and Recommendation

Chapter 8
Fundamental Discoveries

ABSTRACT

This chapter addresses the findings related to the participants' lived experience, the role of choice and culture in shaping the participants' development, and how the participants' lived experience informs understanding about the achievement of social transformation. This chapter also details the important changes, strengths and weaknesses, and limitations of the study. The important changes reflect consideration and planning for achieving representational aims, including the number of participants, their country of origin, and regions of Africa studied. Strengths and weaknesses of the study take a hard look at what methodological elements enhanced or diminished efforts of the study to explore the lived experiences of the participants through narrative inquiry and case study. This deliberate advantages and disadvantages review helps to illuminate the fundamental limitations of study, which relate, positively and negatively, to the research design and sampling approach.

SUMMARY OF FINDINGS

Lived Experience

The findings from this narrative inquiry and case study suggest that the participants make meaning of their lives through storytelling. They each shared how their lives unfolded through a retelling of stories about events and milestones that shaped the direction of their lives. Osie shared fond memories of life in Ghana and the stories behind his relocation to North America. Zhara described growing up in Kenya and she juxtaposed the experience with life in her native Tanzania, where she embarked on a transformational career

DOI: 10.4018/979-8-3693-2403-5.ch008

in music and endured setbacks. Siya shared stories of his activism against apartheid and his eventual foray into diplomacy and business. Amie recounted her experience as a village Chief's daughter, who weathered the expectations of her traditional society to make a life for herself outside of her homeland.

In the retelling of their storied experiences, the trajectory of development, personal agency/action, and social influence were consistent themes that emerged. These themes brought to light the convergence of personal choices and environmental circumstances that manifested in each of the participants' lives. For example, the participants' choices or decision-making related to major and minor life decisions, were greatly influenced by their observations of family and community behaviors, by enduring a traumatic experience, or experiencing a physical relocation from home to another land. The participants' observations of family and community behaviors influenced their perceptions of what was possible for them to achieve. Experiencing trauma or relocating to another land had a similar life altering effect – either helping to set the stage upon which the participants' lives could unfold, forcing the participants to defer their dreams, or stifling the participants' dreams altogether.

Osie experienced the culture shock of moving from Ghana to Canada and elsewhere in Europe very early in his life and again when he immigrated to the US as a husband and father. Each instance led him to emulate others or to change the essence of his own character in an effort to fit in. Zhara was traumatized in her adolescent years by her parents' abusive relationship, leading her to accept as an adult abuse (both verbal and physical) as normal conditions of her romantic relationships. Her community's expectations for women in careers and relationships had an equally negative influence on her development. Siya was born and grew up in abject poverty and was locked up in prison at 16 years of age, an experience that fundamentally altered his outlook and forced him to consider the root cause of his family and peoples' impoverished and unfree predicament. He traveled the world as a diplomat and took part in affecting foreign relations that impacted South Africa's growth as a country. Amie experienced the death of her father as a child, then relocated from her neat village setting to a sprawling urban environment in Freetown. This move precipitated another, one that transplanted her into a country and culture of differences in the US. She was utterly transformed by these experiences, to the point that Amie was able to leverage her new identity to pursue the noble cause of returning home to contribute to her people's development.

The participants' storytelling demonstrated how each of them made meaning of their lives through stories. Their stories were not only about their individual experience, as Clandinin and Rosiek (2007) observed when discussing the importance of narrative inquiry as a research methodology, "but also [about] the social, cultural, and institutional narratives within which individuals' experiences are constituted, shaped, expressed, and enacted" (p. 35). The participants' storytelling provided a well-spring of information, rich data that explained and amplified the human conditions they experienced. The sum total of their experiences was a confluence or convergence of personal choices and environmental circumstances. This overarching theme underscored the baseline theory of social learning: that personal source of control and environmental sources of control – the interplay of the two in the lives of human beings – determines human behavior and ultimately dictates the achievement of human accomplishments (Bandura, 1974).

As we learned through Will Storr's (2020) compelling research, *The science of storytelling*, the human species has long used storytelling for survival, to influence and control the self-interested behaviors of tribe members for the preservation of the tribe. Each participant shared their stories to help shed light on their own experiences within the context of developments unfolding around them as they pursued their education and careers. The participants' narration of their stories featured insights about the behaviors and expectations of their community. While subtle and at times indirect, the same was true about the participants' observations about their governments. They used their storytelling to express positive or negative emotions about their environment and the people within them in order to identify a source of their particular failures or successes. Also obvious from the participants' storytelling was their eagerness to share their stories in support of the overall objective of the study. The participants demonstrated a willingness to "get along" by being open about their lived experiences because they believed their sharing indeed could and would illuminate lessons about some of the underlying causes of Africa's socio-economic struggles.

Choice and Culture

The findings also suggest that choice and culture are instrumental in the socio-economic development process of the participants. Choice and culture was evident in each of the participants' lived experience journeys, especially in their acquisition of formal education, professional training and employment, and their personal/social life. Osie struggled through his Dad and community's influence to settle on engineering as an education and career path. He then left Ghana for the US in pursuit of social mobility, only to be challenged by discrimination, a global pandemic, and his choice not to actively prepare for the job loss he eventually suffered. Zahra overcame the resistance of family and community to embrace a transformational career in music, only to lose this career to choices in relationships and efforts to meet her society's expectations. Siya blazed a trail of political activism while attaining an academic degree in social sciences that he did not plan to acquire. This background and South Africa's political opening in the early 1990s were the catalyst for Siya's successful career in diplomacy, which he eventually left to pursue a career in business. Amie leveraged her humble beginnings in Sierra Leone to harness values and a discipline that would enable her to thrive in the different and enabling environment in the US. Decisions, including whether to keep an unexpected pregnancy, were forced upon her. She responded with determination and, in doing so, amplified how choice and culture can combine to shape the direction of one's life.

Evidence from the exploration of the participants' lives aligned with Bandura's (1974) theory about human behavior, specifically the interplay between or the "bidirectional influence process" of personal control and environmental sources of control. What each of the participants were able to accomplish or not accomplish "[resulted] from reciprocal interaction of external circumstances with a host of personal determinants including endowed potentialities, acquired competencies, reflective thought, and a high level of self-initiative" (p. 867). This interdependency of choice and culture proves significant when the consideration is social development.

To be sure, choice and culture, as established in the literature, are prerequisites for individual and societal transformation (Arendt, 1958; Arnold, 1869; Bandura, 1977; Barker, 1997; Gemmill and Oakley, 1992; Soyinka, 2000). They make change possible through leadership, the type and kind Barker (1997) instructed had to be different from our traditional concept of the construct: a man in a position of authority or one with traits that can turn around a struggling enterprise. Barker (1997) employed us to define leadership as a social process if our goal is freedom, education, or social development – human endeavors that require the navigation of complex social and political processes.

Freedom, education, and social development were precisely what the participants of the study were after. For Osie and Zahra, this meant breaking free from the expectations of their communities in order to chart their own paths. Osie found a way through schooling and employment outside of Ghana, while Zahra relied on her God-giving talent for music to break through the social barriers Tanzania presented for young women. Siya and Amie embraced education with equal zeal in order to overcome the impoverished conditions of their childhoods. Both found employment outside of their countries, which improved their professional development and material condition, and both returned home after many years of life on the outside in order to contribute to the socio-economic life of their nation-states in the private and public spheres.

Their achievement of these goals depended on choice (their decision-making or personal control). Their achievement of these goals was also predicated on the culture (environmental circumstances or sources of control) they experienced. While the participants' personal narratives outlined the family and community pressures each experienced, the country narrative inquiry and case study presented in Chapter 6-7 offered perspective on the influence of the socio-political experience of their nation-states. The common theme in each country was the political instability, brought on by a tug-of-war for power, that greatly diminished the socio-economic development potential of the nation-states and, thereby, the personal and material development of citizens like Osie, Zahra, Siya, and Amie. The citizens' inability to develop as a result of this instability, when examined from a national perspective, equally rendered their nation-states ill-equipped and ill-prepared to advance a national development agenda.

The resulting "bidirectional influence process" of choice and culture, including the nation-state's effect on the individual and the individual's effect on the nation-state, dictated or shaped the course of the lives of each participant as well as the development trajectory of their respective countries. The participants' individual examples, within the context of the environmental challenges presented by their families, communities, and nation-states, underscored the significance of the conceptual framework assumption that if people are empowered to make good choices about our life pursuits, and we are supported, rather than hindered, by our cultural environment, we might be better equipped to navigate the conditions that influence our socio-economic development.

Informing Social Transformation

The findings suggest that the participants of the study are largely disengaged from participation in the national life of their nation-states. The disengagement manifested in one of three ways: (1) participants either elected to or were forced to leave their home country in search of better opportunities in education and employment. Some returned home, while others did not; (2) participants avoided involvement in or were locked out of participation in the life of their nations due to environmental reasons; or (3) participants actively participated in the life of their nations, but eventually elected to discontinue participation for personal and environmental reasons.

Osie left Ghana to develop himself in Canada, then ultimately immigrated to the United States because of poor educational standards and a lack of social mobility in Ghana. The years he spent developing himself in Canada meant that Osie could not take on the civic roles, including voting in local district and regional elections, nor could he directly advocate or canvass for issues germane to his interests. Equally important, Osie could not leverage a platform – any that he might have developed in the country – to galvanize support among Ghanaians for the development of sports in the country, the very field in which Osie believed in his heart that he could have excelled in, even become a professional, had his community cultivated and supported his interest through positive reinforcement and infrastructure development.

Osie's absence from Ghana during his employment in the US resulted in similar abandonment of Ghana's national purpose. In these years, however, the consequences of his absence resolved to Osie not being in a position to contribute to the economic life of the nation, to include putting his skills to work so that others might benefit from his knowledge, or electing to work for the Ghanaian government in the mold of his diplomat mother, or Osie potentially putting his hard-earn income to use in support of social causes or even a political candidate and organization to advance the kind of socio-political agenda that he supports.

Zahra deliberately avoided involvement in the participatory process of nation building in Tanzania because of firsthand experience with the nature of politics in the country. Her popularity as a musician created the opportunity for her to join the ranks of Tanzania's national legislators. Yet, the same love that she had for music, coupled with a quiet distaste for the country's politics and the people in it, persuaded her to let go of the opportunity. In so doing, Zahra leaned further and harder into her music career as her vehicle to help make change in the lives of her fans. This effort was laudable but because life (choice and culture) intervened to cut short her music career, Zahra was not able to sustain participation in Tanzania's socio-economic life, to say nothing of being able to see through some of her own personal endeavors.

Her opportunity to serve in the national parliament was no guarantee for Zahra to positively influence Tanzania's national purpose. The fact that she had the opportunity but elected to focus her energies elsewhere is nonetheless difficult to overlook or ignore given what prevailed in Tanzania at the time and how her own development materialized. The very same societal forces that contributed to Zahra suffering from an abusive and violent relationship, a dead-beat Dad who refused to pay child support for their son, and a non-existent social safety-net that could have prevented her from sleeping with men for money when she was younger or eased her fall when her music career faded, were those Zahra would have had a chance to combat through legislation in Parliament, in addition to using the platform of a public figure with more immediate ties to national leaders to draw attention to the plight of the ordinary man and woman in Tanzania.

Siya actively participated in nation building in South Africa, but elected to discontinue participation in order to pursue business interests. Of particular interest in this sequencing of events is the timing of Siya's decision to leave government service. On the heels of his departure from government the first time around in the mid-to late 2000s, South Africa was taking a full measure of the impact of the black economic empowerment legislation, which gave confidence to Siya and government employees like him to leave their positions for better paying opportunities in the private sector. The immediate impact of the wave of departures that ensued was that government ministries were stripped of valuable skills and experience. It became too difficult, if not impossible, to replace the expertise that the droves of officials who left had gained from their years-long work on issues germane to the creation and implementation of public policy, and this invariably affected the pace and effectiveness of the work of their ministries, the bulk of which were charged with delivering social services to the people. South Africa's primary challenge in those years was (and still remains) figuring out how to effectively marshall resources of the state to the country's communities and to do so with officials at the helm who did not take or hijack the same resources for personal gain.

On the heels of his departure from government the second time around in the mid-to late 2010s, South Africa was coming to grips with the decade or so inner-Party squabbles of the ruling ANC government about positions and the lack of true focus on the people's business that was accompanied by a concerning tendency of officials to fleece money from the public purse. This neglect translated into the existence of a wider socio-economic gap, the juxtaposition of enormous wealth and severe poverty that is the regrettable character of present-day South Africa. Siya had every right to leave the government in order to pursue his private interests, especially given the fact that he had literally paid his dues to the public (twice). His foray into private business allowed him to engage in South Africa's national purpose in a different way: through economic production.

Yet, the reality of Siya's situation was that he had a much deeper influence on South Africa's national development in the public sector (as a student activist and diplomat) than he was ultimately able to realize in private industry. What is more, Siya's departure from government underscores the influence of the public sector environment in South Africa. He was not fulfilled even by all that he experienced and accomplished as a government worker. His environment allowed him to experience the internal workings of the ANC government. It then allowed him to envision a place for himself outside of the same government. What resulted was Siya making the obvious choice to go where he had the best chance to gain materially and to self-actualize. The conditions of the public sector, including no doubt the constant drumbeat of officials in government prioritizing themselves over the public in the aftermath of the Mandela and Mbeki years (1994-2007) persuaded Siya to go his own way.

Amie left Sierra Leone to develop herself in the United States because of the poor conditions in Sierra Leone. Her departure was of little significance to Sierra Leone's national purpose because it occurred when Amie was a young child. This consideration would not matter in fact, for the purpose of the current discussion, until the time Amie became an adult. Once this happened, Amie made the conscious decision to return home rather than stay in the comfort of her US community. She wanted to help advance her homeland given what she witnessed during a visit in 2012: a country in decay in just about every area that concerned human development.

Mirroring the experience of Siya in South Africa, albeit as a private sector employee, not a member of the government, Amie soon gained exposure, upon her return home, to Sierra Leone's public sector environment when she tried her hand at partisan politics. The exposure provoked an epiphany of sorts, a realization that the trajectory of a person's life in Sierra Leone was closely intertwined with the prerogatives of the people in power. The farther one is from partisan politics, the less relevant one becomes. The closer one is to partisan politics, the more relevant one becomes. And when one gets as close as Amie got during the 2018 elections – to the partisan side that did not win, it renders that person vulnerable to manipulation. This is precisely what Amie experienced in not being able to secure meaningful contracts as a business developer after the elections. Amie's take-away from the experience thus became one of regret about and resentment of political participation. It simply does not pay when one is locked out of power in the country of her birth.

Osie, Zahra, Siya, and Amie's examples thus demonstrate a profound truth: choice and culture plays a meaningful role in distancing them from the national purpose of their nation-states – the chores of nation building. The reciprocal interaction of choice and culture hardens their resolve to prioritize personal development over national advancement. This evidence demonstrates the relevance and validity of the theory of social learning, which posits that human behavior is determined by the "bidirectional influence process" of personal control and environmental sources of control. Each participant made a decision to participate or not participate in the life of their nations based on the prevailing conditions in their nations. Conversely, the prevailing conditions in the nations shaped the decisions each participant made regarding the same consideration.

Above findings result from a study that featured important changes, strengths and weaknesses, and limitations. The pertinent considerations therein include planning for achieving representational aims and methods employed that enhanced or diminished efforts of the study.

IMPORTANT CHANGES

An important change in the study involved the number of participants. In the planning phase, the researcher envisioned a range of 5-8 persons participating in the study. This range was deemed appropriate to help satisfy the representational aims of the study, specifically ensuring the inclusion of at least one participant from countries representing each region of Africa. The ultimate number of participants who took part in the study, four, resulted from difficulties securing participation from candidates from regions not represented in the study as well as the countries of Zimbabwe and Tanzania. Many people who were asked to participate declined because of confidentiality concerns. The researcher was finally able to secure participation from a candidate in Tanzania near the end of the data collection process. Her addition in the study compelled further adjustments, namely a reduction in the number of candidates from each country (from 2 to 1), the number of countries (from 5 to 4), and the number of regions (from 5 to 3).

Another change was that all of the participants provided interviews via the online platform Zoom or Whatsapp. The researcher had hoped to be able to sit-down with some of the participants in-person, but logistics for the same did not materialize. The researcher was based on the East Coast of the United States, while all but one participant (Osie) resided in their home countries. Another subtle but nonetheless important change was usage of the thematic analysis approach instead of the content analysis approach, as planned during organization of the study. The change occurred after data collection and at the start of the analysis. The researcher came to understand, through a deeper reading of the literature and consultations with an expert scholar, that a thematic analysis is an optimal way to establish recurring patterns within a data set and to interpret the said patterns for effective presentation in table/graph and narrative format.

A final, important change was the omission of the researcher's own lived experience in parallel with the lived experience of the participants and the inclusion of the same, instead, in the concluding chapter of the study. While the researcher engaged in this process with the participants, whose narratives paralleled the periods in which the researcher resided in the participants' home countries – enabling references and experiences that both participants and the researcher could reflect upon, such as the death of a mutual friend with Osie from Ghana because of the healthcare system in that country, the researcher did not document this part of his own lived experience in parallel with the participants.'

The participants' narratives were rich, substantive, and relevant to the research questions and thus necessitated particular focus for documentation. The participants' narratives offered enough of a layered perspective that rendered unnecessary the retelling/documentation of the researcher's own story in parallel with the participants' in the body of the study. The researcher elected to instead include in the concluding chapter of the study his lived experience that more closely aligned with the study's overarching focus on a comparative approach on development and socio-economics of Africa.

STRENGTHS AND WEAKNESSES OF THE STUDY

The strengths of this study included the research design, the inclusion of participants with incredible narratives, and the acquisition of a rich data set that adequately addressed the pertinent questions of the study. Narrative inquiry and case study design compelled a focus on lived experience narratives, which necessitated the identification and selection of participants whose life stories yielded an inquiry that was germane to the research questions. Engagement of the small sample of participants through the qualitative questionnaire and semi-structured interview resulted in a rich set of data that offered a compelling window into and perspective on the living conditions of the participants and of their home countries.

Focusing solely on the narratives of Osie, Zahra, Siya, and Amie allowed the researcher to examine the full scope of their lives in order to ascertain the relevance of their lived experience to the research questions. The questionnaire, interviews, and case study concerning the participants offered a multi-layered perspective for exploration of the lives of everyday Africans to inform understanding about achieving lasting social transformation on the African continent.

Just as the research design and small sample of participants proved to be strengths of the study, their use also hindered the ability to make broad generalizations about the findings. As the literature makes clear, generalizing findings from qualitative research is difficult to do and even controversial (Johnson and Christensen, 2021; Polit and Beck, 2010). This is because such studies are focused on topics or phenomena that are further narrowed by subjects and context. Generalizing from such studies is not ordinarily an expected attribute. Thus this study's methodology, coupled with use of a small sample size, presented obstacles in drawing broad inferences from the data collected and analyzed. For example, this study demonstrated that the four participants, despite their varying dispositions (two living in their home countries and two living outside of their home countries) were largely disengaged from participation in the national life of their countries – a prerequisite for socio-economic development and nation building. The finding did not provide definitive evidence that can be said to apply to all of the African countries and people because the methodology used and the overall design of the study did not support such theoretical generalizations or applications.

Moreover, the study featured a small sample size of participants relative to the target population under study, which reflects the African continent's population (over a billion people), the number of countries on the continent (54), and the divergent language, heritage and customs, and history of the continent's people. The degree of differences, juxtaposed with the limited number of participants (4 people), made it a challenge to determine, for example, if a particular outcome reflected a true or rigorous finding that can be generally approximated.

The sampling approach of the study was another weakness. Johnson and Christensen (2021) agreed that random sampling is the ideal and optimal type of sampling approach for research studies because of its simplicity and lack of bias, which, depending on the sample size, allows for making generalizations about a population. Random sampling also ensures that sample results approximate findings if the entire population had been measured or tested (Shadish, 2011). The study utilized a purposive sampling approach, which deliberately targeted for participation in the study a subset of Africans, while excluding others, and it further allowed the researcher to discriminate in the selection process of participants by narrowing focus on identified criteria to align with the research design. This discriminant selection opened the door to potential bias (Collier and Mahoney, 1996).

The strengths and weaknesses outlined the fundamental limitations of study, which relate, positively and negatively, to the research design and sampling approach. This latter aspect of the study is discussed at some length in the next chapter within the context of recommendations for future research.

CONCLUSION

Storytelling is the way in which participants described their lived experiences. Choice and culture featured prominently in their storytelling as strong influencers of their behaviors and decision-making. This latter featured character of the participants' lives, the net result of the confluence of choice and culture, compels considerations about Africa that are not always emphasized or even mentioned in the discourse about the continent's woes. The first of these considerations is that there is a need for further exploration of the phenomena of socio-economic struggle in African countries through the qualitative research design of narrative inquiry and case study. The voices of the people in Africa and Africans' storied experiences deserve an airing, far more so than what can be found in the existing literature, because it is the stories about how we persevere to piece our lives together against the odds we face that will more accurately and resoundingly inform the solutions we need to tackle the ills of our societies.

The second consideration is the nature of discourse about national development in Africa. While we cannot generalize or approximate the study findings, they nonetheless surface a need for greater emphasis on human development in conversations about nation-building in Africa. The findings further underscore the significant role of choice (decision-making) and culture (environment) in our lives and how they can harness the power of leadership to affect social transformation. Harnessing the said power of leadership, another point of consideration yielded by the study, is possible through an unambiguous and zealous focus on education and educational leadership. Chapter 9 takes on these important implications of the study findings through consideration of what the said findings mean or tell us.

REFERENCES

Arendt, H. (1958). *The human condition.* The University of Chicago Press.

Arnold, M. (1869). *Culture and anarchy: An essay in political and social criticism.* Macmillan.

Bandura, A. (1974). Behavior theory and the models of man. *The American Psychologist*, *29*(12), 859–869. doi:10.1037/h0037514

Bandura, A. (1977). *Social learning theory*. Prentice Hall.

Barker, R. A. (1997). How can we train leaders if we do not know what leadership is? *Human Relations*, *50*(4), 343–362. doi:10.1177/001872679705000402

Clandinin, D. J., & Rosiek, J. (2007). Mapping a landscape of narrative inquiry: Borderland spaces and tensions. In D. J. Clandinin (Ed.), *Handbook of narrative inquiry: mapping a methodology* (pp. 35–75). Sage. doi:10.4135/9781452226552.n2

Collier, D., & Mahoney, J. (1996). Insights and pitfalls: Selection bias in qualitative research. *World Politics*, *49*(1), 56–91. doi:10.1353/wp.1996.0023

Gemmill, G., & Oakley, J. (1992). Leadership: An alienating social myth? *Human Relations*, *45*(2), 113–129. doi:10.1177/001872679204500201

Johnson, R. B., & Christensen, L. (2020). *Educational research: Quantitative, qualitative, and mixed approaches* (7th ed.). Sage Publications.

Polit, D. F., & Beck, C. T. (2010). Generalization in quantitative and qualitative research: Myths and strategies. *International Journal of Nursing Studies*, *47*(11), 1451–1458. doi:10.1016/j.ijnurstu.2010.06.004 PMID:20598692

Shadish, W. R. (2011). Randomized Controlled Studies and Alternative Designs in Outcome Studies: Challenges and Opportunities. *Research on Social Work Practice*, *21*(6), 636–643. doi:10.1177/1049731511403324

Soyinka, W. (2000). Culture, democracy and renewal. *Trends in Organized Crime*, *5*(3), 110–117. doi:10.1007/s12117-000-1039-2

Storr, W. (2020). *The science of storytelling: Why stories make us human and how to tell them better*. Abrams Press.

Worldatlas. (n.d.). *Least Developed Countries 2022*. World Population Review. https://worldpopulationreview.com/country-rankings/least-developed-countries

Chapter 9
What Does It All Mean?

ABSTRACT

The findings reviewed in the previous chapter offer compelling insights into the lives of the study participants. They shed light on conditions the participants had to navigate in their pursuit of socio-economic development. They also offer a much better vantage point from which to try to make sense of participants' experiences, especially as it relates to implications for the development of the participants, their nation-states, and for the achievement of lasting social transformation. This consideration of the findings' implications is the focus of this chapter, which is written with the aim of elucidating answers about what meaning can be derived from the present study. This chapter deliberates on the important question, what does it all mean? It considers the theoretical and empirical implications of the study findings and offers recommendations for future research and future practice that can be applied to improving outcomes in African countries.

THEORETICAL IMPLICATIONS

Evidence of social learning (Bandura, 1977) at play in the experience of the participants, as it relates to their involvement in the national purpose of their nations, highlights the importance of the intersectionality between choice (personal control), culture (environmental sources of control), and socio-economic development (human accomplishments). The reciprocal interaction of the first two constructs, choice and culture, is what determines both human behavior and human accomplishments. The latter includes socio-economic

DOI: 10.4018/979-8-3693-2403-5.ch009

development, which, in keeping with the definition of the term by (Oaks et al., 2003), is a function of one's or a country's material, human, and social capital in relation to others (p. 776).

There is evidence of personal, professional, material growth each participant experiences when we examine their individual narratives. This growth is both hindered and enabled by the choices made by the participants and the cultures (environments) in which they lived and made those choices. Osie and Amie were hindered by their community and the poor conditions of their countries. They were enabled by their decision to leave their countries for education and work on the outside. Zahra was hindered by her community and the poor conditions of her country. She was enabled by her decision to pursue music at whatever cost and a transformative career that gave her a platform to chart her own course. Siya was hindered by apartheid. He was later enabled by South Africa's political opening to become a diplomat and government legislation that helped him to amass a modest fortune.

There is equal evidence of the revulsion against or quiet abandonment of the national purpose of their nation-states that each participant experiences when we examine the parallel narratives of their nation-states. Despite his earlier departure, Osie remained keen on returning to contribute to Ghana's national purpose. Yet the poor conditions that encouraged him to leave the first time, including politics that deprioritized the public interest, were the same ones that were discouraging Osie from making good on his intent to return. Zahra out-right declined entry into Tanzania's national parliament because politics in Tanzania, the route she would have to take to get there, was inconsistent with her values. She would instead lean into her music career to contribute to Tanzania's national purpose through socially inspiring songs until this avenue was taken away by life events.

Siya made the choice to step-away from service in government to make money in the private sector. While contributing to South Africa's national purpose in this way through involvement in the country's economy, Siya's impact in the private sector, given his expertise and the deteriorating condition of South Africa's body politic at the time he left government, did not measure up to the impact Siya had in the public sector. Amie similarly withdrew from direct participation in Sierra Leone's national purpose because the winning side of the country's partisan politics blacklisted her from business opportunities.

This confluence of choice and culture in the lived experience of the participants' lives, wherein conditions within their environments prevail on them to make the choice to rebel against participation in the national purpose of their countries, greatly centers focus on the validity of the study's conceptual framework. If people are empowered to make good choices about our life pursuits, and we are supported, rather than hindered, by our cultural environment, we might be better equipped to navigate the conditions that influence our socio-economic development. This was evidently true for the participants when they excelled in their educational and career pursuits after making some tough choices, in response to their environments, that positioned them to excel. And it was also true when the participants turned away from direct participation in the national purpose of their home countries because the means to do so, influenced by their environments, had either been denied to them, made difficult to access, or proved too toxic to be a part of.

But here is where we bridge the gap that exists in the literature whenever the focus turns to development in Africa. This interdependency of choice and culture is a constant in the human condition, but it proves particularly significant when our focus turns to social development. The literature tells us that choice and culture reciprocally enable individual and societal transformation (Arendt, 1958; Arnold, 1869; Bandura, 1977; Barker, 1997; Gemmill and Oakley, 1992; Soyinka, 2000). This choice and culture empowerment makes change possible through the social process of leadership (Barker, 1997), which encourages people to negotiate, compromise, and sacrifice in the name of nation building – the equivalent of what Barker (1997) prescribed when he identified freedom, education, and social development as goals that require the navigation of complex social and political processes.

Thus, the interplay of choice and culture, as reflected in the examples of the lived experience of the participants and the parallel narratives of their nation-states, negatively influenced the participants' involvement in the national life of their countries. It hindered the achievement of socio-economic development (human accomplishments) at the national level because participants did not or could not engage in the social process of leadership that would have enabled them to prioritize participation in the national life of their nations. As their narratives demonstrated, Osie and Zahra clearly opted out of direct participation in the national life of their nations. Osie left the country. While he desires a return, he has delayed the decision as a result of the conditions in Ghana. Zahra participated in the life of her country through music, but this was short-lived. She later declined the opportunity for direct engagement in Tanzanian politics when the opportunity was presented in the form of joining the national assembly.

Siya and Amie elected to participate in the life of their nations but the absence of their engagement in the social process of leadership, which was denied to them by a confluence of choice and culture, influenced the breadth of their participation. They ultimately discontinued their participation because, in Siya's example, self improvement proved more important to him and, in

Amie's example, the politics of her country proved more inhibiting for her. Since they were not entirely empowered to make good choices about their life pursuits and they were hindered by their cultural environment, they were not better equipped to navigate the conditions that influenced their decisions to participate in the social development project of their nation-states.

EMPIRICAL IMPLICATIONS

Understanding African countries' socio-economic development struggles requires a deeper examination of the role of the people. The peoples' lived experiences help us make sense of the challenges of development and national advancement. This is so because nation building, the purpose of which is the achievement of lasting social transformation, is not possible without the active involvement and participation of the individuals who comprise the nation. When we take a closer look at our lives, we see our agency (choice and decision-making) and environment (culture) converging to influence our condition, including our ethics and disposition (relationship) with one another. Ethics and relationships have considerable relevance because they form the basis of trust and respect required among a people for achievement of a common or greater good. This relevance is reflected in the literature, including Barker's (1997) idea of leadership — how this social process comes about through the ethics and social realities of a people to encourage them to negotiate, compromise, and sacrifice in order to affect change.

The relevance of ethics and relationships to social progress is equally transparent in *The tyranny of experts: Economics, dictators, and the forgotten rights of the poor*, a book in which William Easterly (2013) dissected the relationship between poverty and the lack of freedom and concluded that poor societies generally suffered from acute oppression. This oppression induces a trust deficit that renders trade and development difficult to accomplish. Easterly wrote in this vein about early China, Latin America and Africa (giving firm consideration to the latter's history of the slave trade, in which Africans sold Africans to Europeans) and concluded that "a history of autocracy and oppression breeds values like lack of trust and respect for others, fostering an insider/outsider distinction in which the insiders place little value on the rights or well-being of the outsiders" (p. 166). Said another way, mistrust and lack of respect between people and ethnic groups in Africa and elsewhere in the world, where poverty is endemic and the rule of law is an afterthought, has manifested in the politics and civic participation of the very same people so forcefully that it has rendered for them political stability and economic development a difficult, if not impossible national goal to attain.

There is no greater indication of this for Africa than the sheer number of attempts, since the post-independence days of 1950, in the overthrowing of governments: 214 attempts, with 106 having succeeded and 108 having failed, according to researchers Jonathan Powell and Clayton Thyne (2011). There is no greater evidence for African countries of the mistrust and lack of respect between people inhibiting political stability and economic development than the wave of Africans opting out of civic participation or leaving the region in search of self-development and economic opportunities elsewhere in the world, as demonstrated in the lived experience of participants of this study.

This view of African countries' present-day predicament, what the study findings tell us, thus compels particular focus on a few fronts about the continent, namely narrative inquiry as a useful research design for better understanding of the conditions therein; a reorientation of the concept of leadership in our discourse; the need for human capacity development; and a reframing of our priorities for national development.

Narrative Inquiry

Examining the lived experience of the people in Africa demonstrates the value of narrative inquiry as an important research design for understanding the human condition in Africa as it relates to development. The literature has continuously demonstrated that what leads our nations to fail in advancing the lives of our people are external or internal impediments. There is little evidence of how these impediments converge, in the way social learning theorists describe the determinants of human behavior and accomplishments, to influence African countries' socio-economic predicament. Failure of the literature to tell the whole story about Africa's predicament through a concise examination calls for re-examination of the problem through a different lens: an exploration of the lived experience of everyday Africans. So, what exactly is the value of narrative inquiry or storytelling?

Narrative inquiry is important because of the power and significance of storytelling to the human experience and its capacity to help us make meaning out of our lives (Barrett and Stauffer, 2009; Clandinin and Rosiek, 2007; Storr, 2020). Use of the research design to explore the socio-economic challenges in African countries broadens understanding of the phenomenon through the telling of true life stories of Africans. Stories and storytelling are the well-spring of information, the rich sources of data that explain and amplify the human condition as it is experienced and recorded for posterity.

Storytelling is the format the participants of this study used to describe their lived experience. They each shared how their lives unfolded through a retelling of stories about events and milestones that shaped the direction of their lives.

The experience of the participants mirrored what Will Storr (2020) observed in his account about humans using storytelling for survival. Storr shared with us that storytelling was how early humans influenced and controlled behaviors of tribe members for the preservation of the tribe, and how individuals communicated their motivations. Hutson and Johson (2016) offered a more immediate rationale for storytelling's usefulness to humans. In times of crisis, the authors observed, storytelling is an imperative, especially for leaders. "In chaos or calamity, the greatest loss an organization [or a people] can experience is the loss of meaning. When meaning is disrupted, we feel unsafe, out of control, baffled, or dazed. Without meaning, we don't trust our ability to understand what is going on or to imagine what could happen next. We need coherence. We need a story" (p. 3).

African countries' experience with socio-economic development qualifies, at least for those enduring it, as chaotic and cataclysmic. The people make this chaos and calamity easier to understand and to digest through the stories they tell, much like in the examples contained in this study. In our participants' retelling of their storied experiences, the trajectory of development, personal agency/action and social influence were consistent themes that emerged. These themes offered meaning about what was experienced and, in so doing, brought to light the convergence of personal choices and environmental circumstances that manifested in each of the participants' lives. The sum total of their experiences (revealed through the stories they shared) enabled us to see how choice and culture determined the participants' behaviors and actions and, ultimately, what they were able to accomplish.

Leadership

The findings underscored the important role of choice (decision-making) and culture (environment) in our lives and how these constructs can harness the power of leadership to affect social transformation. As reflected in their narratives, what each of the participants were able to accomplish or not accomplish "[resulted] from reciprocal interaction of external circumstances with a host of personal determinants including endowed potentialities, acquired competencies, reflective thought, and a high level of self-initiative" (Bandura, 1974, p. 867). This interdependency of choice and culture is critical in social development because choice and culture are prerequisites for individual and societal transformation (Arendt, 1958; Arnold, 1869; Bandura, 1977; Barker,

1997; Gemmill and Oakley, 1992; Soyinka, 2000). They make change possible through leadership.

But this leadership is not the kind we have been conditioned to embrace. Rather, we have collectively subscribed to leadership as a man in a position of authority or one with traits that can turn around a struggling enterprise or a nation. Our embrace of this concept of leadership in the discourse about Africa's predicament has led us to point fingers and to absolve ourselves of responsibility of the conditions in which we find ourselves, as Gemmill and Oakley (1992) eloquently observed about how society has come to use the existing myth about leadership as a crutch. They explained that,

When members of a group are faced with uncertainty and ambiguity regarding direction, they often report experiencing feelings of anxiety, helplessness, discomfort, disappointment, hostility, and fear of failure. Frightened by these emerging emotions and impulses, which are ordinarily held in check by absorption into the prevailing social system, they collude, largely unconsciously, to dispel them by projecting them onto "leadership" or the "leader" role. The projection allows organizational members to avoid directly confronting the emerging emotions and regress to a form of social order with which they are familiar (Gemmill and Oakley, 1992, p. 2).

The leadership that we ought to instead subscribe to is the kind Barker (1997) employed us to embrace if our goals are freedom, education, or social development – human endeavors that require the navigation of complex social and political processes. Relying on people in positions of authority for leadership of our affairs is backward thinking. "It is not the leader who creates leadership [or cultural norms and our achievements], it is leadership that creates the leader" [and our norms and achievements] (Barker, 1997, p. 354). Thus, the social process of leadership, driven by ethics, enables people in society to negotiate, compromise, and sacrifice to create a vision of a future good so that our development goals can materialize.

Our growth and transformation in African countries requires each of us to engage in the social process of leadership. In so doing, we acknowledge that we have a common destiny for which we have shared responsibility. We rid ourselves, once and for all, of the false belief that our national leaders are the ones who have failed us. We acknowledge that our failures lay not in what our so-called leaders have done or not done but in our collective disengagement from one another and from the life of our nation-states, as the narratives of the participants of this study revealed. We come to terms with the reality that the failure of leadership in African countries that is so often faulted for

Africa's predicament has less to do with the people in positions of authority and more to do with our collective lack of engagement in leadership.

Human Development

The findings emphasized the important role of choice and culture for human beings, how, as magnified by the study's theoretical and conceptual frameworks, one influences the other to yield the social process of leadership that makes change possible. Harnessing the said power of leadership is an important study implication, as it speaks directly to the often underrated need for human development in the context of Africa's socio-economic challenges. As previously stated, nation building, the purpose of which is the achievement of lasting social transformation, is not possible without the active involvement and participation of the individuals who comprise the nation. Thus, our discourse on and efforts to transform communities in Africa must feature considerations about developing the men, women and children of African countries. Our discourse and efforts must promote the kind of education and training that increases the capacities of our people for the work of self and community betterment.

In the literature, we met Matthew Arnold (1869), who viewed culture as a transformative change agent for England at the height of the industrial revolution when England was floundering. The culture Arnold promoted was rooted in the general expansion of the mind, wherein the individual ensures his best self permeates all that he says and does, and that he puts his energies not on "having something but in becoming something." In this way, his drive for personal development will be purposeful and free of infringement on the similar efforts of his neighbors. He will contribute to the collective advancement of his people without the slightest apprehension or concern that doing so might lead to setbacks in his own individual development.

The ability of individuals to develop such an "inward condition of the mind and spirit," Arnold explained, depended on the availability of an enabling environment. People need the space to develop the ability to analyze and think critically; to develop an understanding of who we are, how best we can relate to our world and how to give meaning and purpose to our lives. Arnold's answer was a more refined and systemic process of learning for England, a system of education administered by the State to replace the religious-based learning of his day that compelled individuals to follow a strict moral code, rather than focus on critical thinking and community service.

The education and training Arnold (1869) advocated for his people centuries ago for individual development is the same education and training we saw reflected in Barker's (1997) clarion call for a reassessment of our views on leadership and how to impart the practice to others. In sum, Barker (1997) concluded that the social process that is leadership emerges within individuals when the said individuals are provided training in skills such as communication, building coalitions and compromising. It emerges through development of individual emotional and intellectual capabilities, and also through education in the "social patterns and moral orders that produces an integration of conceptual knowledge, ideals, insights, experiences, and sources of behavior" – all of which contribute to the "process of integrating individual ethics into community mores" (Barker, 1997, p. 360).

The acquisition of this training, development and education Barker (1997) outlined raises greater awareness and responsibility in the individual through a focus on choice (decision-making) and the consolidation of an enabling culture that aligns thinking and behavior toward personal growth and service for a common good (Arnold, 1869). The narratives of the study's participants made it abundantly clear how self-development improved the participants' material conditions. The same narratives also helped us to understand the limits of education and training on the social transformation agenda when the said education and training are not centered on human development through educational leadership – the acquisition of the soft skills of awareness, active listening, communication, coalition building, negotiation, compromise, and service to others that enables individuals to contribute to affecting change beyond our own self-interests.

National Development

The study findings direct focus on the need for human capacity development as a driver for socio-economic development and the achievement of lasting social transformation. This orientation suggests a need for reframing our priorities for national development, including related policies that seek to spur growth of the national economy. Just as nation building is not possible without involvement of the nation's people, so too is socio-economic development not possible without the creativity and ingenuity of the people. National development considerations must therefore be informed and rooted in the perspective that development transpires *only* when we invest in the development of the people. National strategies for transforming the agricultural sector, improving infrastructure, or reforming the private sector to attract foreign investment, for example, will have minimal impact on the ultimate goal of lasting social transformation without proper investment in the souls who will carry-out the work.

To be sure, we return to Bandura (1977) and the social learning theorists who demonstrated that "Human accomplishments result from reciprocal interaction of external circumstances with a host of personal determinants including endowed potentialities, acquired competencies, reflective thought, and a high level of self-initiative" (p. 867). The underlying message here is that individuals make decisions in relation to the circumstances of their environment in order to influence the course of their lives. It is the individual's creativity and ingenuity, in response to the stimulus of his environment, that sparks the actions necessary to change or shape his or her living condition. This spark-plug of creativity and ingenuity within human beings is the reason development experts make the case for nations to give adequate attention to the development of their economies through individual initiative rather than through state or national planning.

This idea of "conscious design" being inferior to "spontaneous solutions" in the development context is what William Easterly (2013) convincingly postulated in *The tyranny of experts: Economics, dictators, and the forgotten rights of the poor*. Conscious design is state or national planning of the economy, whose fixtures are binding decisions of the national authorities and their expert advisors on economic policy. Spontaneous solutions, on the other hand, is simply allowing the people and the marketplace to drive the economy through the creativity and ingenuity people regularly rely upon to address their individual, family, and community needs.

A fundamental difference between "conscious design" and "spontaneous solutions" is that the former restricts decision-making to a small, often powerful elite, while the latter promotes individual freedom for the masses. As demonstrated through this study's theoretical framework and study findings, human accomplishments are possible through the interplay of environmental sources of control and personal control (choice and decision-making). Thus, freedom – one's ability to make choices about the direction of his or her life – ought to be a paramount consideration in national development planning.

National development requires a free society in which individuals have the liberty to exercise agency for personal and material development. Public policy thus has to be strongly focused on the development of human capacity, not solely or predominantly on technical economic or trade reform. The necessity of human development and freedom correlates to the need for adequate attention to be given to development of the economy through individual initiative, which is supported by education and training of the individual.

SUMMARY

The areas of focus outlined all present opportunities for tangible improvements, notably for the people, our communities and our governing bodies. In the case of narrative inquiry, the improvement is the perspective of a different lens to explore Africa's condition, as well as the ability to create a roadmap for change that is derived from and tethered to the experiences of the people who matter. For reorientation of leadership, the improvement is individuals embracing awareness and responsibility toward the path of positive engagement with others for the common good. This social process of leadership will spark a cultural shift in how problems are addressed both at the individual or personal and national level.

Human capacity development, namely training and education keyed to skills and emotional intelligence development, will improve the competence and moral outlook of individuals, many of whom will take-on roles in organizing and running society's governing bodies. Reframing national development, to ensure a priority is placed on supporting individual initiative and freedom, will drive improvements in the social, political and economic spheres of life. This respect for individual rights – a foundation for any human development initiative, coupled with a concerted focus on increasing the capacities of our people through education and leadership – is a path for positive and lasting change in Africa.

Let us now consider the recommendations that the research findings compel us to think about, including recommendations for future research and recommendations for future practice.

RECOMMENDATIONS

Future Research

The cause of African countries' perennial low-income status and failure to achieve lasting social transformation has proven to be a consistently vexing puzzle. This study was an exploration of a conceptual framework that addressed this important query. The framework was informed by existing literature, including the ideas of social learning theory, leadership as a social process, and choice and culture as the catalyst for change in society. The study's findings proved difficult to approximate to the entire continent of Africa because of sample size and limited data collected relative to the target population of Africa. Yet, the findings make a strong case for conducting more studies about socio-economic development in Africa that are grounded in narrative inquiry and case study of the lived experience of African people.

Future studies could aid in the approximation of findings and strengthen validity, including the integrity of the conceptual framework of this study, through use of a larger sample of participants, either concentrated in one country or spread through-out multiple countries representing each region of Africa. Random sampling of a larger sample size would also greatly promote validity and efforts to more broadly generalize the findings.

One of the shortcomings of this particular study related to sample size and scope, including the exclusive use of Africa's urban dwellers as participants. While some of the participants of this study grew up in rural areas, they largely spent their adult lives in urban settings, where they focused on achieving social mobility through formal education, rather than through a vocation or trade. Future studies would thus benefit from an inclusion of Africa's rural masses (farmers, fisherman, carpenters, shoemakers, seamstress, and so on) who make-up the bulk of Africa's labor force and whose socio-economic pursuits might be more internally focused or driven, compared with current study participants, because of a lack of interest or opportunity to immigrate outside of their homeland.

An exploration of the lived experience of Africa's rural masses will offer perspective on the ideas presented in this study and aid in the approximation of the findings. Furthermore, a similar consideration could be given for Africa's divergent make-up of linguistic and cultural heritages, namely the Francophone, Anglophone, Arabic, Spanish, Portuguese, and Creole speaking peoples of the continent, whose perspectives are dissimilar for the very reasons their languages and cultural influences are dissimilar.

In light of the fact that the established literature offers limited perspective on the intersectionality between choice (personal control), culture (environmental sources of control), and socio-economic development (human accomplishments) as it relates to developments in Africa – the conceptual framework of this study, the research community can now be charged with the work of conducting further inquiries in this area and examine the validity of the ideas presented in this study. There is an urgent need to examine further the assumption, as it relates to developments in Africa, that if people are empowered to make good choices about our life pursuits, and we are supported, rather than hindered, by our cultural environment, we might be better equipped to navigate the conditions that influence our socio-economic development.

The urgency for Africa in this regard is palpable because of the dire human conditions that prevail on the continent. To navigate our way out of the malaise and shed the label of "the third world of the third world," the research community must help practitioners gain a better understanding of our present, collective condition through an examination of our individual roles in the struggle.

Future Practice

An important takeaway from this study for individuals to implement within the real world is reframing our outlook on the problem space. Socio-economic development and the achievement of lasting social transformation in Africa is a condition of the people, by the people, and for the people. The citizens of African countries work to improve our living conditions, and the work that we do is manifestly in the investments we make and in our engagement with one another. This reframing or recognition of the problem implies awareness and responsibility, which are the hallmarks of leadership as a social process.

If our goals are freedom, education, or social development – human endeavors that require the navigation of complex social and political processes, as Barker (1997) observed, we need to embrace our individual and collective leadership roles in the struggle for advancement. National development is a condition of human development which is a condition of education and leadership.

The education required for human development must be centered around awareness and responsibility cultivated through skills development and a focus on emotional and social intelligence to build and sustain relationships among community members. Self-awareness, communication, coalition building, and compromising are thus prerequisites for this learning, as is education in the "social patterns and moral orders that produces an integration of conceptual knowledge, ideals, insights, experiences, and sources of behavior" – all of which contribute to the "process of integrating individual ethics into community mores" (Barker, 1997, p. 360).

The leadership required is an orientation to service that enhances a person's capacity for improvement and achievement. Stainer (2016) and Whitmore (2017) emphasized the 'unlocking of people's potential' as the foundation of coaching leadership. It is, the authors contended in their respective works, training one's focus on the content of a situation or issue as well as on the relationship with the people involved in order to help remove or reduce the barriers standing in the way of achievement and self-actualization. The positive impact of this leadership orientation is not limited to the individual. Organizations and nation-states similarly benefit from adoption of this leadership orientation, notably in the creation of a culture that sheds dependency and creates conditions for high performance.

One of the greatest challenges for our communities in African countries is our conformist nature and restrictions on individual liberty, as demonstrated in *Values and development in Southern Africa*, (Müller, Mekgwe, & Mhloyi, 2013), wherein decisions that impact social mobility and national development fall in the hands of a select-few in the name of consensus building. The lack of freedom and inclusion that such a values orientation generates inevitably negates our growth; it discourages trust and it creates a culture of dependence. It also sets up scenarios for blame and criticism when things go wrong. As Whitmore (2017) observed, blame and criticism "breaks down relationships and blocks learning" (p. 34). The people of our nation-states must therefore find a way to disperse responsibility, and this requires the cultivation of trust based on a shared purpose, which engenders commitment from and between people.

The success of our nation-states depends on the performance of individuals, who must integrate said performance with the performance of the families and communities to which they belong. This integration speaks to the need for coalition-building and collaboration. These elements are what bind group members together. They cultivate what Margaret Heffnan (2015) highlighted as an important element of successful teams: social sensitivity toward each other. Heffnan reminded us that "companies [nations] don't have ideas, only people do. And what motivates people are the bonds, loyalty, and trust developed between each other." This social capital, as Heffnan described it (the reliance and interdependency that builds trust) enables teams (or communities within nation-states) to both perform at a high level and be resilient during times of complexity and uncertainty.

In considering the development and socio-economic challenges of Africa, we (Africans) are obliged to appreciate and to train our focus on the central role we all play in our communities in promoting betterment and social mobility. This recognition points to the importance of individual awareness and responsibility, coupled with our engagement with each other in the social process of leadership to affect change where we stand. Harnessing this leadership is the work of education, educational leadership to be more precise, which strengthens individual development through the cultivation of skills (awareness, active listening, communication, empathy, relationship and coalition building, and service to/investment in others) that enable individuals to contribute to affecting change beyond our own self-interests.

Allowing for such an orientation permits or enables the reframing of our thoughts about the problem space concerning the achievement of lasting social transformation in Africa. We evolve from the position of needing to find answers to a set of questions to the understanding of having an opportunity to help change lives through awareness, learning, as well as all of us making a genuine investment in the development of our people to help maximize our potential.

The socio-economic struggles in African countries are neither unique nor insurmountable. We can overcome our struggles with self-reflection, service and engagement with one another. The spirit we embody as a people is evidence enough for us to believe, just as study participant Siya reminded us about the way out of the struggles in his home country. In his words,

While we have made some bad choices, the strength we have to effect positive change and to reverse the effects of those bad choices lies in our culture. Our culture demands self-reflection, the ability to engage in robust self-criticism, to admit wrongs and to find ways to correct those wrongs. This way of being and doing is captured in the ideals of Ubuntu (humanity) – the generosity of spirit, the willingness to forgive and to give people a second chance at redemption. Ubuntu, a sprite of humanness and humanity that permeates all over Africa, is the reason slavery and colonialism in Africa could not thrive. "I am because we are," the ubuntu philosophy, is a powerful deterrent against the disempowerment of a people and a catalyst for uniting them (Siya, personal interview, September 14, 2022).

The contours for change in South Africa can be seen in Siya's comments, and they are underpinned not by a focus on the mechanics of institutional or economic reform, even as these are important elements for affecting change, but rather on the capacity of individuals to be self-aware and to embrace service to community. These are the very same elements that Albert Bandura (1977) and social learning theorists distilled as the determinants of human behavior and achievement: the reciprocal interaction of external circumstances with a host of personal determinants – choice and culture as lived and experienced by individuals in a society. This central focus on the individual – the facilitation of his or her growth, initiative and freedom through education and leadership is a path to achieving lasting social transformation in Africa.

An exemplary evidence of just how precise this observation is are the lives of the people who made this study possible. Osie, Zahra, Siya, and Amie's lived experiences told in parallel and within the context of the narratives of their nation-states offer a unique window through which to observe the building blocks and gradual formation of the social elements that either discouraged and stifled or enabled and furthered their growth.

But a nagging question remains. Are the participants' experiences unique to them for reasons not uncovered in this study such as, perhaps, the timing of their development, separate personal dispositions, or other extenuating circumstances? Chapter 10 offers perspective on this question through illumination of the larger story about Africa, which our participants' lived experiences have shown to be an alarming pattern since African countries began to gain their political independence and right to self-determination.

REFERENCES

Arendt, H. (1958). *The human condition*. The University of Chicago Press.

Arnold, M. (1869). *Culture and anarchy: An essay in political and social criticism*. Macmillan.

Bandura, A. (1974). Behavior theory and the models of man. *The American Psychologist*, *29*(12), 859–869. doi:10.1037/h0037514

Bandura, A. (1977). *Social learning theory*. Prentice Hall.

Barker, R. A. (1997). How can we train leaders if we do not know what leadership is? *Human Relations*, *50*(4), 343–362. doi:10.1177/001872679705000402

Barrett, M. S., & Stauffer, S. L. (2009). *Narrative inquiry in music education: Troubling certainty*. Springer. doi:10.1007/978-1-4020-9862-8

Clandinin, D. J., & Rosiek, J. (2007). Mapping a landscape of narrative inquiry: Borderland spaces and tensions. In D. J. Clandinin (Ed.), *Handbook of narrative inquiry: mapping a methodology* (pp. 35–75). Sage. doi:10.4135/9781452226552.n2

Easterly, W. (2013). *The tyranny of experts: Economics, dictators, and the forgotten rights of the poor*. Basic Books.

Gemmill, G., & Oakley, J. (1992). Leadership: An alienating social myth? *Human Relations*, *45*(2), 113–129. doi:10.1177/001872679204500201

Heffernan, M. (2015, May). Forget the pecking order at work. Youtube. https://www.ted.com/talks/margaret_heffernan_forget_the_pecking_order_at_work?language=en

Hutson, H., & Johnson, M. (2016, May 2). *To recover from a crisis, retell your company's story*. Harvard Business Review Digital Archives.

Oakes, J.M., & Rossi, P. H. (2003). The measurement of SES in health research: current practice and steps toward a new approach. *Social Science & Medicine (1982), 56*(4), 769–784. . doi:10.1016/S0277-9536(02)00073-4

Powell, J., & Thyne, C. (2011). Global Instances of Coups from 1950-Present. *Journal of Peace Research, 48*(2), 249–259. doi:10.1177/0022343310397436

Soyinka, W. (2000). Culture, democracy and renewal. *Trends in Organized Crime, 5*(3), 110–117. doi:10.1007/s12117-000-1039-2

Stanier, M. B. (2016). *The coaching habit: Say less, ask more & change the way you lead forever*. Box of Crayons Press.

Storr, W. (2020). *The science of storytelling: Why stories make us human and how to tell them better*. Abrams Press.

Whitemore, J. (2017). *Coaching for performance: The principles and practice of coaching and leadership* (5th ed.). Nicholas Barely Publishing.

Chapter 10
Narrative Inquiry

ABSTRACT

Chapter ten offers concluding perspectives through the researcher's engagement in the obligatory practice of narrative inquirers, wherein "researchers also engage in narrative inquiry into their own lived and told stories as part of the process of coming alongside research participants" (Johnson and Christensen). The aim of this effort is to expound upon and contextualize the lessons of this study through a personal example, which draws attention to the larger story in Africa of the peoples' migration and detachment from one another. This larger story offers hope – a roadmap for change in Africa that centers on understanding and navigating the confluence of choice and culture in our lives.

INTRODUCTION

In narrative inquiry the researcher has an obligation to accurately tell the lived experience of the study participants. This obligation requires relational listening, which compels the researcher to share his own living, telling, retelling, and reliving of life in the same manner that participants share their lived experience narratives. As Johnson and Christensen (2020) contend, "Narrative inquirers…come alongside participants and begin to engage in narrative inquiry into participants' lived and told stories. Of necessity, researchers also engage in narrative inquiry into their own lived and told stories as part of the process of coming alongside research participants" (p. 406). This responsibility is an important and compelling one that I take on in this final, concluding chapter as a way to expound upon and contextualize the lessons of this study.

DOI: 10.4018/979-8-3693-2403-5.ch010

I include my lived experience with Dad and Mom in these pages because it is a story that so plainly encapsulates the lessons of the connection between the lives we lead and the full measure of the environments in which we lead them – what social learning theory tells us about the determinants of human behavior and our accomplishments. Our family's experience proves to be a precursor of the general arc of the lived experience of present-day Africans, including study participants Osie, Zahra, Siya, and Amie, wherein, as a consequence of Africans' decision to try to overcome the conditions of our environments at home, we see the emergence of the larger story of African migration and of our socio-political distancing from one another – even as some of us remain in the country of our birth.

This larger story of migration and detachment from one another illustrates some of the basic truths about our problems – problems that are not in any way unique to the experiences of Osie, Zahra, Siya, and Amie. This larger story magnifies the base nature of humanity. It demonstrates in profound depth how our frailties can manifest in the worst ways when (1) we allow our drive for personal development to cloud our judgment or overtake the responsibility that we have for each other, and (2) when we develop a sense of indifference to such an extent that we feel neglected, locked-out of the prevailing system, or we feel empowered by the same system to prey on others.

This larger story, in which we demonstrate our humanity for all the right and wrong reasons, also offers hope for lasting change – a roadmap that centers on understanding and navigating in our lives the bidirectional influence process of choice and culture that determines both our behavior and accomplishments.

* * *

Dad was convulsing, gasping for air. He had no idea of what possessed him just hours from his rest at the guest house. His heart was pounding inside his chest. The stomach ache, nausea, made him fatigued. He was vomiting, on the verge of keeling over. MK sat across the table watching, his dark brown eyes transfixed. He let some time pass, not bothering to consider, as anyone in his position might have, that he ought to rush Dad to the hospital. Only after the conditions pleased him did MK move to place Dad inside his late model sedan. They were on the way, "to get help," along the potholed streets of Conakry. But MK didn't make the turn for the hospital nearby, as he navigated the car under the cover of darkness. He turned instead in the direction of his personal physician.

MK was orderly, businesslike in his movements, uttering not a single word to comfort or reassure his sickened guest in the backseat. His plan was coming together. All he had to do was wait just a little longer. Inside, as his medic took over, MK poured himself a drink, sat down on a brown leather sofa and began skimming through the day's newspaper. He was patient. Minutes went by, then an hour until evening blended into night. It was ten-thirty P.M. when Dad stopped breathing. MK had moved him yet again by this hour, and Dad's body was now in the hands of the medical staff at Clinique Medico-Chirugicale de Sanoyah—the very hospital Dad should have been taken to when he fell ill. He was pronounced dead in the moment of their arrival.

The hospital staff turned their attention to protocol in search of next of kin. A nephew named Musa hurried to the hospital. The young man of 23 years was a shell of himself, nearing a state of madness when he saw the lifeless body of his uncle. The two of them had just spoken a few short hours earlier–Dad retelling plans for Musa to help Dad manage a new business. Musa would have to stew in his confusion and anger for a bit longer in the waiting room, however. The hospital insisted that he wait in order to hand him a terse, to-the-point death certificate in French language–Dad's first and last names woefully misspelled in the document in the same cavalier manner as his final moments had been handled.

An able-bodied forty-four year old man doesn't just collapse and die, Musa thought out loud. He was at a loss for what he'd been told had happened. "You really don't know?" Memuna asked him, with her stunning face bulging in mild disbelief. She'd been in the house several nights before when it happened, playing the familiar role of a lady for the night. Now, she stood with Musa outside the aging, four-story flat, where she rented a room, pacing, with a look of despair. "It was the salad," Memuna said, unable to hide what so deeply tormented her. Dad had been fed a local poison. The substance severed his vital organs and caused him to bleed to death.

This wasn't how it was supposed to end, certainly not for the man who'd defied the odds to overcome his humble beginnings.

Just a few years earlier in 1988, Dad had joined a precious metals, stones, and commodities company headquartered in Riverdale, Maryland, mere miles from our home across the Potomac River in Falls Church, Virginia. Goldstone Limited was the brainchild of John Okra and Bruce Piedt, entrepreneurs whose business interests appealed to Dad as much as Dad's background and ambition appealed to them. The businessmen hired Dad to be their representative in West Africa, for a venture to expand the company's fledgling efforts on the continent, where quality gold and diamonds could be sourced far less expensively for lucrative sale in the US market.

Dad was the ideal hire—a man who had made it out of Africa to settle in a place, America, that many in his homeland could only dream of. Along the way, he developed a network of people who were themselves connected to the political elites of his home region, in countries like Senegal, Guinea, Ivory Coast, Liberia and beyond.

The plan for Dad was, first, to incorporate and grow Goldstone in Sierra Leone. This effort would later serve as the basis for expansion in the neighboring states. But as Mom endured throughout their marriage, Dad elected to put more faith in the advice of others instead of in that of his own wife—in this case, a distant cousin and business associate based in Conakry. Mohamed Kamara, or MK as he was commonly known, was at the time in the Guinean capital, the beneficiary of lucrative public tenders owing to his political ties and shrewd business reputation.

Hailing from the same Susu tribe as Dad, but from opposite sides of the Sierra Leone-Guinea border, MK and Dad could not have been more different in the way they lived and touched the lives of others. Dad sought and reveled in contact with people. He wanted to get to know them, even if that knowledge came to nothing. MK was reclusive, coming around to people only when it suited a purpose. Dad was quick to trust, and he tended to take people at their word. MK never allowed himself to put faith in others, as if he'd been victimized and as if he himself had victimized others. Yet, they both loved being entrepreneurs. They relished taking risks; benefiting from the independence and power that flowed from being the master of one's own destiny.

They also bonded over the opposite sex, ascribing to the view that, as the French military leader Napoléon Bonaparte once crudely put it, "Women are the occupation of idle men [but they can also be for] the relaxation of the warrior." When their wives were not around, and the two were done discussing business or politics, they turned their attention to the joys of physical pleasure with women for whom they did not have deep feelings and to whom they had, at best, only a surface commitment. These commonalities drew them closer together. It explained why, despite having the means, MK lodged in the Virginia apartment of his distant cousin whenever he visited the US, rather than stay in a hotel.

Dad told MK about Goldstone's plans for West Africa. Sensing an opportunity, MK made the case that the company should start its efforts in Conakry, not Freetown. From there, MK claimed he could help grow the business by leveraging his influence in the country. Dad must have reflected hard on MK's suggestion, if only to anticipate questions that might arise from people like John, Bruce, and Mom. In the end, he let MK convince him that they were on to something. Conakry, they both would come to believe, was the better market. The company executives thus put plans in motion. They purchased mining trucks and other auxiliary materials for shipping to Conakry. They even sent a sedan from Brussels to serve as the company car.

Goldstone was well established in Guinea by March 1990. This upward trajectory bolstered the case for expansion and neighboring Sierra Leone was the obvious choice. Dad was dispatched to Freetown to start the process. He was by now a regular traveler for the company to the region, and he knew exactly what he needed to secure approvals. He took thousands of dollars with him, inconspicuously stashed away in his briefcase, along with a letter from Goldstone's executives, which implored cooperation from those whom Dad sought out for assistance. Dad went prepared, never mind that he was venturing into a world he thought he could easily navigate because of his roots.

Dad made his way up north to Conakry to check in on the company after his meetings in Freetown. MK was waiting for him with a plan of his own. In fact, he had designs on getting more involved with the company's operations from the time Dad had told him about Goldstone. His interests were not in making money for the company but rather in wresting control of its assets in order to incorporate them into his own business empire. But MK would have a difficult, if not impossible, go at seeing his plans through since Dad was in charge of the company's operations.

MK had made a fortune on the backs of unsuspecting people who were starting out in business and who were inclined to trust him for not only what he promised them but also for the strength of his ties to powerful men. To be sure, MK enjoyed a direct line to the country's leaders, including then-President Lansana Conté, who ruled Guinea with an iron fist from 1984 until his death in 2008. MK used these ties to lure people in, to make them believe that, with the right connections, they too could amass the fortunes they saw in the cars and houses MK flaunted all over Conakry.

But MK also used these ties as an insurance policy against potential reprisal. He knew that once he made his move, his victims would think twice about retaliating because of the protection afforded to him by men like Conté. Dad played right into his hands. Not only did Dad work to amass Goldstone's investments in Conakry; he further insulated himself in the mirage of MK's world, in which wealth was staged as a platform to beget more wealth with the blessing of those who made and enforced the rules. Dad could have it all in this world whenever he visited: a new house to stay in, cars to chauffeur him around, proximity to political power, prestige, and women—lots of women.

So Dad must have thrown caution to the wind as he thought about the good time that awaited him in Conakry. He elected to travel alone instead of taking along one of his nephews. They were three young men, each not more than twenty-five years of age, who availed themselves to Dad for whatever he might need when he traveled back home. On this particular trip, north to a place they'd all lived for a time, each was aware of the need to be by Dad's side. They'd experience Conakry both at its best and at its worst far more times than they cared to remember. Yet Dad wouldn't have it any other way. He insisted on going alone—a decision that not only reflected arrogance but also a misplaced trust in a world he'd long ceased to know.

MK sat patiently in a luxury SUV with a driver at the wheel as Dad's flight touched down from Freetown. Dad walked to the waiting car–with immigration formalities behind him.

"Welcome, my Brother. It is so good to see you," MK offered in greeting.

"Happy to see you, my Brother," Dad responded, reaching out for MK's hand with a grin as expansive as the thoughts in his head about the good times awaiting him.

"What are you in the mood for?"

"You know, I am so tired from all the traveling. Tonight, I just want some good food and the chance to unwind." Dad's words must have rung loudly in MK's ears, for he had already organized a sumptuous dinner.

"We are going to the guest house," MK told him. "You will have time to rest there. The driver will come for you in a few hours for dinner." Dad nodded his head in agreement as he surveyed from inside the chauffeured car a city that had fallen on hard times.

Conakry, at the start of the 1990s, was a shell of a city compared to earlier years of the 1940s and 1950s, when it bustled with development activity designed to enrich colonizers in France. Much of the city's infrastructure was dilapidated. The roads were in bad shape. Electric power was unreliable. Public buildings needed structural repair and even a coat of paint. Safe drinking water was scarce, as was indoor plumbing and adequate housing in which such a "luxury" could even be constructed.

The city was grossly overcrowded, on account of a mass exodus of people from outside regions of the country in search of employment opportunities that did not exist. The city had indeed taken an even sharper nosedive economically than the one precipitated years earlier by the country's nationalist leaders (namely Ahmed Sekou Toure, who famously gave France's Charles de Gaulle the middle finger when France, during pre-independence talks in 1958, offered Guinea the choice of membership in the French Community or complete independence).

Toure's decision for Guinea to go it alone was brazen in and of itself, but also for the fact that he made it at a time when all the other French West African colonies embraced the opposite position in order to ensure their nations' economic survival. Toure so angered the French that they pretty much took everything—light fixtures and even the kitchen sink—on their way out the door. France gutted Guinea in material terms, but also created a brain-drain that severely strained the country's ability to move on, even thirty years after Toure's seminal decision.

The downward spiral could have been avoided if not for Toure's political and economic mismanagement. He killed and jailed opponents in order to force acceptance of his ruling party as the government, then used legislation to codify the symbiotic relationship in law. He centralized control of the economy, which led to a loss of even basic services and to average Guineans being unable to put bread and butter on the table.

Toure's death in 1984 did not help matters. Rather than usher in a new beginning, the ones he left behind allowed the country to succumb to a military coup and another prolonged rule by MK's friend, Lansana Conté, that featured a move away from centralized economic planning but nonetheless yielded the same dismal output. It was no surprise that life for the average man on the street decades after independence was rendered nearly impossible. As a consequence, people's hearts and minds hardened against their own countrymen and, even more so, against outsiders.

People preyed on each other with reckless abandon, and none did it better than the country's political elites and those with ties to them. The pair seemed to work in tandem to perpetuate the political power of one while advancing the economic interests of the other. In the process, they combined to construct lifestyle amenities like luxury hotels, upscale restaurants, and boutique services that few in the country but themselves could afford.

Dad was an example of the kind of person who could benefit from the economic imbalance that plagued the country. He was a businessman whose foreign currency stretched far in the local market, whose foreign ties made him difficult to ignore. He had the advantage of a local host in MK, whose own influence in the city expanded the aperture of possibilities for unadulterated fun.

Unfortunately, he was also the kind of person that Guineans like MK took for a fool—someone who was there for the taking.

"Do you want Memuna to join us," MK asked Dad, not long after they took off in the car from the airport.

"Yes, I'd like that very much," came Dad's response. He had no idea that his life would end in just a few short hours.

It was Saturday, May 19, 1990...

* * *

Mom sat at the dining room table, opposite the sliding glass door of the balcony, as she got her hair braided for the work-week ahead. I could make out her outstretched arms from my seat in the living room, where I sat soaking in cartoon shows on our television set. She reached for the telephone, its ringing blaring through the apartment, then dropped the handset within seconds, as if she had been startled by someone or had accidentally touched a hot pan. The calm in the house on that day, before the sound of that phone ringing and then cratering against the floor, belied the fact that ours was typically the apartment in the building that blared music on Saturday mornings at the expense of our neighbors' peace and tranquility.

It was Dad's way of relaxing when he was in a good mood. He got up at a reasonable hour and, while waiting for his breakfast, squatted right on the coffee table in the living room and turned to his music sets. He sat there with his headphones on like an amateur DJ, playing music chosen from his crates of vinyl LP records. His collection was an eclectic mix of genres and musicians, and he got as excited about listening to Tracy Chapman's "Fast Car" as he did about getting down to his favorite African Soukous.

"Foday, dun die. Papa God, oh, Foday dun die." Mom's voice screeched higher with every syllable. It was Bruce from Goldstone. Dad, he told Mom, was no longer with us.

Our apartment was filled with mourners by nightfall, some traveling tens of miles from corners of Washington, D.C. Metro area to offer their condolences. I found myself among the sea of people in our living room that night, crouched on the same ottoman I occupied when I observed Mom reaching for the phone earlier in the day.

There I sat, listening to testimonies about the last time each person had seen or talked with Dad. I did not cry. Instead, I was moved by the actions taking place around me. An aunt demanded that all of Dad's photographs in the house be covered out of respect for the deceased. I looked on with curiosity as Uncle Sumah, a man we hardly ever saw during normal times because he worked so much, logged the names of those offering a donation, then quietly made arrangements for a meeting to decide which male family member would travel with our family for the funeral.

Days on, the Guinean authorities allowed Dad's body, along with his briefcase, now containing nothing more than some company papers, two dollars tucked underneath the base, and his wedding band, to be transported to Sierra Leone. There would be no official investigation and, therefore, no real chance to render justice for Dad—not in a place like Guinea, where MK was connected to power brokers and where the rule of law proved to be only an aspiration. It was an ending that no one in our family ever saw coming, but it came, and the motive behind his killing could not have been more clearer to us, even before Dad was laid to rest.

Bruce planned to attend the funeral in Lungi, Sierra Leone. He had developed over the years a special bond with Dad, whose untimely death was proving to be difficult to come to terms with. Standing beside his late friend's family in their greatest hour of need might, therefore, help ease the pain of the loss, if only a little. There was also the matter of Goldstone's business in Conakry. Someone had to account for and take control of the company's assets, a process needed to help inform decisions about the future of the business without its deceased West African Representative. And so, Bruce began to take the steps necessary for his trip. One of the first people he spoke to was MK. Their conversation did not go well.

MK wanted no part of Bruce's reclamation project. He wasted no time making his feelings known after Bruce made what, in Bruce's mind, was a reasonable attempt to negotiate getting back what rightfully belonged to the company. "You see what happened to someone from here. Just imagine what will happen to you," MK said to Bruce with an air of invincibility rooted in his ties to the country's decision-makers. He put into the universe words that confused no one. "Just imagine what will happen to you" was all Bruce had to hear to convince him that staying home in America was really the only option available to him, so long as his friend's funeral took place in Africa.

Goldstone's subsequent demise doubled the pain we all felt, for it was a venture that held the kind of promise immigrant families like ours dreamed about as a path to financial independence and social mobility. Dad's fingerprints had been all over it, which in and of itself was a remarkable turn of events considering the struggles he and Mom endured from the time they left Sierra Leone for the US in the early 1970s.

Dad worked in construction for a time after he arrived in Washington, DC in 1972 with the help of a friend, another Sierra Leonean immigrant who invited him, earning pennies on the dollar, until he found another way to make money driving a taxi. His savings purchased a one-way ticket for Mom to join him over a year later in 1973. Together, with Mom waitressing and cleaning hotels, they managed to make enough money to move into an apartment of their own and to afford Dad the chance to pursue a college degree in hotel management.

But starting a family–with the birth of my sister, then me a year and some months later in the last days of 1975–upended their fragile stability. Months of struggling with childcare, monthly rent, household expenses, and caring for extended relatives, took its toll. So, Mom and Dad made the decision to send their two children to Sierra Leone. It was a temporary solution, a year or two of separation so that they could gather their financial bearings. The decision seemed prudent, even if their lives together remained a constant struggle.

By 1981, nearly a decade after he arrived from Freetown, Dad, with Mom's support, could count among his accomplishments a college degree and the signposts of a steadily rising income, which reinforced that he too was well on his way to fulfilling the American dream. The family still lived in an apartment, but their material wealth was demonstrable by the location of the apartment in the suburbs of Falls Church, Virginia, rather than the crowded inner city of Northwest, DC, where they started out–Dad sleeping on a friend's sofa before being able to rent a room of his own to share with Mom.

The rise in their standard of living was evident in the cars they regularly leased, through the frequency of Dad's travels back to Sierra Leone, and through the number of associations Dad made on these trips. In yet another sign of upward mobility, the family itself grew. My older sister returned to the US due to severe illness and another baby girl was born into the family in the summer of 1979. It was quite an impressive distance that Dad had traveled from his farming days in his childhood home not far from the border with Guinea.

But Dad was not satisfied. He abandoned his training in hotel management without warning. Many of his contemporaries believed hotel management did not offer a level playing field for minorities at the time, so when Dad decided to walk away, they concluded that it was because of discrimination. Those times in the US were hard even for African Americans born in the country. But it really was Dad's personality and determination to be his own boss that drove him to leave the relatively stable conditions in the US (where he would always be someone else's subordinate) for a business opportunity that offered him a considerable measure of independence. The opportunity came in the form of Goldstone Limited in 1987-88.

Dad's venture with Goldstone was supposed to be a turning point, a chance to establish a safety net and to gain a degree of financial independence that alleviated the pressures barreling down on him and Mom. It was supposed to ensure my siblings' and my own path toward a good education. Immigrating from Sierra Leone and laboring in odd-end jobs while attending night school were great teachers. Dad did not want his children to go through what he went through, and he knew the difference between achieving success and falling into the trap of mediocrity because of failures in the classroom.

Dad also never abandoned his idea of returning home. Considering Sierra Leone's worsening economy, however, he believed that their return could only be made possible if they did not have to rely on said economy. What better way was there for him to do that than to establish himself in the US, build up savings, construct a home in Sierra Leone, and maintain a business that ensured a constant revenue stream to accommodate his family? Dad was on course on many of these fronts. But his aspirations ran deeper still. In the world in which he grew up, family included more than just the individual, his spouse, and their children. The more well-to-do someone becomes, the greater one's responsibility to all relatives, both near and far.

Having the financial means to give money on demand to relatives was one thing, but the ability to offer them jobs was an unparalleled opportunity to help change the course of their lives. This sense of obligation was the reason our small apartments in Northern Virginia seemed always to be full of visitors—a few staying for extended periods at a time to get acclimated after Dad helped them to get a visa to immigrate to the US. It was the reason Dad took a step toward the Goldstone venture. He knew helping to establish a profitable company in his home country would fundamentally alter the economic fortunes of the people who depended on him most, given their own limited opportunity for advancement.

But belying all these aspirations was the recurring theme of Dad allowing other people to influence his decisions—often to his own detriment—and his willful disregard for the advice of his wife when it mattered most. "Stick to the plan," Mom offered wisely. She had concerns about his involvement in a country he did not know well. But she was also worried about MK. "You don't know this man, not like you think you do. There is a lot at stake." Hers was an intuitive reaction, she would later say. She had no foresight, yet she could not get herself to stop thinking about the ways she had seen people change over money. Dad would not listen. He paid for this mistake with his life and our future without him in it…

Back home in our Alexandria, Virginia apartment weeks after Dad's funeral, Mom faced the reality of our situation. We had no life insurance or savings to depend on. What we did have were mounting bills and thousands of dollars in unpaid loans Mom did not know even existed. Our only way to survive was through a bankruptcy filing and moving in with relatives. Yet, Mom refused to allow us to go on living while dependent on others, even as our troubles mounted. She found work as a home health assistant, what was fast becoming a growth industry for Sierra Leone immigrants at the time. Her $450 bi-weekly paycheck proved just enough for us to secure public housing six months after our return from Sierra Leone.

Our new apartment on South Reynolds Street, just a few blocks from where we lived on North Ripley Lane when Dad was alive, was a far cry from what we were accustomed to. Essex House was not a garden-style apartment but a concrete block high-rise of 210 units subsidized for low-income families. While many residents there turned to honest work for a living, a few settled for selling drugs and prostitution. These activities were not overtly public for obvious reasons, but a walk around the building in the mornings—especially around the back where the parking lot bridged the adjacent 7-Eleven, gas station, and shopping plaza—provided a window into what happened when day turned into night. Used condom wrappers and drug needles were strewn about—some found not too far from bloodstains and random pocket litter from the very people who were either being serviced or providing the service.

The four of us felt like we were on top of each other in the small apartment we shared, a place designed simply with a living room that was attached to a kitchen, which was connected to a nook just big enough for a small dining table. The walls separating the apartments were razor-thin, making family quarrels, roaches and rodents something of a shared experience. Yet the $500 a month rental was a bargain. Mom was able to make rent, pay utilities, and—without fail—send at least $40 dollars to her family in Sierra Leone after each pay.

We managed with the food and other basics she could afford with the balance of her paycheck. Some of our needs and many of our wants were unmet, however. Children have a hard time understanding such difficult realities, and we were no different. Our struggle was never laid more bare for me outside the four walls of our home than when I was 15 years old on a day some neighborhood friends and I played basketball at the nearby court.

I remember running down the court at full speed to get back on defense during an intense 5-on-5 scrimmage when all of a sudden my feet buckled. My right shoe dangled off, exposing the outsole of my shoe. There was nothing there but the newspapers I'd tucked inside to compensate for the fact the rubber soles on both sneakers had been worn out from overuse. Boy, did the other kids have a field day! "Damn Yo, you can't afford sneakers," I heard one of the kids blurt out. The others began pointing and laughing. One even picked up the tattered shreds of the newspaper and tossed them in my direction, as I sat on the court fiddling with my toes. I wanted to crawl under a rock. The shame was too much. I went home that night and vented to Mom, not about the incident but about not having money like other families.

Mom had a way of centering us whenever we complained or compared ourselves to other children. "We are better off than you think," she said, purposely leading me to thoughts about our family back home in Sierra Leone. "Life is about making the most of your opportunities. From where we've come, we can be thankful for where we are." She was resolute.

But every so often, when she was alone in her bedroom by nightfall, when she believed we were asleep, she'd kneel down by her bed, next to the table lamp where she kept a cup of water that she'd used in prayer, and acknowledge her doubts. She'd ask aloud why she was left alone with three kids to care for; how she'd be able to make it through. She'd pray for answers, for guidance, for anything that might help her steer us through the choppy waters of the life we knew. I'd watch her from the bathroom stall, through a small opening of her bedroom door, wondering with her if we'd make it.

Despite our collective doubts, we managed to stay together in that apartment for six long years, living and witnessing through Mom's eyes what it meant to struggle. Those years molded us, they gave us perspective on life, particularly with the backdrop of the deeply distressing experiences Mom would share with us about her life with Dad.

I was too young to know or was absent for much of it. Dad and Mom's decision to send their children to Sierra Leone during their early years in the US resulted in me staying in the country for a decade. I rejoined the family just as I was nearing my 11th birthday, 3 years before Dad's death. My immersion in Sierra Leone was life changing and it would, in unbelievable irony, provide me with the awareness necessary to truly grasp Mom's ordeal.

One of the many lessons I absorbed about Sierra Leone was the country's rich and deeply embedded values and way of life, which was often on display during my childhood years in the form of mascot processions. Men chanting and dancing usually happened when we least expected. They'd storm the lone street in and out of town, go door to door, and showcase their charm. Central to these surprise visits were men dressed in traditional mascots in the form of devils. My earliest recollection of these processions growing up was the day one appeared as we sat with Mom's brother, Uncle Abdullah, in the front veranda of our compound. I was seven. Sitting next to me were several of Uncle's sons. It was a lazy late afternoon, well before sunset. We'd just returned from a day's work on Uncle's farm, where rice plants and root vegetable crops consumed our thoughts and labor.

Uncle's wives were preparing dinner as he held court on random affairs. Someone was moving to the big city, Freetown; another had returned for a short visit; yet another had agreed to help advance plans to build a brick annex or second home at our compound that was to become a model for the neighborhood. As Uncle spoke, our short-wave radio blared the soft sound of Susu music—socially conscious songs set to the rhythm of traditional instruments made out of wood and strings.

Uncle's slow drawl began to coincide with the faint sounds of an organized chant as we sat listening to him. The chant drowned him out not too long after, putting us in plain sight of the direction and people from which it came. We could see men blowing whistles, beating drums and whatever other instruments they could get their hands on to create a rhythmic accompaniment to their chants. The mascots wore scary, devilish masks, colorful customs with straws streaming all over on their upper and lower bodies. They paraded about in this heap of body covering, dancing one moment and playing to the gathering crowd the next.

To my young eyes, this play always seemed threatening, as if the deviled mascots planned to jump on their subjects and send them to the ends of the world in a blink of an eye. It so frightened the other kids and me that we ran into the house, abandoning Uncle on the veranda. Feeling protected inside, we gathered around the nearest window to watch the performers as they danced and prostrated in front of Uncle.

Any other person would have been scared, we thought. But Uncle sat still, seemingly unfazed by what we perceived as intimidation. The scene played out for several minutes, with the chants, musical instruments, and gathering crowd all reaching a critical mass, until finally the deviled mascots made the decision to move on to other victims. Uncle then turned his eyes to us, our faces crowded against the window pane, to ensure we were safe and that we had not followed the procession before settling back in his chair.

None of us understood the significance of these processions at the time. To us, they just seemed like occasions for the deviled mascots and the men behind them to get what they wanted, which often turned out to be money thrown at their feet as they danced and prostrated in a manner only they understood. But we caught on eventually, due in no small part to a bit of maturing and lessons from Uncle about the cultural significance of what appeared to us to be spur-of-the-moment events.

Uncle taught us that Sierra Leone has an entrenched tradition of using masked devils to convey the emotions, unity, and pride of her communities. He told us it is the way of our people to express our collective feelings—be it joy over a harvest, sadness over the death of an important member of the community, or a show of strength in the face of a potential danger or power struggle. It is, he'd say, a display of the reverence for and connection to the spiritual world that Sierra Leoneans are known to have, not unlike in many other places across Africa.

This poignant and often misunderstood idea about the peoples of Africa is what Richard Dowden tried to capture in his seminal book *Africa: Altered States, Ordinary Miracles*. Africans, Dowden explained, have a numinous feel for the world. We have a deep sense of the supernatural, wherein the present, objective world also bears a relationship to the spirit.

The spirits are powerful but can be assuaged or placated by offerings. In a world ordered by destiny and spirits, it is important to know who is employing which spirits and how to counteract their influence. Everyone wants to know the future and obtain charms and fetishes to bring success and happiness, to honor the ancestors, gain the love of someone, pass exams or win at football. They also want to ward off evil or bring it upon their enemies. (Dowden, 2009, p. 315)

To illustrate, Dowden tells the story of a man in Zambia who was kicked out of his village because he had "become too successful and created jealousy." The man was married with children. When his wife died, he married a younger woman, changed his profession from teaching to farming, and expanded his farm to grow food for the nearest town. The changes brought some measure of success, but rumors soon began to swirl. It was said that the man killed his first wife by witchcraft and that his new wife was a witch herself, hence the reason for his recent success. Thus, "The man was forced to flee [the village and abandon] his business" (318).

In Sierra Leone's version of "a world ordered by destiny and spirits," it is little wonder Mom turned to a soothsayer when Dad proposed marriage in the early 1970s. Her decision to do so was based on culture—namely the prevailing practice of consorting with those in the community with the power to tap into the spiritual sphere for a better sense of one's future, fortune, and misfortune. Mom didn't particularly like what she heard. The soothsayer spoke of a life of pain and suffering. Mom began to see the light a few years after that fateful encounter. The life she lived with Dad edged dangerously close to the one the soothsayer foretold, and it continued in this manner for years until Mom could no longer deny the prophecy.

One of the earliest indications that hard times were coming was the unevenness of their responsibilities in the home and Dad's proclivity for control. At daybreak, Mom woke up to prepare breakfast, then got my sister and me ready for daycare. Dad avoided these responsibilities and helped himself to breakfast before leaving for work in the one car the family owned. He left behind a few coins on the kitchen table for Mom's bus fare on his way out. Mom put me in a stroller and strapped my sister on her arms for the journey to daycare. The winter months were the hardest. Mom had to plow through the elements with us in tow to make the drop-off time. From the daycare, she walked farther to catch a different bus for the ten-mile ride to her minimum-wage job, where she spent eight hours waitressing or cleaning hotel rooms.

Mom reversed her commute at the day's end to pick us up and head home, completing the travel pattern Dad forced upon her, regardless of the weather. Once home, Mom prepared dinner while tending to our needs for the night. Dad arrived home from work just as Mom was busy with these chores. His arrival was always a source of anxiety for her. She never knew what to expect—whether he would be happy or upset, in a mood to talk or solely interested in keeping his silence and thus demonstrating the depths of his indifference.

The slightest thing set him off: the smell of the trash in the house or an overcooked dinner. His mood swings were notorious, and they often led to violent outbursts. He did not eat left-overs, so Mom prepared a fresh meal every single night to keep him satisfied. He was unbelievably demanding despite the fact that he never helped around the house.

Dad was just as demanding when it came to the family's finances. Mom had to give up her check each payday. He'd cash it, then decide what to do with the funds. Mom had to make a case for groceries or upkeep of the house, and Dad would often overrule her. Then, every five months or so, Dad announced his plans to travel home. His pocket money for these trips were the funds they saved, while he'd charge the cost of his round-trip ticket to one of several credit cards in Mom's name. He rarely explained why he was traveling home, nor did he plan for how Mom would manage the bills and household expenses in his absence. News of his travel brought only blame for Mom when Dad touched down in Sierra Leone. Her family saw extravagance in Dad's frequent trips. They also felt disrespect on the occasions Dad did not visit the family compound whenever he traveled home.

These insults were minor when compared to what gradually began to settle in their marriage. Dad's verbal abuse gave way to physical assaults. He beat

Mom many times for reasons he believed were justified. Sometimes, it was because she called him out on withholding the monies she'd earned. Other times, it was because she'd confronted him about the women he kept. Their confrontations went on for years and, while Mom never spoke out about them, I knew, within my first few months of rejoining the family, that the subject of women was a source of routine conflict between them.

Their arguments in those early years always seemed under control to me—until they weren't. I witnessed it quietly one cold autumn morning, in the warmth of our apartment in Alexandria. I heard the first rumblings from their bedroom as I sat alone in the living room watching Saturday morning cartoons, a ritual for kids in those days. The sound of their conversation gradually moved through the hallway when one of them opened their bedroom door. "She is not sleeping here tonight," Mom boldly proclaimed. She now made it clear what so upset her, and she was drawing a line in the proverbial sand.

Dad walked out of the room, seemingly unwilling to engage in the conversation any longer. It was a mistake he didn't yet know he'd made. He walked casually to the kitchen to peruse the refrigerator for something to eat or drink. Mom followed right behind him. She was going to get his attention, regardless of whether he wanted to give it to her. I sat uncomfortably on the couch, viewing what was now happening from the half-wall that separated the kitchen and living room.

"This is too much. I am your wife. You're not going to disrespect me in my own house. Your girlfriend has to go. She is not coming back here." Mom spoke these words with vigor and determination as she stood holding the edge of the countertop closest to the dining room table. She faced Dad, as if ready to charge at any given moment.

"What are you going to do about it? What are you going to do if she doesn't leave?" Dad was taunting her. It was the only logical explanation for why he said what he said. Mom had apparently had enough of the arrangement Dad made for the young woman he helped immigrate to the US. She was staying with us to get settled in the same way that other men whom Dad helped did when they first arrived. But something about this woman just didn't sit well with Mom. She felt a need to say or do something, so she confronted her husband.

This woman, who was away visiting relatives, had to go, she told him. From their back-and-forth in the bedroom, Mom probably thought, "This man dared to bring this woman into my home. Instead of making things right when I confront him about it, he gets defensive."

"What are you going to do?" Dad responded. "What are you going to do if she doesn't leave?"

Mom showed him. She reached for the handle of the kitchen drawer closest to where she was standing and pulled out a butcher knife. "If your girlfriend comes back here, it's because you and I are both dead." Mom waved the knife in Dad's face as she spoke with such force that it startled Dad and caused him to move back several feet in unprecedented fear.

Dad probably would have grabbed her by the throat had Mom challenged him in this manner just a few months earlier. But he wouldn't dare do it now. Several months before, Dad had eased into his usual pattern of putting his hands on Mom.

He grabbed her by the hair one afternoon in our Falls Church, Virginia apartment and began mashing her head against the walls. The trigger was an argument over food. She hadn't prepared the soup the way he liked and had been cavalier about it when he confronted her. My sisters and I looked on in horror from a distance. He was going to split her head open, Mom thought, as her mind bounced from concern for herself to the safety of her children, whose screams she could now hear from underneath Dad's firm hold.

Back and forth her head went, as the pounding continued, until Mom was able to get free of his hold. She bolted from the house with nothing but underclothes—no shoes or an overcoat to protect her from the winter's cold. She crossed the street to the adjacent hotel in a state of panic, in search of a public phone. Into the booth she went, with blood smearing her face and the pain from the blows she suffered blurring her vision to a point that she could hardly make out the digits on the phone. Luckily, she only needed to place one of them: the digit 0, which she pressed to get through to an operator for a collect call.

The call to her cousin was unsuccessful. He wasn't home, his wife told Mom. She tried to reach others. None of her male relatives were home.

Cell phones and pagers were not in wide circulation then, so she'd have to wait until they returned home for them to get her message. But time was something she didn't have. She feared going back to the house, and yet was also completely seized with thoughts of what Dad might do to us in the house. She was desperate. She picked up the receiver once more and dialed 911. It was a decision she'd contemplated before, yet never followed through on because she didn't think anything consequential would result from calling the police— not given her status as an African immigrant, anyway. But she had no other choice. She was desperate. Her husband just might kill her this time. So, she waited in the phone booth for the police to arrive. She was afraid to exit because of fear that he might come looking for her, because of shame that her neighbors might see her.

The police cruiser pulled up to the hotel at last. Out came Mom from the phone booth in a still disheveled state. "Are you the one who called us, Ma'am?" one of the officers asked. Mom identified herself. "My kids," she tried to explain, "are in there with him. Please help me." The officers agreed. They walked up the flight of stairs to the third floor. They knocked on the door. Mom stood meters away on the second floor platform from what she thought was going to be a confrontation. She could hear Dad's responses, "yes" and "no" answers.

He was unfazed, which had the effect of making it seem as if there was nothing the police needed to be concerned about. Dad shut the door after a few minutes of questioning. The police walked down the flight of stairs to speak with Mom. "There is nothing else we can do here, Ma'am. He denies what you said happened."

Mom was in shock. They were going to leave her there with him. "You have to help me. I can't go in there. I can't leave my kids with him," she pleaded.

"Ma'am, the only way we can help is if you come with us to the station and file a report. You can press charges. The courts will make sure you and your children are protected." She thought long and hard about the option being presented to her. She and her kids would be protected, but at what cost? She could not dwell on this thought at that moment. Right then and there, she needed physical protection.

"Can you come with me inside while I check on the kids and pick up a few clothes?" Mom asked.

"Certainly, Ma'am; take all the time you need. We'll be right beside you."

Into the apartment they went. Mom made a passing glance at Dad as she walked through the front door. She had to place the source of her fear; it was instinctive. He sat in complete silence, his hand on the remote, watching television. He made no attempt to look her way or to figure out why she'd returned to the house with the cops. Mom hurriedly found us in our room. "Are you okay?" she asked, kissing each of us on the forehead as we embraced in a bear hug.

"What happened, Mommy?"

"Where did you go, Mommy?"

"Why was Daddy hitting you, Mommy?"

There was little time to explain. We were old enough to understand that the beating happened. But the underlying reason for why Dad would turn so violent against our mother—that would take more time than Mom had to talk through, assuming she could even find the words or overcome the shame she felt to do it.

"I'll be back for you, don't worry. Just take care of each other. I'll be back, I promise."

Mom left us in the room. She gathered a few belongings and walked out the door with the policemen for the station. There she filed a complaint, then sat in a holding area, waiting for instructions on what to do next.

Some time passed. She tried to numb her pain with a little sleep—the kind that tends to overcome the body when the mind is exhausted with anxiety. But he wouldn't let her have even that brief moment of peace. His stern voice, coming from the front of the station, roused her from her sleep. Dad wanted to know the whereabouts of his wife. She hadn't come home, he told the police officer, who was now asking Dad for his identification.

He'd calculated wrong this time. His cool demeanor, what he used to dismiss the police's earlier attempts to intervene, would no longer serve him.

"Mr. Yilla, you are under arrest for domestic battery." The policeman placed Dad in handcuffs. Mom, now observing what she never fathomed that day through an opening from where she sat, got a glimpse of Dad being walked to a detention room in handcuffs.

The image of him being restrained in that manner was surreal, almost unbelievable. He couldn't hurt her anymore—at least not anymore on that day. But this comforting feeling quickly evaporated with thoughts about home. In all the commotion, she realized Dad must have just left us in the house by ourselves while he came looking for her at the station. She alerted the police to this fact and gained their permission for her to return to the apartment. By this late hour, the cousin Mom tried to reach earlier at the phone booth had gotten the news from his wife. He came straight to the apartment.

"Bintu, wotin hapen (Bintu, what happened)?" he asked, still fuzzy on the details his wife had shared. Mom told him everything: the nonsense about the soup, the ensuing beating, the mashing of her head against the walls, the run for her life, the phone calls, the police, and finally Dad's arrest. He felt for his cousin—he really did. But with the ability to process the situation from a distance, he latched on to the fact of Dad's arrest and what he knew would be demands by the authorities for Mom to press charges against him. This, he thought, could in effect trigger a downward spiral, wherein Dad was thrown in prison for a time and likely deported, which could potentially lead to the disintegration of our family. For the next several days the cousin and others thus prevailed on Mom to reconsider.

"I didn't call the police to have him arrested," Mom explained to her relatives. "I called to get protection for myself and my kids. I don't want him to go to jail, but I need the beatings to stop. I need for him to never put his hands on me again." The relatives got the message. They then turned their attention to Dad, who sat in a detention cell, uncertain of his fate.

It didn't take long for the authorities to ask Mom to declare her intentions in front of a Judge. A decision had to be made. The court hearing took place in a matter of days. Mom, with the advice of her relatives playing over in her mind, didn't mince words when she addressed the court. She wouldn't press charges, but neither would she ever again put up with Dad's physical abuse. He needed to stop.

The court had to make him stop.

The judge was sympathetic. "Mr. Yilla," he directed his attention at Dad, "if your wife ever again files a complaint against you, rest assured this court will do everything in its power to put you away in prison for as long as the law will allow; and when you're through serving that sentence, you will be on the next plane back to your home country. Is that understood?" Dad muttered a "yes" to the question, but he knew as well that the question was as rhetorical as it was logical.

So, months later, when he stood in the kitchen with Mom wielding a knife in his face, Dad had a very good reason to restrain himself. He could do nothing but listen, as his wife made it clear to him that she would not allow his girlfriend to return to the house, even if it meant putting an end to both of their lives.

Looking at them in that moment, as a thirteen-year-old, I got a much clearer understanding of what divided them as a married couple. The young woman never returned to our house. I learned just a few years later that she and others like her were a recurring theme in their marriage, to the point that Dad had fathered other children, a girl and a boy, with two different women. The fact of their existence only emerged at his funeral in Lungi, of all places, where the family gathered to lay him to rest.

The talk then was that both women came to pay their respects and to ensure they were part of any conversation involving the wealth Dad might have left behind. It is difficult to imagine how any mother could have a conversation on such a topic with her children, especially one with a conservative upbringing like our mother. Mom kept the facts of Dad's transgressions to herself for a long time, perhaps out of shame, or perhaps out of concern that such knowledge would tarnish our memory of him.

As we grew older and struggled through life in our public housing apartment, Mom occasionally found the will to reflect on past years. These conversations were always spur-of-the-moment, triggered by memories too painful for her to hold back or events unfolding right in front of our own eyes.

One was the divorce of one of Mom's friends. Once a bridesmaid in Mom and Dad's wedding, she had finally made the bold decision to leave her husband after thirty years of abuse. The friend had been coerced into accepting the abuse for years. She feared that striking out on her own, as an immigrant from Sierra Leone with young kids to care for, would only lead to her demise. So she remained in the same two-bedroom apartment they'd lived in for all those years until one day she decided she'd had enough and would rather die trying life on her own than to live out the miserable one she endured with her husband.

Yet, it was visits to Mom's longtime friend in the capital city that triggered Mom's deepest and most enduring reflections. Carol, a woman then in her late fifties, was the first African-American to befriend Mom in the US. She and her husband lived in the same apartment building as Mom and Dad. They spent much of the early 1970s together, bonding over their youth and Mom's story of a fresh-off-the-boat immigrant from Africa.

Carol schooled Mom in the ways of America. She babysat when my sister and I were born, and even gave Mom bus fare on occasion for trips to the daycare and to work. Mom reciprocated with kindness reflective of her upbringing. She regularly cooked for her neighbor, whose exposure to our family opened her to the tantalizing tastes of some of West Africa's popular dishes like Jollof rice, fried sweet plantain, and fufu—pounded cassava served with groundnut or light soup.

But it was their marriages—namely the turbulence each experienced in those relationships—that brought them even closer. Dad's beatings were so severe and constant, Mom would say, that she developed the habit of sleeping inside the hallway bathroom at night. She'd store spare clothes and undergarments on the small shelves. At nightfall, after having served him dinner and waiting for him to turn in, she'd creep inside the bathroom, lock the door, and stretch out on the floor to get whatever sleep she could get.

She'd wake up early, clean herself, make sure breakfast was made, then head out to her job. This routine might go on for two, three days, until Dad found a reason to snap once more. Carol would be there after he did, offering Mom a shoulder to cry on while recounting the tumult in her own marriage.

The two of them looked out for and nurtured each other when their husbands failed them, developing in the process a bond so deep that Mom felt moved on any given weekend, even some twenty years later, to drive the distance from Virginia to Washington, DC and pay her friend a visit, complete with a cooked meal and one of us by her side.

On the way back in the car, after her nostalgic trip down memory lane with her old friend, Mom invariably recounted the experiences that infused her relationship with Carol with so much meaning. Carol, she'd say, saw her through some of her darkest days in America, the times she felt most vulnerable, abandoned, and unsure of her self-worth and her ability to survive life with a man who had uprooted her from all that she had known in Lungi. She'd wonder aloud how she managed to make it through all those years.

Hearing about Dad's philandering and his abusive behavior made me angry. I felt sorry for the pain Dad caused Mom. I wondered why Mom put up with it all and why she didn't pick up and leave. But she had an answer—one that didn't really surprise me given her nature.

"I stayed," she conceded during a ride home from Carol's one spring afternoon, "because I didn't want another woman to raise you all."

"But you could have gotten help, Mom," I responded with what now sounds like empty words.

"I was young, new to the country. Your Dad had all my documents, and he made all the decisions. I was not confident I'd be able to stop him. I didn't want to lose you guys."

"So you stayed," I said to stress the point.

"I stayed," Mom said as she exhaled.

She had the look of someone troubled by a nagging thought. Her hands were on the steering wheel, and her eyes were fixed on the road ahead. But her mind seemed far removed from our conversation inside the four doors of her champagne-colored Toyota Camry.

"I don't know how much longer I would have stayed, to be honest. I wouldn't have survived with your Dad. I was losing myself and I didn't even know it."

"What do you mean?" I asked. Mom took a deep breath.

"I left the house one morning with your sister before you were born. She was a little over a year old. We walked from our apartment on 16th Street to a nearby clinic on 14th and R. Your sister needed shots. The weather was really nice that day, and I remember there was so much activity around: cars passing by; people on foot, running errands; others out for a stroll to enjoy the warm sun. As I observed this bustling activity, my mind suddenly veered off course to the previous night, and all the other nights before, when your father would just make my life a living hell. I got consumed with thoughts about his beatings, his verbal attacks, his mental and emotional abuse, his complete control of my life—to a point I felt like I was given to him as property or as a child he did not want but had to raise. What would he do to me next? Was this nightmare ever going to end? How would it end? Absorbed in these thoughts, with your sister holding my hand, I walked into the middle of the intersection at 14th and R. I was supposed to have turned left on 14th. I could hear the sounds of car horns blaring, people screaming for me to get out of the way, but I was frozen in place and in time, paralyzed to move. It felt like I was in a dream. It must have been only a few seconds, but anything could have happened in those seconds. I remember finally hearing, in real time, the sound of the horns and the voice of a man, when I came out of the trance. He said, from the inside of his car as he drove past me, 'Lady, what's wrong with you? If you want to die, go and die somewhere else.'

"I tell you, Baimba, I was completely out of my mind. It was all because of your father. There was no way I would have made it. I would have eventually left him."

Dad's murder absolved her of that decision.

And this very fact, which Mom seldom failed to emphasize whenever she talked about her marriage to help steer our own relationships on the right course, was the point about life. She was always emphatic about her belief that

"Tomorrow takes care of itself. You just have to be willing to learn from the past, accept that the person you are and the choices you make will determine what comes next for you…It will determine the impact you have on the lives of those around you, and none will be more important than your family."

Mom's words only truly registered at a much later age for me, well after I'd become a husband and a father and I'd begun to chart a course for my family in much the same way Dad tried to do for us. Her words, I came to realize, were silent echoes of her own past, the years that shaped the wisdom she imparted.

Character and decision-making were paramount for anyone, she observed, not least those responsible for others. She suffered needlessly during her tumultuous years with Dad because he failed to be an example, and yet she became one when she was forced into raising us on her own. The jobs she took and the hours she worked, for instance, all had to offer the flexibility she sought to care for her kids. She gave up night school, which would have improved her chances for better employment, for this reason. She sacrificed relationships with men for the same reason, with no better example than her decision to let go of a man we all admired.

This man had invested his time in us as a family. He showered us with gifts—the tangibles that readily stand out for young kids beyond anything else. Some of his gifts—a large television set for the family, and a pair of $100 Nike Air Jordans for me—were impressive for the early 1990s. But he also showed he cared for us as children through conversation and, as a result, engendered an unquestionable bond. He was beyond our wildest expectations, and yet he could not overcome Mom's resolve. When he asked her to relocate to another state, Mom made the painful decision to turn him down because she feared the transition would uproot her children from the stability we knew. She was certain she needed to raise us free of the baggage that a man who didn't father us might bring. She was afraid to surrender her parental rights to this new love in an environment in which he would dictate the terms of their relationship, so she let go of her chance at love to continue leading us through our struggles well into our adult years.

This thoughtful, self-effacing character Mom demonstrated was rooted in her perseverance in Lungi as the youngest sibling among many, at a time and in a place where young girls could only dream as far as their male relatives would permit. Her time in the United States reinforced the value of hard work and dedication. She observed early on that people in her neighborhoods maintained a certain discipline in pursuing their goals. Even sometimes at the cost of their comfort, they pushed through, regardless of the barriers they faced. In living outside of the land of her birth, Mom was thus able to create a new harmony. She was able to take advantage of opportunities not offered in her ancestral home, even when her husband stunted her growth and, years later, when his sudden death changed the direction of her life.

Mom's experiences helped her to cope and persevere, to accept that none were caused by where she had come from or the pain she endured in her life. It was about the will she had to keep going—to grab hold of her roots and keep planting. She could have complained, but she didn't. She could have given up; she chose not to. She made ways when there seemed to be no way. She sought out and revealed her purpose and, with it, infused light into others, demonstrating that while the scars of the past are still visible, through perseverance, even old wounds can heal.

Mom showed us, on top of everything else she did, that change, especially those that involve healing of some sort, begins with a decision to face ourselves in the mirror and to embrace our power to evolve.

REFERENCES

Arieff, A. (2009). Still standing: Neighborhood wars and political stability in Guinea. *The Journal of Modern African Studies*, *47*(3), 331–348. doi:10.1017/S0022278X09004108

Dowden, R. (2009). *Africa: Altered States, Ordinary Miracles*. Public Affairs.

Meredith, M. (2006). *The state of Africa: A history of fifty years of independence*. Free Press.

Polgreen, L. (2007). Discontent in Guinea Nears Boiling Point. *The New York Times*.

Appendix

RECRUITMENT LETTER

Dear (Potential Participant)

I am writing to inform you about an opportunity to help increase understanding about the challenges in achieving social transformation in Africa. You have the chance to be part of a small group of participants in a qualitative research study for a dissertation in practice. The study I plan to conduct will explore the intersectionality and impact of choice and culture on individual development and how this analysis informs our understanding of Africa's struggles to achieve social transformation at the community and national level.

As the thrust of the study will be narrative inquiry (an exploration of the lived experience of ordinary African citizens like yourself), your participation in the study will include an oral interview and your completion of an open-ended qualitative questionnaire. These data collection methods will focus exclusively on learning, through the stories you share about your life experiences, about the constructs of choice/decision-making and culture on socio-economic development of participants.

I formally request your participation in this study, as you are uniquely representative of the study's broader target population. You are a citizen of (name of country); you have the lived-experience in Africa that can inform about choice and culture; you have experienced personal challenges that parallel the contours of the struggles of your country; and you offer a demographic consideration (age and locale in Africa) that enables the study to have a multi-generational and geographic representation of Africa's core regions.

I thank you in advance for your consideration and look forward to your positive response.

Sincerely,

INFORMED CONSENT FORM

Marymount University Informed Consent for Participation in Research

Research Study Title: Lived experience: Narratives of struggle and transformation.

Researcher(s): This research is being carried out by Baimba Yilla, EdD candidate, Marymount University.

Research Purpose: The purpose of this study is to explore the relationship between the lived experience of ordinaryAfricans and the challenges of socio-economic development in African countries. Does the lived experience of average citizens (decision-making and cultural context) reveal impediments to individual growth that might inform our understanding of Africa's struggles to achieve social transformation at the community and national level? The study will be grounded in the qualitative research methods of narrative inquiry and case study of ordinary men and women from select countries in Africa, namely Tanzania, South Africa, Zimbabwe, Ghana, and Sierra Leone. The study will begin with a deductive analysis of the established literature on what has been identified as impediments to development in this part of the world. The study will then aim to measure, through narrative inquiry and case study, the impact of decision-making or choice on socio-economic development of participants, and the impact of culture/social standards on socio-economic development of participants.

Study Expectations: If you agree to participate in this study, here is what will be asked of you: complete an open-ended qualitative questionnaire, which will include four-five questions that aim to get your perspective on the constructs under study: choice and culture and their impact on your socio-economic development. You will also be asked to take part in a 1.5 hour sit-down, semi-structured interview in which you will be asked questions about your lived experience in your home country. The questions will engage you on the experiences of your formidable years, your transition into adulthood, your efforts to build your life and navigate the challenges you encountered along the way, including pivotal decisions you made, cultural expectations you shouldered, and the social, economic, and political conditions prevailing at the time of your lived experience.

The interview and an open-ended qualitative questionnaire are important because the study is focused on a social phenomenon and aims to gain an understanding of your storied experience through narrative inquiry and case study. This effort necessarily implies talking with you, getting to know you and your experiences, and having the ability to deeply understand the conditions and contexts underpinning your experiences. The interviews provide the time, access, and flexibility to conduct this exploratory work.

The time commitment for both the interview and questionnaire will not be more than two hours combined. The questionnaire will be provided to you via email, and the interviews can either take place in person or via an online platform such as Zoom or FaceTime. The study will likely commence in the late 2022/early 2023 timeframe in the continental United States.

Risks: We do not anticipate that participating in this study poses any risks greater than those encountered in day-to-day life. Exploring your lived experience might surface unpleasant memories or even evoke a psychological or emotional reaction. To minimize this risk, I will be sensitive to the potential intrusiveness of my interview questions and allow you the space necessary to determine what you feel comfortable with or deem too invasive.

Benefits: The benefit to you for your participation in this study is that you will contribute in efforts to educate and broaden understanding of our larger community about a phenomenon that has troubled people for generations. The proposed study aims to leverage the true life stories of real people to enlighten and offer a road-map for change in Africa. It is a deep examination of the lives of some of the very people who continue to experience the region's socio-economic struggles, and it offers a contrast to the established literature's reliance on theories or theoretical arguments that are based on geography, history, and politics to explain Africa's challenges. You will also stand to deepen your understanding of your own experiences and to use reflection or look-back to better inform your contemporary, living experience.

Compensation: There is no compensation for participation in this study.

Privacy and Confidentiality: If you agree to participate in this research we will protect your privacy (no one outside of the research team will know that you participated in this study). We will do this through use of aliases and/or first names only, and also refrain from including any identifiable information about you in the study. We will also protect the confidentiality of your data (when we share study findings we will present the data in such a way that no one will be able to associate you with your data). We will do this through the maintenance of your information on a secure computer laptop (stored with the requisite security measures) and the storage of field notes, interview and questionnaire responses in a similarly safe location. We will de-identifying the data from participant names and store the list of participants separate from the data.

Identifiers might be removed from the identifiable private information or identifiable biospecimens and that, after such removal, the information or biospecimens could be used for future research studies or distributed to another investigator for future research studies without additional informed consent from the subject or the legally authorized representative, if this might be a possibility;

Sharing Study Findings: The results of this study will be a dissertation in practice (DiP), submitted to Marymount University for eligibility for a Doctorate in Education. The findings will also be considered for sharing via conference presentation and/or academic journal article.

Voluntary Participation: Taking part in this study is completely your choice. If you decide to participate, you are free to skip parts or stop participating at any time for any reason. Your participation or lack of participation will not affect your current or future relationship with the researcher(s) or with Marymount University.

Questions: Please ask any questions you have now before signing the consent form. If you have questions later, you may contact Baimba Yilla at 703.459.8259 or bmyilla@yahoo.com. If you have any questions or concerns regarding your rights as a participant in this research, you may contact Marymount University's Institutional Review Board (IRB) via email, irb@marymount.edu, or phone, (703) 526-6898.

You will be given a copy of this form to keep for your records.

Statement of Consent:

I understand the above statements and all of my questions have been answered. I am at least 18, and freely consent to participate in the research as it has been explained to me.

Your Signature ________________________________ Date _______
Your Name (printed)______________________________________
Written Informed consent form template. Last revised 11-6-2021

If you are applying for a waiver to document consent due to anonymous study design (see Worksheet for Informed Consent), signature and date lines will be replaced by Agree / Disagree buttons for online forms or by a statement that indicates completion of the data collection tool constitutes consent for the study.

This consent form will be kept by the researcher for at least three years beyond the end of the study and was approved by the Marymount IRB on insert date of IRB approval.

INTERVIEW QUESTIONS

Greetings, and thank you for your time and interest in this research study, which aims to explore the relationship between the lived experience of everyday Africans and the challenges of socio-economic development in African countries. The constructs of interest to the study are choice (decision-making) and culture – what impact, if any, these have on an individual's socio-economic development.

We will explore these themes through a semi-structured interview that will focus on your lived experience. This includes pertinent stories – those you consider significant – about your maturation into an adult, your professional career, and your social life. Providing the story of your lived experience in this 60-90 minutes interview would be of great benefit to this educational research effort. Understanding that this interview is voluntary and that you can elect to stop at any time and decline to answer any question, do I have your permission to continue?

Thank you. Let's get started.

1. Tell me about your childhood. Where did you grow up and what events/ moments left an indelible mark on you as a child?
2. What events were unfolding at the time in your country? How did those events impact the decisions your parents had to make for your family's welfare?
3. What impressions did these events and your parents' decisions in reaction to them have on you growing up? Did they have any influence on how you viewed the world and what you needed to do to prepare to live in it?
4. Give me your impression of your community, the culture you grew up in, and the expectations for community members.
5. Describe your professional development and career; how did you settle on what you do now to earn a living? What influenced your decision and what roadblocks, if any, did you experience?
6. How did social and political conditions in your country impact your work-life experience?

7. Describe the approach you took to meet expectations for having your own family. What challenges did you encounter, if any? What choices did you make based on or because of those expectations?
8. What were some of the most difficult choices or decisions you had to make? Why?
9. What was the impact of your choices on yourself and on those around you?
10. What are your thoughts about where you are now in life? What would you do or would have done differently? Do you believe you had the agency or freedom to pursue your dreams – to live your life in the way you envisioned? What enabled or prevented you from exercising agency or freedom?

SURVEY QUESTIONNAIRE

Greetings, and thank you for your time and interest in this research study, which aims to explore the relationship between the lived experience of everydayAfricans and the challenges of socio-economic development in African countries. The constructs of interest to the study are choice (decision-making) and culture – what impact, if any, these have on an individual's socio-economic development.

Providing your experience and perspective in this 15-25 minutes survey would be of great benefit to this educational research effort. Please do not put your name on this questionnaire so that your responses will be completely anonymous. Please respond to the following prompts in narrative form.

1. Events in my life were primarily the result of my own actions.
2. Events in my life were primarily the result of external factors.
3. The choices that I made in my life shaped the direction of my socio-economic development.
4. The culture in which I lived shaped the direction of my socio-economic development.
5. Events in my home country were primarily the result of the actions of the people of my home country.
6. Events in my home country were primarily the result of external factors.

IRB APPROVAL LETTER

Attachments:

Exemption Verified - IRB ID: 712.pdf

Exemption Verified - IRB ID: 712
Date: 08/18/2022
To: Baimba Yilla
From: Marymount University IRB

Project: IRB ID: 712 - Lived Experience: Narratives of struggle and transformation in Africa

Submission Type: Initial: Exemption
Action: **EXEMPT**
Category: (2) Tests, Surveys, Interviews, (4) Secondary Research Uses of Data or Specimens
Determination Date: 08/18/2022
Study Status Report
Due Date:08/17/2023

The materials submitted for the above-referenced study have been reviewed and determined to qualify for exemption from federal regulations.

However, if you plan on amending your research in any way, you must first submit a **modification** to the Marymount University IRB for a determination of whether or not the exemption referenced above is still met, unless the change is necessary to eliminate an apparent immediate hazard to a subject(s), in which case it must be immediately reported. **Annual Check-In:** You will be asked to complete a Study Status Report to satisfy Marymount University institutional requirements. Once your study has concluded, please submit the final status report and set the continuation status to "Study Closed" and complete the study closure form.

Based on the information provided, this research is subject to the following requirements:

- The policies and procedures of Marymount University IRB and Marymount University
- State law, as applicable

As the Principal Investigator you are responsible for ensuring compliance with all applicable regulations and requirements. If you have any questions or comments about this correspondence, please contact the IRB Office at swarna.pothur@marymount.edu. In addition to the IRB Application form, the following documents were submitted:

Protocol Description 08/01/2022 Protocol Description DiP 2022.pdf
Consent Form 08/17/2022 Informed Consent Form.docx
08/17/2022 Informed Consent Form.docx
Data Collection Instruments 08/01/2022 Data Collection Instruments.pdf

CODE BOOK: LIVED EXPERIENCE (EARLY WORKING TITLE)

Semi-Structured Interview Protocol

Data Analysis

Codes

Impact and Role of Choice (41)
Transition (5)
Personal Development (12)
Impact and Role of Culture/Environment (45)
Achievements (10)
Condition of Country (14)
Lived Experience and Awareness (14)
Public Service (14)
Coming of Age (7)
Childhood (6)

Order of Code in List	Nested Level	Code Name	Number of Snippets	Code Description	Code URL
1	>	Impact and Role of Choice	41	Reflection on the role and impact of the choices (decisions) participants made in living their lives and pursuing their goals.	https://app.delvetool.com/projects/11579/codes/398627
2	>>	Transition	5		https://app.delvetool.com/projects/11579/codes/398617
3	>>	Personal Development	12		https://app.delvetool.com/projects/11579/codes/398631
4	>	Impact and Role of Culture/ Environment	45	Reflection on the role and impact of participants' culture (environment) during the course of their lives and in pursuit of their goals.	https://app.delvetool.com/projects/11579/codes/398624
5	>>	Achievements	10		https://app.delvetool.com/projects/11579/codes/398634
6	>>	Condition of Country	14		https://app.delvetool.com/projects/11579/codes/398637
7	>	Lived Experience and Awareness	14	Reflection on the experiences and milestones that shaped and influenced the direction of participants' lives, including childhood and coming of age.	https://app.delvetool.com/projects/11579/codes/398611
8	>>	Public Service	14		https://app.delvetool.com/projects/11579/codes/401241
9	>>	Coming of Age	7		https://app.delvetool.com/projects/11579/codes/398616
10	>>	Childhood	6		https://app.delvetool.com/projects/11579/codes/398608

Compilation of References

Acemoglu, D., & Robinson, J. A. (2013). *Why nations fail: The origins of power, prosperity, and poverty (Pbk* (C. Business, Ed.).

Achebe, C. (1994). *Things fall apart*. Anchor Books.

Achebe, C. (1998). *The trouble with Nigeria*. Fourth Dimension Publishing.

Ajah, A. (2014). On Truthful narrative-identity and a development model for Nigeria. *Open Journal of Philosophy*, *4*(4), 531–540. doi:10.4236/ojpp.2014.44055

Ake, C. (1996). *Democracy and development in Africa*. Brookings Institution.

Allen, P. J., Lahai, S. B. S., & O'Connell, J. (2003). *Sierra Leone's Truth & Reconciliation Commission and Special Court: A Citizen's Handbook*. International Center for Transitional Justice & Freetown, Sierra Leone.

Arendt, H. (1958). *The human condition*. The University of Chicago Press.

Arieff, A. (2009). Still standing: Neighborhood wars and political stability in Guinea. *The Journal of Modern African Studies*, *47*(3), 331–348. doi:10.1017/S0022278X09004108

Arnold, M. (1869). *Culture and anarchy: An essay in political and social criticism*. Macmillan.

Ayittey, G. (1998). *Africa in chaos*. St. Martin's Press.

Bandura, A. (1974). Behavior theory and the models of man. *The American Psychologist*, *29*(12), 859–869. doi:10.1037/h0037514

Bandura, A. (1977). *Social learning theory*. Prentice Hall.

Barker, R. A. (1997). How can we train leaders if we do not know what leadership is? *Human Relations*, *50*(4), 343–362. doi:10.1177/001872679705000402

Barrett, M. S., & Stauffer, S. L. (2009). *Narrative inquiry in music education: Troubling certainty*. Springer. doi:10.1007/978-1-4020-9862-8

BBC News. (2008). *Tanzanian PM to resign over graft*. BBC News. http://news.bbc.co.uk/2/hi/africa/7232141.stm

BBC. (2009). South Africa's Congress of the People party facing "leadership" crisis. *BBC Monitoring Africa*. BBC Worldwide Limited.

Bengtsson, M. (2016). How to plan and perform a qualitative study using content analysis. *NursingPlus Open*, *2*, 8–14. doi:10.1016/j.npls.2016.01.001

Bolden, R., & Kirk, P. (2006). Transforming communities through leadership development: A Pan-African example. *British Academy of Management Conference.*

Bolden, R., & Kirk, P. (2006). Transforming communities through leadership development: A Pan-African example. *British Academy of Management Conference.* British Academy of Management.

Bonsu, O. K. (2002). *Leadership: The missing variable in the economic development of sub-Saharan Africa*. ProQuest Dissertations Publishing.

Braun, V., & Clarke, V. (2006). Using thematic analysis in psychology. *Qualitative Research in Psychology*, *3*(2), 77–101. doi:10.1191/1478088706qp063oa

Brickstone. (n.d). *Oil and gas in developing positive growth in economies in Africa*. Brickstone. https://brickstone.africa/oil-and-gas-in-africa-positive-growth-economies

Britannica. (2023). *Tanzania*. https://www.britannica.com/place/Dodoma

Bruijn, D. R. & Gewald, J.B. (2007). Strength beyond structure social and historical trajectories of agency in Africa. Brill.

Butler, A. (2010). *Paying for politics : party funding and political change in South Africa and the global South*. Jacana.

Callaci, E. (2016). Chief Village in a Nation of Villages: History, Race and Authority in Tanzania's Dodoma Plan. *Urban History*, *43*(1), 96–116. doi:10.1017/S0963926814000753

Camilli, E. P. B., & Green, J. L. (2006). Handbook of complementary methods in education research. Lawrence Erlbaum Associates.

Cappelen, A., Fest, S., Sørensen, E. Ø., & Tungodden, B. (2022). Choice and Personal Responsibility: What Is a Morally Relevant Choice? *The Review of Economics and Statistics*, *104*(5), 1110–1119. doi:10.1162/rest_a_01010

Castaneda Dower, P., Gokmen, G., Le Breton, M., & Weber, S. (2021). Did the Cold War Produce Development Clusters in Africa? *IDEAS Working Paper Series from RePEc.*

Chapman, G. (1992). *The 5 love languages: The secret to love that lasts*. Northfield Publishing.

Clandinin, D. J., & Rosiek, J. (2007). Mapping a landscape of narrative inquiry: Borderland spaces and tensions. In D. J. Clandinin (Ed.), *Handbook of narrative inquiry: mapping a methodology* (pp. 35–75). Sage. doi:10.4135/9781452226552.n2

Collier, D., & Mahoney, J. (1996). Insights and pitfalls: Selection bias in qualitative research. *World Politics*, *49*(1), 56–91. doi:10.1353/wp.1996.0023

Connelly, F. M., & Clandinin, D. J. (1990). Stories of Experience and Narrative Inquiry. *Educational Researcher*, *19*(5), 2–14. doi:10.2307/1176100

Darawsheh, W. (2014). Reflexivity in research: Promoting rigor, reliability and validity in qualitative research. *International Journal of Therapy and Rehabilitation, 21*(12), 560– . doi:10.12968/ijtr.2014.21.12.560

Denny, E., & Weckesser, A. (2019). Qualitative research: What it is and what it is not: Study design: qualitative research. *BJOG*, *126*(3), 369–369. doi:10.1111/1471-0528.15198 PMID:29916201

Dieckmann, O. (1996). Cultural determinants of economic growth: Theory and evidence. *Journal of Cultural Economics*, *20*(4), 297–320. http://dx.doi.org.proxymu.wrlc.org/10.1007/s10824-005-7320-0. doi:10.1007/s10824-005-7320-0

Dowden, R. (2009). *Africa: Altered States, Ordinary Miracles*. Public Affairs.

Du Bois, W. E. B. (William E. B. (2007). The Negro. Oxford University Press.

Easterly, W. (2013). *The tyranny of experts: Economics, dictators, and the forgotten rights of the poor*. Basic Books.

Ekeh, P. (1986). Development theory and theAfrican predicament. *Africa Development. Afrique et Developpement*, *11*(4), 1–40. https://www.jstor.org/stable/24486618

Fanon, F. (1963). *The wretched of the earth*. Grove Press.

Feinstein, A. (2009). *After the party: Corruption, the ANC and South Africa's uncertain future*. Verso.

Forsyth, F. (1969). *The Biafra story: The making of anAfrican legend*. Penguin Books.

French, H. (2015). *China's second continent: How a million migrants are building a new empire in Africa*. Vintage Books.

Gemmill, G., & Oakley, J. (1992). Leadership: An alienating social myth? *Human Relations*, *45*(2), 113–129. doi:10.1177/001872679204500201

Goldin, I. (2018). *Development: A very short introduction*. Oxford University Press. doi:10.1093/actrade/9780198736257.001.0001

Guenther, J., & Falk, I. (2019). Generalizing from Qualitative Research (GQR): A New Old Approach. *The Qualitative Report*, *24*(5), 1012–1033. doi:10.46743/2160-3715/2019.3478

Hammarlund, C., & Andersson, A. (2019). What's in it for Africa? European Union fishing access agreements and fishery exports from developing countries. *World Development*, *113*, 172–185. doi:10.1016/j.worlddev.2018.09.010

Harris, D. (David J. (2014). Sierra Leone : a political history. Oxford University Press.

Harris, J. H. (1912). *Dawn in darkest Africa*. E.P. Dutton.

Haugen, D. M., & Musser, S. (2012). *Africa*. Greenhaven Press.

Heffernan, M. (2015, May). Forget the pecking order at work. Youtube. https://www.ted.com/talks/margaret_heffernan_forget_the_pecking_order_at_work?language=en

Hodder, M. (2023). *Africa's agricultural revolution: From self-sufficiency to global food powerhouse*. White & Case. https://www.whitecase.com/insight-our-thinking/africa-focus-summer-2023-africas-agricultural-revolution#:~:text=Africa%20has%2060%20percent%20of,Africans%20than%20any%20other%20sector

Hutson, H., & Johnson, M. (2016, May 2). *To recover from a crisis, retell your company's story*. Harvard Business Review Digital Archives.

Hutson, H., and Johnson, M. (2016, May 2). *To recover from a crisis, retell your company's story*. Harvard Business Review Digital Archives.

Jackson, R. L. II, Drummond, D. K., & Camara, S. (2007). What Is Qualitative Research? *Qualitative Research Reports in Communication*, *8*(1), 21–28. doi:10.1080/17459430701617879

Johnson, C. (2021). *Meeting the ethical challenges of leadership: Casting light or shadow* (7th ed.). Sage Publications.

Johnson, R. B., & Christensen, L. (2020). *Educational research: Quantitative, qualitative, and mixed approaches* (7th ed.). Sage Publications.

Juma, T. O., & Oluoch, K. K. (2013). System failure causes of conflict in Africa as a social transformation. *International Affairs and Global Strategy*, *17*, 2013.

Kabbah, A. T. (2010). *Coming Back from the Brink in Sierra Leone*. EPP Book Services.

Kincaid, J. (1988). *A small place*. Penguin.

Kuada, J. (2010). Culture and leadership in Africa: A conceptual model and research agenda. *African Journal of Economic and Management Studies*, *1*(1), 9–24. doi:10.1108/20400701011028130

Legatum Institute. (n.d.). *The Legatum Prosperity Index 2023*. Legatum Institute. https://prosperity.com/about-prosperity/prosperity-index

Leotti, L. A., Iyengar, S. S., & Ochsner, K. N. (2010). Born to choose: The origins and value of the need for control. *Trends in Cognitive Sciences*, *14*(10), 457–463. doi:10.1016/j.tics.2010.08.001 PMID:20817592

Lin, J. Y. (2014). *The Quest for prosperity: How developing economies can take off*. Princeton University Press.

Lusigi, A. (2022). *Harnessing Africa's creativity and innovation to drive human development*. United Nations Development Program. https://www.undp.org/ghana/blog/harnessing-africas-creativity-and-innovation-drive-human-development

Manby, B. (1995). *South Africa: threats to a new democracy: continuing violence in KwaZulu-Natal.* Human Rights Watch/Africa.

Marshall, B., Cardon, P., Poddar, A., & Fontenot, R. (2013). Does Sample Size Matter in Qualitative Research?: A Review of Qualitative Interviews in Research. *Journal of Computer Information Systems*, *54*(1), 11–22. doi:10.1080/08874417.2013.11645667

Mawere, M., & Mwanaka, T. R. (2015). Democracy, good governance and development in Africa (Mawere & T. R. Mwanaka, Eds.). Langaa Research & Publishing CIG.

Meredith, M. (2005). *The fate of Africa: from the hopes of freedom to the heart of despair: a history of fifty years of independence*. Public Affairs.

Meredith, M. (2006). *The state of Africa: A history of fifty years of independence*. Free Press.

Meredith, M. (2011). *Born in Africa the quest for the origins of human life* (1st ed.). PublicAffairs.

Minorities at Risk Project. (2003, December 31). *Assessment for Zulus in South Africa.* RefWorld. https://www.refworld.org/docid/469f3ad2c.html

Müller, H., Mekgwe, P., & Mhloyi, M. (2013). *Values and development in Southern Africa.* Council for the Development of Social Science Research in Africa. doi:10.2307/j.ctvk8vz4z

Mutiiria, O. M., Ju, Q., & Dumor, K. (2020). Infrastructure and inclusive growth in Africa: An empirical analysis. *Progress in Development Studies*, *20*(3), 187–207. doi:10.1177/1464993420927507

Nakatani, H. (2023). Aging and shrinking population: The looming demographic challenges of super-aged and super-low fertility society starting from Asia. *Global Health & Medicine*, *5*(5), 257–263. doi:10.35772/ghm.2023.01057 PMID:37908514

Njoh, A. J. (2006). *Tradition, culture and development in Africa: Historical lessons for modern development planning*. Ashgate Publishing.

Noble, H., & Smith, J. (2015). Issues of validity and reliability in qualitative research. *Evidence-Based Nursing*, *18*(2), 34–35. doi:10.1136/eb-2015-102054 PMID:25653237

Nugent, T. (1949). *The spirit of the laws (trans.).* MacMillan.

Nyerere, J. (1985). Africa and the debt crisis. *African Affairs (London), 84*, 337.

Nyerere, J. (1985). Africa and the debt crisis. *African Affairs (London), 84*, 493–4. Google Scholar.

Oakes, J.M., and Rossi, P. H. (2003). The measurement of SES in health research: current practice and steps toward a new approach. *Social Science & Medicine (1982), 56*(4), 769–784. . doi:10.1016/S0277-9536(02)00073-4

Odhiambo, N. M. (2021). Health expenditure and economic growth in Africa: An empirical investigation. *Development Studies Research, 8*(1), 73–81. doi:10.1080/21665095.2021.1892500

Olopade, D. (2014). *The bright continent: breaking rules and making change in modern Africa*. Houghton Mifflin Harcourt.

Olopade, D. (2014). *The bright continent: Breaking rules and making change in modern Africa*. Houghton Mifflin Harcourt.

Overview. (n.d.) World Bank. https://www.worldbank.org/en/topic/poverty/overview

Polgreen, L. (2007). Discontent in Guinea Nears Boiling Point. *The New York Times*.

Polit, D. F., & Beck, C. T. (2010). Generalization in quantitative and qualitative research: Myths and strategies. *International Journal of Nursing Studies, 47*(11), 1451–1458. doi:10.1016/j.ijnurstu.2010.06.004 PMID:20598692

Powell, J., & Thyne, C. (2011). Global Instances of Coups from 1950-Present. *Journal of Peace Research, 48*(2), 249–259. doi:10.1177/0022343310397436

Prasad, D. (2021, November 24). *Regional integration and the African Continental Free Trade Agreement: from parallelism to harmonisation*. International Bar Association. https://www.ibanet.org/regional-integration-afcfta#:~:text=The%20African%20Continental%20Free%20Trade%20Area%20agreement%20%28AfCFTA%29,across%2054%20members%20of%20the%20African%20Union.%20

Proxy Wars During the Cold War . (2018). Atomic Heritage Foundation. https://www.atomicheritage.org/history/proxy-wars-during-cold-war-africa

Riddell, J. (1992). Things fall apart again: Structural adjustment programs in Africa. *The Journal of Modern African Studies, 30*(1), 53–68. doi:10.1017/S0022278X00007722

Russell, A. (2009). *Bring me my machine gun: The battle for the soul of South Africa from Mandela to Zuma* (1st ed.). PublicAffairs.

Sachs, J. B. (2006). *The end of poverty: Economic possibilities for our time*. Penguin.

Saul, J. S. (2012). Tanzania fifty years on (1961-2011): Rethinking ujamaa, Nyerere and socialism in Africa. *Review of African Political Economy, 39*(131), 117–125. doi:10.1080/03056244.2012.662386

Scanlon, T. M. (1986). The significance of choice. *The Tanner Lectures on Human Values, 7*, 149–216.

Settles, J. D. (1996). *The impact of colonialism on African economic development.* Chancellor's Honors Program Projects. https://trace.tennessee.edu/utk_chanhonoproj/182

Shadish, W. R. (2011). Randomized Controlled Studies and Alternative Designs in Outcome Studies: Challenges and Opportunities. *Research on Social Work Practice*, *21*(6), 636–643. doi:10.1177/1049731511403324

Shaw, A. (2020, March 15). *President Bio Appoints Sierra Leone Police Chief & Female Deputy from his Mende Tribe*. The Organiser.net. https://theorganiser.net/sierra-leone/1143-president-bio appoints-sierra-leone-police-chief-female-deputy-from-his-mende-tribe.

Siebolds, P., & Steinberg, F. (1980). Dodoma: A future African Brasilia? *Habitat International*, *5*(5-6), 681–690. doi:10.1016/0197-3975(80)90008-9

Sierra Leone State House. (2022). *The Republic of Sierra Leone State House*. Sierra Leone State House. https:// statehouse.gov.sl/

Singh, R. (2019). *Education: An effective engine and catalyst of social transformation.* Eurasiareview.com.

Slevin, E., & Sines, D. (2000). Enhancing the truthfulness, consistency and transferability of a qualitative study: Utilizing a manifold of approaches. *Nurse Researcher*, *7*(2), 79–98. doi:10.7748/nr2000.01.7.2.79.c6113

South African History Online. (2023). *Athlone or Cape Flats, Cape Town*. https://www.sahistory.org.za/place/athlone-or-cape-flats-cape-town

Sowell, T. (2005, July 14). Geography and man have all but killed Africa. *Deseret News*. https://www.deseret.com/2005/7/14/19902079/thomas-sowell-geography-and-man-have-all-but-killed-africa

Soyinka, W. (1975). *Death and the king's horseman*. Hill and Wang.

Soyinka, W. (1976). *Myth, literature and theAfrican world*. Cambridge University Press.

Soyinka, W. (2000). Culture, democracy and renewal. *Trends in Organized Crime*, *5*(3), 110–117. doi:10.1007/s12117-000-1039-2

Stanier, M. B. (2016). *The coaching habit: Say less, ask more & change the way you lead forever*. Box of Crayons Press.

Storr, W. (2020). *The science of storytelling: Why stories make us human and how to tell them better*. Abrams Press.

The Mail & Guardian. (2009, May 15). Zuma's Cabinet Inc. *The Mail and Guardian*. https://mg.co.za/article/2009-05-15-zumas-cabinet-inc/

The Sierra Leone Web. (2003). *A Statement by President Ahmad Tejan Kabbah Made Before the Truth and Reconciliation Commission on Tuesday 5th August 2003*. Sierra Leone State House. http://www.sierra-leone.org/Speeches/kabbah-080503.html

UN. (2019). Selected Results of the 2019 UN World Population Projections. *Population and Development Review, 45*(3), 689–694. . doi:10.1111/padr.12288

UNICEF. (n.d.). *Sierra Leone - education.* UNICEF. https://www.unicef.org/sierraleone/education

United Nations. (n.d.). *The sustainable development goals report 2023.* UN. https://sdgs.un.org/sites/default/files/2023-07/The-Sustainable-Development-Goals-Report-2023_0.pdf

Ventures Africa. (2021, December 28). Seven notable innovations in Africa in 2021. *Ventures Africa.* https://venturesafrica.com/five-notable-innovations-in-africa-2021/

Ventures Africa. (2021, July 29). Meet Noel N'Guessan. The innovator helping farmers monetize biowaste in Cote d'Ivoire. *Ventures Africa.* https://venturesafrica.com/meet-noel-nguessan-the-ivorian-innovator-helping-farmers-generate-an-income-from-waste/

Wang, F. (2023, January 18). Why China's shrinking population is a big deal – counting the social, economic and political costs of an aging, smaller society. *The Conversation.* https://theconversation.com/why-chinas-shrinking-population-is-a-big-deal-counting-the-social-economic-and-political-costs-of-an-aging-smaller-society-198056

WaterAid. (n.d.). *Nigeria.* https://www.wateraid.org/uk/where-we-work/nigeria

Whitemore, J. (2017). *Coaching for performance: The principles and practice of coaching and leadership* (5th ed.). Nicholas Barely Publishing.

Williams, A. S. (2021). *White malice : the CIA and the covert recolonization of Africa* (1st ed.). PublicAffairs.

Williams, A. S. (2021). *White malice: The CIA and the covert recolonization of Africa* (1st ed.). PublicAffairs.

World Bank. (2020, Jul 27). *The African continental free trade area.* World Bank. https://www.worldbank.org/en/topic/trade/publication/the-african-continental-free-trade-area

World Bank. (2022). *Understanding Poverty.* World Bank. https://www.worldbank.org/en/news/factsheet/2022/05/02/fact-sheet-an-adjustment-to-global-poverty-lines

World Bank. (n.d.). *World Poverty Overview 2023.* World Bank. https://www.worldbank.org/en/topic/poverty/overview

Worldatlas. (n.d.). *Least Developed Countries 2022.* World Population Review. https://worldpopulationreview.com/country-rankings/least-developed-countries

Worldatlas. (n.d.). *Least Developed Countries 2022.* World Population Review. https://worldpopulationreview.com/country-rankings/least-developed-countries

Ziorklui, E. Doe. (1989). Ghana : Nkrumah to Rawlings (Revised edition.). Em-zed Books Centre.

Related References

To continue our tradition of advancing academic research, we have compiled a list of recommended IGI Global readings. These references will provide additional information and guidance to further enrich your knowledge and assist you with your own research and future publications.

Ababio, G. K. (2018). Nutraceuticals: The Dose Makes the Difference – It's All in the Dose. In A. Verma, K. Srivastava, S. Singh, & H. Singh (Eds.), *Nutraceuticals and Innovative Food Products for Healthy Living and Preventive Care* (pp. 24–47). Hershey, PA: IGI Global. doi:10.4018/978-1-5225-2970-5.ch002

Adams, M. G. (2018). Systematically Investigating Instructor Impact on Student Satisfaction in Graduate Programs. In D. Polly, M. Putman, T. Petty, & A. Good (Eds.), *Innovative Practices in Teacher Preparation and Graduate-Level Teacher Education Programs* (pp. 200–214). Hershey, PA: IGI Global. doi:10.4018/978-1-5225-3068-8.ch012

Akgül, Y., & Tunca, M. Z. (2018). Proliferating View of Knowledge Management and Balanced Scorecard Outcome Linkage. In N. Baporikar (Ed.), *Global Practices in Knowledge Management for Societal and Organizational Development* (pp. 168–193). Hershey, PA: IGI Global. doi:10.4018/978-1-5225-3009-1.ch008

Alcaraz-Valencia, P. A., Gaytán-Lugo, L. S., & Gallardo, S. C. (2018). An Exploratory Study on the Interaction Beyond Virtual Environments to Improve Listening Ability When Learning English as a Second Language. In F. Cipolla-Ficarra (Ed.), *Optimizing Human-Computer Interaction With Emerging Technologies* (pp. 306–331). Hershey, PA: IGI Global. doi:10.4018/978-1-5225-2616-2.ch013

Altıntaş, F. Ç., & Kavurmacı, C. (2018). Value Statements in Web Pages of Turkish State Universities: A Basic Classification. In U. Thomas (Ed.), *Advocacy in Academia and the Role of Teacher Preparation Programs* (pp. 302–316). Hershey, PA: IGI Global. doi:10.4018/978-1-5225-2906-4.ch017

Amoroso, D. L. (2018). The Importance of Advocacy on Reputation and Loyalty: Comparison of Japanese, Chinese, and the Filipino Consumers. In P. Ordóñez de Pablos (Ed.), *Management Strategies and Technology Fluidity in the Asian Business Sector* (pp. 114–125). Hershey, PA: IGI Global. doi:10.4018/978-1-5225-4056-4.ch007

Atiku, S. O., & Fields, Z. (2018). Organisational Learning Dimensions and Talent Retention Strategies for the Service Industries. In N. Baporikar (Ed.), *Global Practices in Knowledge Management for Societal and Organizational Development* (pp. 358–381). Hershey, PA: IGI Global. doi:10.4018/978-1-5225-3009-1.ch017

Ayoola-Amale, A. (2018). Women in Leadership: Why We Need More Women Leaders. In B. Cook (Ed.), *Handbook of Research on Examining Global Peacemaking in the Digital Age* (pp. 211–222). Hershey, PA: IGI Global. doi:10.4018/978-1-5225-3032-9.ch015

Baran, A. G. (2018). Through the Syrians Refuge in Turkey Towards the Creation of the War Migration Theory. In Ş. Erçetin (Ed.), *Social Considerations of Migration Movements and Immigration Policies* (pp. 178–196). Hershey, PA: IGI Global. doi:10.4018/978-1-5225-3322-1.ch011

Beckett-Camarata, J. (2018). Public Choice and Financing Local Government Fiscal Reform in Albania. In H. Levine & K. Moreno (Eds.), *Positioning Markets and Governments in Public Management* (pp. 197–208). Hershey, PA: IGI Global. doi:10.4018/978-1-5225-4177-6.ch015

Bedford, D. A. (2018). Sustainable Knowledge Management Strategies: Aligning Business Capabilities and Knowledge Management Goals. In N. Baporikar (Ed.), *Global Practices in Knowledge Management for Societal and Organizational Development* (pp. 46–73). Hershey, PA: IGI Global. doi:10.4018/978-1-5225-3009-1.ch003

Benaouda, A., & García-Peñalvo, F. J. (2018). Towards an Intelligent System for the Territorial Planning: Agricultural Case. In F. García-Peñalvo (Ed.), *Global Implications of Emerging Technology Trends* (pp. 158–178). Hershey, PA: IGI Global. doi:10.4018/978-1-5225-4944-4.ch010

Beneventi, P. (2018). When Technology Becomes Popular: A Multimedia, Shared Production for the Information Age. In *Technology and the New Generation of Active Citizens: Emerging Research and Opportunities* (pp. 23–44). Hershey, PA: IGI Global. doi:10.4018/978-1-5225-3770-0.ch002

Bernal, L. D., & Cusi, M. L. (2018). Corporate Entrepreneurship in Colombia: Contrast Cases of Two Colombian Manufacturing SMEs. In R. Perez-Uribe, C. Salcedo-Perez, & D. Ocampo-Guzman (Eds.), *Handbook of Research on Intrapreneurship and Organizational Sustainability in SMEs* (pp. 368–390). Hershey, PA: IGI Global. doi:10.4018/978-1-5225-3543-0.ch017

Berning, S. C., & Ambrosius, J. (2018). How the Human Resource Practices of Chinese MNEs in Africa Create Economic Growth and Livelihood Options. In S. Hipsher (Ed.), *Examining the Private Sector's Role in Wealth Creation and Poverty Reduction* (pp. 85–109). Hershey, PA: IGI Global. doi:10.4018/978-1-5225-3117-3.ch005

Bharti, A., & Mittal, A. (2018). Perishable Goods Supply Cold Chain Management in India. In A. Kumar & S. Saurav (Eds.), *Supply Chain Management Strategies and Risk Assessment in Retail Environments* (pp. 232–246). Hershey, PA: IGI Global. doi:10.4018/978-1-5225-3056-5.ch013

Bhattacharya, S., Kumar, R. V., & Dutta, A. (2018). Exploring Kapferer's Brand Identity Prism Applicability in Indian Political Marketing Aspect With Special Focus to Youth Voters. In Rajagopal, & R. Behl (Eds.), Start-Up Enterprises and Contemporary Innovation Strategies in the Global Marketplace (pp. 136-152). Hershey, PA: IGI Global. doi:10.4018/978-1-5225-4831-7.ch010

Bhattarai, R. K. (2018). Enterprise Immune System. In *Enterprise Resiliency in the Continuum of Change: Emerging Research and Opportunities* (pp. 88–111). Hershey, PA: IGI Global. doi:10.4018/978-1-5225-2627-8.ch003

Bhattarai, R. K. (2018). Enterprise Philosophy. In *Enterprise Resiliency in the Continuum of Change: Emerging Research and Opportunities* (pp. 1–43). Hershey, PA: IGI Global. doi:10.4018/978-1-5225-2627-8.ch001

Bhattarai, R. K. (2018). Enterprise Resiliency. In *Enterprise Resiliency in the Continuum of Change: Emerging Research and Opportunities* (pp. 112–137). Hershey, PA: IGI Global. doi:10.4018/978-1-5225-2627-8.ch004

Bisen, S. S., & Deshpande, Y. (2018). The Impact of the Internet in Twenty-First Century Addictions: An Overview. In B. Bozoglan (Ed.), *Psychological, Social, and Cultural Aspects of Internet Addiction* (pp. 1–19). Hershey, PA: IGI Global. doi:10.4018/978-1-5225-3477-8.ch001

Biswal, S. K. (2018). Branding Culture: A Study of Telugu Film Industry. In S. Dasgupta, S. Biswal, & M. Ramesh (Eds.), *Holistic Approaches to Brand Culture and Communication Across Industries* (pp. 1–23). Hershey, PA: IGI Global. doi:10.4018/978-1-5225-3150-0.ch001

Blake, S., & Burkett, C. M. (2018). Individual Creativity: Predictors and Characteristics. In *Creativity in Workforce Development and Innovation: Emerging Research and Opportunities* (pp. 88–104). Hershey, PA: IGI Global. doi:10.4018/978-1-5225-4952-9.ch005

Blomeley, S., & Hamilton, A. H. (2018). Writing Partners: Bridging the Personal and Social in the Service-Learning Classroom. In O. Delano-Oriaran, M. Penick-Parks, & S. Fondrie (Eds.), *Culturally Engaging Service-Learning With Diverse Communities* (pp. 202–222). Hershey, PA: IGI Global. doi:10.4018/978-1-5225-2900-2.ch012

Bohra, M., & Visen, A. (2018). Nutraceutical Properties in Flowers. In A. Verma, K. Srivastava, S. Singh, & H. Singh (Eds.), *Nutraceuticals and Innovative Food Products for Healthy Living and Preventive Care* (pp. 217–235). Hershey, PA: IGI Global. doi:10.4018/978-1-5225-2970-5.ch010

Boyd, L. N. (2018). Fortifying Parent Partnerships Through the Black Church Space. In K. Norris & S. Collier (Eds.), *Social Justice and Parent Partnerships in Multicultural Education Contexts* (pp. 118–137). Hershey, PA: IGI Global. doi:10.4018/978-1-5225-3943-8.ch007

Bozoglan, B. (2018). The Role of Family Factors in Internet Addiction Among Children and Adolescents: An Overview. In B. Bozoglan (Ed.), *Psychological, Social, and Cultural Aspects of Internet Addiction* (pp. 146–168). Hershey, PA: IGI Global. doi:10.4018/978-1-5225-3477-8.ch008

Briz-Ponce, L., Juanes-Méndez, J. A., & García-Peñalvo, F. J. (2018). Current Situation and Appraisal Tendencies of M-Learning. In F. García-Peñalvo (Ed.), *Global Implications of Emerging Technology Trends* (pp. 115–129). Hershey, PA: IGI Global. doi:10.4018/978-1-5225-4944-4.ch007

Brkljačić, T., Majetić, F., & Wertag, A. (2018). I'm Always Online: Well-Being and Main Sources of Life Dis/Satisfaction of Heavy Internet Users. In B. Bozoglan (Ed.), *Psychological, Social, and Cultural Aspects of Internet Addiction* (pp. 72–89). Hershey, PA: IGI Global. doi:10.4018/978-1-5225-3477-8.ch004

Brown, M. A. Sr. (2018). Defining Your Team. In *Motivationally Intelligent Leadership: Emerging Research and Opportunities* (pp. 1–22). Hershey, PA: IGI Global. doi:10.4018/978-1-5225-3746-5.ch001

Brown, M. A. Sr. (2018). Empowering Leaders With Tools. In *Motivationally Intelligent Leadership: Emerging Research and Opportunities* (pp. 72–96). Hershey, PA: IGI Global. doi:10.4018/978-1-5225-3746-5.ch006

Brown, M. A. Sr. (2018). Sensemaking Theory. In *Motivationally Intelligent Leadership: Emerging Research and Opportunities* (pp. 46–55). Hershey, PA: IGI Global. doi:10.4018/978-1-5225-3746-5.ch004

Brown, S., & Bousalis, R. (2018). Best Practices in K-12 Arts Integration: Curricular Connections. In *Curriculum Integration in Contemporary Teaching Practice: Emerging Research and Opportunities* (pp. 95–124). Hershey, PA: IGI Global. doi:10.4018/978-1-5225-4065-6.ch004

Brown, S., & Bousalis, R. (2018). Interdisciplinary Curriculum in K-12 Schools: Current Practices in the Field. In *Curriculum Integration in Contemporary Teaching Practice: Emerging Research and Opportunities* (pp. 125–143). Hershey, PA: IGI Global. doi:10.4018/978-1-5225-4065-6.ch005

Bullock, C. A. (2018). Collaboration: Academes, Government, and Community to Drive Economic Uplift and Empowerment. In S. Burton (Ed.), *Engaged Scholarship and Civic Responsibility in Higher Education* (pp. 1–24). Hershey, PA: IGI Global. doi:10.4018/978-1-5225-3649-9.ch001

Burdenko, E. V., & Mudrova, S. V. (2018). Indicators System as a Measure of Development Level of Knowledge Economy: Application of World Bank Methodology. In N. Baporikar (Ed.), *Global Practices in Knowledge Management for Societal and Organizational Development* (pp. 74–105). Hershey, PA: IGI Global. doi:10.4018/978-1-5225-3009-1.ch004

Burston, B., & Collier-Stewart, S. (2018). STEM for All: The Importance of Parent/School/Community Partnerships Across the K-12 Pipeline and Beyond. In K. Norris & S. Collier (Eds.), *Social Justice and Parent Partnerships in Multicultural Education Contexts* (pp. 274–288). Hershey, PA: IGI Global. doi:10.4018/978-1-5225-3943-8.ch015

Carboni, M., & Perelli, C. (2018). "Beyond" Religious Tourism: The Case of Fez. In H. El-Gohary, D. Edwards, & R. Eid (Eds.), *Global Perspectives on Religious Tourism and Pilgrimage* (pp. 71–83). Hershey, PA: IGI Global. doi:10.4018/978-1-5225-2796-1.ch005

Cascella, M., Muzio, M. R., Bimonte, S., & Cuomo, A. (2018). Nutraceuticals for Prevention of Chemotherapy-Induced Peripheral Neuropathy. In A. Verma, K. Srivastava, S. Singh, & H. Singh (Eds.), *Nutraceuticals and Innovative Food Products for Healthy Living and Preventive Care* (pp. 236–259). Hershey, PA: IGI Global. doi:10.4018/978-1-5225-2970-5.ch011

Cena, F., Rapp, A., Likavec, S., & Marcengo, A. (2018). Envisioning the Future of Personalization Through Personal Informatics: A User Study. *International Journal of Mobile Human Computer Interaction, 10*(1), 52–66. doi:10.4018/IJMHCI.2018010104

Chandiramani, J., & Airy, A. (2018). Urbanization and Socio-Economic Growth in South Asia Region. In U. Benna & I. Benna (Eds.), *Urbanization and Its Impact on Socio-Economic Growth in Developing Regions* (pp. 130–154). Hershey, PA: IGI Global. doi:10.4018/978-1-5225-2659-9.ch007

Chang, Y., Choi, S. B., Lee, J., & Jin, W. C. (2018). Population Size vs. Number of Crimes: Is the Relationship Superlinear? *International Journal of Information Systems and Social Change, 9*(1), 26–39. doi:10.4018/IJISSC.2018010102

Chaudhary, N. S., & Yadav, R. (2018). Cross-Cultural Conflicts: Concept, Causes, and Elucidations. In N. Sharma, V. Singh, & S. Pathak (Eds.), *Management Techniques for a Diverse and Cross-Cultural Workforce* (pp. 79–96). Hershey, PA: IGI Global. doi:10.4018/978-1-5225-4933-8.ch005

Chirisa, I., Mukarwi, L., & Matamanda, A. R. (2018). Social Costs and Benefits of the Transformation of the Traditional Families in an African Urban Society. In U. Benna & I. Benna (Eds.), *Urbanization and Its Impact on Socio-Economic Growth in Developing Regions* (pp. 179–197). Hershey, PA: IGI Global. doi:10.4018/978-1-5225-2659-9.ch009

Chitima, S. S., & Ndlovu, I. (2018). Incorporating Indigenous Knowledge in the Preservation of Collections at the Batonga Community Museum in Zimbabwe. In P. Ngulube (Ed.), *Handbook of Research on Heritage Management and Preservation* (pp. 396–407). Hershey, PA: IGI Global. doi:10.4018/978-1-5225-3137-1.ch019

Choudhury, D. K., & Rao, P. (2018). Determinants of FDI Inflows in Developing Countries: A Dynamic Panel Approach. In V. Malepati & C. Gowri (Eds.), *Foreign Direct Investments (FDIs) and Opportunities for Developing Economies in the World Market* (pp. 25–45). Hershey, PA: IGI Global. doi:10.4018/978-1-5225-3026-8.ch002

Cipolla-Ficarra, F. V., Carré, J., Quiroga, A., & Ficarra, V. M. (2018). Anti-Models for Architectural Graphic Expression and UX Education. In F. Cipolla-Ficarra, M. Ficarra, M. Cipolla-Ficarra, A. Quiroga, J. Alma, & J. Carré (Eds.), *Technology-Enhanced Human Interaction in Modern Society* (pp. 218–233). Hershey, PA: IGI Global. doi:10.4018/978-1-5225-3437-2.ch011

Cipolla-Ficarra, F. V., Ficarra, V. M., & Cipolla-Ficarra, M. (2018). Inverted Semanteme Into Financial Information Online. In F. Cipolla-Ficarra, M. Ficarra, M. Cipolla-Ficarra, A. Quiroga, J. Alma, & J. Carré (Eds.), *Technology-Enhanced Human Interaction in Modern Society* (pp. 263–283). Hershey, PA: IGI Global. doi:10.4018/978-1-5225-3437-2.ch013

Cipolla-Ficarra, F. V., Quiroga, A., & Ficarra, V. M. (2018). Kernel of the Labyrinths Hypertextuals. In F. Cipolla-Ficarra, M. Ficarra, M. Cipolla-Ficarra, A. Quiroga, J. Alma, & J. Carré (Eds.), *Technology-Enhanced Human Interaction in Modern Society* (pp. 122–142). Hershey, PA: IGI Global. doi:10.4018/978-1-5225-3437-2.ch006

Coffey, S. M. (2018). Unveilings Through Transformative Pedagogy: Striving for Realization of Du Bois' Educational Paradigm. In U. Thomas (Ed.), *Advocacy in Academia and the Role of Teacher Preparation Programs* (pp. 206–224). Hershey, PA: IGI Global. doi:10.4018/978-1-5225-2906-4.ch012

da Rocha, J. P. (2018). Process Outcomes. In *Political Mediation in Modern Conflict Resolution: Emerging Research and Opportunities* (pp. 155–164). Hershey, PA: IGI Global. doi:10.4018/978-1-5225-5118-8.ch004

Dahiya, K., & Dhankhar, R. (2018). Role of Nutraceuticals in Cancer. In A. Verma, K. Srivastava, S. Singh, & H. Singh (Eds.), *Nutraceuticals and Innovative Food Products for Healthy Living and Preventive Care* (pp. 176–194). Hershey, PA: IGI Global. doi:10.4018/978-1-5225-2970-5.ch008

Dasgupta, S., & Kothari, R. (2018). The Impact of Digital Word-of-Mouth Communication on Consumer Decision-Making Processes: With Special Reference to Fashion Apparel Industry. In S. Dasgupta, S. Biswal, & M. Ramesh (Eds.), *Holistic Approaches to Brand Culture and Communication Across Industries* (pp. 176–198). Hershey, PA: IGI Global. doi:10.4018/978-1-5225-3150-0.ch010

Dávila, F. A. (2018). Relationship Lending and Entrepreneurial Behavior: A Game-Theoretic-Based Modeling. In Rajagopal, & R. Behl (Eds.), Start-Up Enterprises and Contemporary Innovation Strategies in the Global Marketplace (pp. 65-86). Hershey, PA: IGI Global. doi:10.4018/978-1-5225-4831-7.ch006

de Sousa, J. C. (2018). Memory. In *Neuromarketing and Big Data Analytics for Strategic Consumer Engagement: Emerging Research and Opportunities* (pp. 92–100). Hershey, PA: IGI Global. doi:10.4018/978-1-5225-4834-8.ch006

de Sousa, J. C. (2018). Sensory and Motor System. In *Neuromarketing and Big Data Analytics for Strategic Consumer Engagement: Emerging Research and Opportunities* (pp. 68–91). Hershey, PA: IGI Global. doi:10.4018/978-1-5225-4834-8.ch005

Deka, D. B., & Jadeja, M. (2018). Childhood Sexual Abuse: Prevention and Intervention. In R. Gopalan (Ed.), *Social, Psychological, and Forensic Perspectives on Sexual Abuse* (pp. 127–146). Hershey, PA: IGI Global. doi:10.4018/978-1-5225-3958-2.ch010

Dobell, E., Herold, S., & Buckley, J. (2018). Spreadsheet Error Types and Their Prevalence in a Healthcare Context. *Journal of Organizational and End User Computing, 30*(2), 20–42. doi:10.4018/JOEUC.2018040102

Donert, K., & Papoutsis, P. (2018). School on the Cloud: Connecting Education to the Cloud for Digital Citizenship. In K. Koutsopoulos, K. Doukas, & Y. Kotsanis (Eds.), *Handbook of Research on Educational Design and Cloud Computing in Modern Classroom Settings* (pp. 157–182). Hershey, PA: IGI Global. doi:10.4018/978-1-5225-3053-4.ch008

Downton, M. P. (2018). Preparation for Future Teaching: Authentic Activities in a Teacher Education Classroom. In D. Polly, M. Putman, T. Petty, & A. Good (Eds.), *Innovative Practices in Teacher Preparation and Graduate-Level Teacher Education Programs* (pp. 293–305). Hershey, PA: IGI Global. doi:10.4018/978-1-5225-3068-8.ch016

Drivas, G., Sotiriou, C., Bonanou, H., Saliari, S., Balafouti, M., & Tsevi, H. (2018). The Sky Is the Limit! In K. Koutsopoulos, K. Doukas, & Y. Kotsanis (Eds.), *Handbook of Research on Educational Design and Cloud Computing in Modern Classroom Settings* (pp. 101–121). Hershey, PA: IGI Global. doi:10.4018/978-1-5225-3053-4.ch006

Erçetin, Ş. Ş., & Bisaso, S. M. (2018). Migration and Refugee Crisis: Structural and Managerial Implications for Education. In Ş. Erçetin (Ed.), *Educational Development and Infrastructure for Immigrants and Refugees* (pp. 47–71). Hershey, PA: IGI Global. doi:10.4018/978-1-5225-3325-2.ch003

Erçetin, Ş. Ş., & Kubilay, S. (2018). Educational Expectations of Refugee Mothers for Their Children. In Ş. Erçetin (Ed.), *Educational Development and Infrastructure for Immigrants and Refugees* (pp. 171–195). Hershey, PA: IGI Global. doi:10.4018/978-1-5225-3325-2.ch009

Erçetin, Ş. Ş., Potas, N., Açıkalın, Ş. N., Özdemir, N., & Doğan, A. M. (2018). Municipalities and Refugee Crisis: Ansar Policies and Numbers. In Ş. Erçetin (Ed.), *Social Considerations of Migration Movements and Immigration Policies* (pp. 46–57). Hershey, PA: IGI Global. doi:10.4018/978-1-5225-3322-1.ch003

Erkekoğlu, L. C., & Madi, İ. (2018). The Hashemite Kingdom of Jordan. In S. Ozdemir, S. Erdogan, & A. Gedikli (Eds.), *Handbook of Research on Sociopolitical Factors Impacting Economic Growth in Islamic Nations* (pp. 95–121). Hershey, PA: IGI Global. doi:10.4018/978-1-5225-2939-2.ch006

Essien, E. D. (2018). Strengthening Performance of Civil Society Through Dialogue and Critical Thinking in Nigeria: Its Ethical Implications. In S. Chhabra (Ed.), *Handbook of Research on Civic Engagement and Social Change in Contemporary Society* (pp. 82–102). Hershey, PA: IGI Global. doi:10.4018/978-1-5225-4197-4.ch005

Feza, N. N. (2018). The Socioeconomic Status Label Associated With Mathematics. In I. Tshabangu (Ed.), *Global Ideologies Surrounding Children's Rights and Social Justice* (pp. 186–203). Hershey, PA: IGI Global. doi:10.4018/978-1-5225-2578-3.ch012

Fleener, J., Lu, L., Dun, J., & Mingquan, Y. (2018). Sustaining a Teacher Professional Learning Community in China Through Technology. In H. Spires (Ed.), *Digital Transformation and Innovation in Chinese Education* (pp. 80–99). Hershey, PA: IGI Global. doi:10.4018/978-1-5225-2924-8.ch005

Forge, J. (2018). Defence. In *The Morality of Weapons Design and Development: Emerging Research and Opportunities* (pp. 52–77). Hershey, PA: IGI Global. doi:10.4018/978-1-5225-3984-1.ch004

Forge, J. (2018). Justification. In *The Morality of Weapons Design and Development: Emerging Research and Opportunities* (pp. 78–93). Hershey, PA: IGI Global. doi:10.4018/978-1-5225-3984-1.ch005

Forge, J. (2018). Projectile Weapons. In *The Morality of Weapons Design and Development: Emerging Research and Opportunities* (pp. 94–117). Hershey, PA: IGI Global. doi:10.4018/978-1-5225-3984-1.ch006

Forge, J. (2018). Proportionality, Just War Theory, and Weapons Design. In *The Morality of Weapons Design and Development: Emerging Research and Opportunities* (pp. 139–154). Hershey, PA: IGI Global. doi:10.4018/978-1-5225-3984-1.ch008

Forge, J. (2018). Purposes and Means. In *The Morality of Weapons Design and Development: Emerging Research and Opportunities* (pp. 34–51). Hershey, PA: IGI Global. doi:10.4018/978-1-5225-3984-1.ch003

Fudge, M. (2018). The Inequity of User Fees and the Overreliance by Communities to Generate Revenue. In H. Levine & K. Moreno (Eds.), *Positioning Markets and Governments in Public Management* (pp. 147–158). Hershey, PA: IGI Global. doi:10.4018/978-1-5225-4177-6.ch011

Furumoto, R. R. (2018). Mexican-American Parents Using Critical Literacy to Address Climate Change. In K. Norris & S. Collier (Eds.), *Social Justice and Parent Partnerships in Multicultural Education Contexts* (pp. 187–208). Hershey, PA: IGI Global. doi:10.4018/978-1-5225-3943-8.ch010

Gabay, D. (2018). Who's Represented in Canadian Teaching and Learning Centres? In B. Blummer, J. Kenton, & M. Wiatrowski (Eds.), *Promoting Ethnic Diversity and Multiculturalism in Higher Education* (pp. 172–198). Hershey, PA: IGI Global. doi:10.4018/978-1-5225-4097-7.ch010

Garner, G. (2018). Foundations for Yoga Practice in Rehabilitation. In S. Telles & N. Singh (Eds.), *Research-Based Perspectives on the Psychophysiology of Yoga* (pp. 263–307). Hershey, PA: IGI Global. doi:10.4018/978-1-5225-2788-6.ch015

Geethanjali, P. (2018). Bio-Inspired Techniques in Human-Computer Interface for Control of Assistive Devices: Bio-Inspired Techniques in Assistive Devices. In D. Lopez & M. Durai (Eds.), *HCI Challenges and Privacy Preservation in Big Data Security* (pp. 23–46). Hershey, PA: IGI Global. doi:10.4018/978-1-5225-2863-0.ch002

Gharote, M. (2018). Common Features Between Findings in Traditional Texts and Contemporary Science: Yoga Texts and Contemporary Science. In S. Telles & N. Singh (Eds.), *Research-Based Perspectives on the Psychophysiology of Yoga* (pp. 309–315). Hershey, PA: IGI Global. doi:10.4018/978-1-5225-2788-6.ch016

Giosi, A., Zaccaro, E., & Testarmata, S. (2018). Social Responsibility, Shared Value, and Business Modelling: An Integrated Approach. In M. Risso & S. Testarmata (Eds.), *Value Sharing for Sustainable and Inclusive Development* (pp. 100–121). Hershey, PA: IGI Global. doi:10.4018/978-1-5225-3147-0.ch005

Grădinaru, C., Toma, S. I., & Marinescu, P. I. (2018). Entrepreneurial Thinking in the Educational System. In M. Risso & S. Testarmata (Eds.), *Value Sharing for Sustainable and Inclusive Development* (pp. 29–48). Hershey, PA: IGI Global. doi:10.4018/978-1-5225-3147-0.ch002

Güler, A. (2018). PKK-Related Asylum Applications from Turkey: Counter-Terrorism Measures vs. Refugee Status. In Ş. Erçetin (Ed.), *Social Considerations of Migration Movements and Immigration Policies* (pp. 117–142). Hershey, PA: IGI Global. doi:10.4018/978-1-5225-3322-1.ch008

Gupta, S. K. (2018). Sexual Abuse of Children and Adults With Intellectual Disabilities: Preventive, Supportive, and Intervention Strategies for Clinical Practice. In R. Gopalan (Ed.), *Social, Psychological, and Forensic Perspectives on Sexual Abuse* (pp. 197–206). Hershey, PA: IGI Global. doi:10.4018/978-1-5225-3958-2.ch014

Gürcan, Ö. F., & Gümüşsoy, Ç. A. (2018). Factors Influencing Effective Knowledge Transfer in Organizations. In N. Baporikar (Ed.), *Global Practices in Knowledge Management for Societal and Organizational Development* (pp. 271–292). Hershey, PA: IGI Global. doi:10.4018/978-1-5225-3009-1.ch013

Hagen, I., Kofoed, S., & Nayar, U. (2018). Yoga for Psychological Wellbeing in Modern Life and Contexts. In S. Telles & N. Singh (Eds.), *Research-Based Perspectives on the Psychophysiology of Yoga* (pp. 316–334). Hershey, PA: IGI Global. doi:10.4018/978-1-5225-2788-6.ch017

Handayani, B. (2018). The Paradox of Authenticity and Its Implications for Contemporary and "Bizarre" Tourism Campaigns. In S. Sarma (Ed.), *Global Observations of the Influence of Culture on Consumer Buying Behavior* (pp. 48–65). Hershey, PA: IGI Global. doi:10.4018/978-1-5225-2727-5.ch003

Huamaní, G. A., Fernández-López, S., Gómez, I. N., Rey-Ares, L., Rodríguez-Gulías, M. J., & Rodeiro-Pazos, D. (2018). The Role Models as Determinants of New Technology-Based Firms: An Exploratory Study. In A. Carrizo Moreira, J. Guilherme Leitão Dantas, & F. Manuel Valente (Eds.), *Nascent Entrepreneurship and Successful New Venture Creation* (pp. 272–288). Hershey, PA: IGI Global. doi:10.4018/978-1-5225-2936-1.ch013

Hucks, D., Sturtz, T., & Tirabassi, K. (2018). Building, Shaping, and Modeling Tools for Literacy Development and Civic Engagement. In *Fostering Positive Civic Engagement Among Millennials: Emerging Research and Opportunities* (pp. 22–35). Hershey, PA: IGI Global. doi:10.4018/978-1-5225-2452-6.ch002

Hucks, D., Sturtz, T., & Tirabassi, K. (2018). Insights, Next Steps, and Future Research. In *Fostering Positive Civic Engagement Among Millennials: Emerging Research and Opportunities* (pp. 65–72). Hershey, PA: IGI Global. doi:10.4018/978-1-5225-2452-6.ch005

Iguisi, O. V. (2018). Comparative Analysis of Hofstede's Culture Dimensions for West African Regions (WAF) and Nigeria. In S. Sarma (Ed.), *Global Observations of the Influence of Culture on Consumer Buying Behavior* (pp. 190–205). Hershey, PA: IGI Global. doi:10.4018/978-1-5225-2727-5.ch012

Islam, M. R. (2018). Abuse Among Child Domestic Workers in Bangladesh. In I. Tshabangu (Ed.), *Global Ideologies Surrounding Children's Rights and Social Justice* (pp. 1–21). Hershey, PA: IGI Global. doi:10.4018/978-1-5225-2578-3.ch001

Ito, K., & Hilliker, S. M. (2018). Supporting University International Students Through Supportive ESL Instruction and Corrective Feedback. In B. Blummer, J. Kenton, & M. Wiatrowski (Eds.), *Promoting Ethnic Diversity and Multiculturalism in Higher Education* (pp. 40–58). Hershey, PA: IGI Global. doi:10.4018/978-1-5225-4097-7.ch003

Iurato, G. (2018). A Brief Account of Ignacio Matte Blanco Theory and Other Related Psychoanalytic Themes. In *Computational Psychoanalysis and Formal Bi-Logic Frameworks* (pp. 114–135). Hershey, PA: IGI Global. doi:10.4018/978-1-5225-4128-8.ch003

Iurato, G. (2018). First Attempts to Formalize Some Main Aspects of Psychoanalysis: Towards a Computational Psychoanalysis. In *Computational Psychoanalysis and Formal Bi-Logic Frameworks* (pp. 136–205). Hershey, PA: IGI Global. doi:10.4018/978-1-5225-4128-8.ch004

Jacobsen, M., Friesen, S., & Brown, B. (2018). Teachers' Professional Learning Focused on Designs for Early Learners and Technology. In D. Polly, M. Putman, T. Petty, & A. Good (Eds.), *Innovative Practices in Teacher Preparation and Graduate-Level Teacher Education Programs* (pp. 417–438). Hershey, PA: IGI Global. doi:10.4018/978-1-5225-3068-8.ch022

Jensen, A. A., & Thomassen, A. O. (2018). Teachers' Reflective Practice in Lifelong Learning Programs. In Z. Djoub (Ed.), *Fostering Reflective Teaching Practice in Pre-Service Education* (pp. 25–45). Hershey, PA: IGI Global. doi:10.4018/978-1-5225-2963-7.ch002

Jiang, K., Barnett, G. A., Taylor, L. D., & Feng, B. (2018). Dynamic Co-Evolutions of Peace Frames in the United States, Mainland China, and Hong Kong: A Semantic Network Analysis. In B. Cook (Ed.), *Handbook of Research on Examining Global Peacemaking in the Digital Age* (pp. 145–168). Hershey, PA: IGI Global. doi:10.4018/978-1-5225-3032-9.ch010

Jiménez-González, S. G., Mendoza-González, R., & Luna-García, H. (2018). Guidelines Based on Need-Findings Study and Communication Types to Design Interactions for MOOCs. In F. Cipolla-Ficarra (Ed.), *Optimizing Human-Computer Interaction With Emerging Technologies* (pp. 210–231). Hershey, PA: IGI Global. doi:10.4018/978-1-5225-2616-2.ch008

Johnson, N. N. (2018). Effectively Managing Bias in Teacher Preparation. In U. Thomas (Ed.), *Advocacy in Academia and the Role of Teacher Preparation Programs* (pp. 146–160). Hershey, PA: IGI Global. doi:10.4018/978-1-5225-2906-4.ch008

Joseph, C. (2018). The Role of Government in a Liberal Market Economy: A Double-Edge Sword. In H. Levine & K. Moreno (Eds.), *Positioning Markets and Governments in Public Management* (pp. 53–61). Hershey, PA: IGI Global. doi:10.4018/978-1-5225-4177-6.ch005

Kade, D., Lindell, R., Ürey, H., & Özcan, O. (2018). Supporting Motion Capture Acting Through a Mixed Reality Application. In F. Cipolla-Ficarra (Ed.), *Optimizing Human-Computer Interaction With Emerging Technologies* (pp. 248–273). Hershey, PA: IGI Global. doi:10.4018/978-1-5225-2616-2.ch010

Karataş, S., Kukul, V., & Özcan, S. (2018). How Powerful Is Digital Storytelling for Teaching?: Perspective of Pre-Service Teachers. In D. Polly, M. Putman, T. Petty, & A. Good (Eds.), *Innovative Practices in Teacher Preparation and Graduate-Level Teacher Education Programs* (pp. 511–529). Hershey, PA: IGI Global. doi:10.4018/978-1-5225-3068-8.ch027

Kavaklı, N. (2018). Hate Speech Towards Syrian Refugees in Turkish Online Reader Comments. In C. Akrivopoulou (Ed.), *Global Perspectives on Human Migration, Asylum, and Security* (pp. 127–142). Hershey, PA: IGI Global. doi:10.4018/978-1-5225-2817-3.ch007

Kaynak, S. (2018). Pakistan. In S. Ozdemir, S. Erdogan, & A. Gedikli (Eds.), *Handbook of Research on Sociopolitical Factors Impacting Economic Growth in Islamic Nations* (pp. 293–313). Hershey, PA: IGI Global. doi:10.4018/978-1-5225-2939-2.ch015

Korstanje, M. E. (2018). Thana-Capitalism and the Sense of Reality: Lessons Unlearned. In C. Akrivopoulou (Ed.), *Global Perspectives on Human Migration, Asylum, and Security* (pp. 1–20). Hershey, PA: IGI Global. doi:10.4018/978-1-5225-2817-3.ch001

Korstanje, M. E. (2018). The Lost Paradise: The Religious Nature of Tourism. In H. El-Gohary, D. Edwards, & R. Eid (Eds.), *Global Perspectives on Religious Tourism and Pilgrimage* (pp. 129–141). Hershey, PA: IGI Global. doi:10.4018/978-1-5225-2796-1.ch008

Korstanje, M. E., & George, B. P. (2018). Emotionality, Reason, and Dark Tourism: Discussions Around the Sense of Death. In M. Korstanje & B. George (Eds.), *Virtual Traumascapes and Exploring the Roots of Dark Tourism* (pp. 1–25). Hershey, PA: IGI Global. doi:10.4018/978-1-5225-2750-3.ch001

Kougioumtzis, G. A., & Louka, D. (2018). Advocacy and Teacher Mentoring. In U. Thomas (Ed.), *Advocacy in Academia and the Role of Teacher Preparation Programs* (pp. 65–87). Hershey, PA: IGI Global. doi:10.4018/978-1-5225-2906-4.ch004

Kousar, H. (2018). Gender Violence in Academia. In N. Mahtab, T. Haque, I. Khan, M. Islam, & I. Wahid (Eds.), *Handbook of Research on Women's Issues and Rights in the Developing World* (pp. 144–155). Hershey, PA: IGI Global. doi:10.4018/978-1-5225-3018-3.ch009

Koutsafti, M., & Politi, N. (2018). Career Counseling: The "Model of Personal Career Management". In K. Koutsopoulos, K. Doukas, & Y. Kotsanis (Eds.), *Handbook of Research on Educational Design and Cloud Computing in Modern Classroom Settings* (pp. 410–429). Hershey, PA: IGI Global. doi:10.4018/978-1-5225-3053-4.ch020

Koutsopoulos, K. (2018). From Ground to Cloud: The School on the Cloud. In K. Koutsopoulos, K. Doukas, & Y. Kotsanis (Eds.), *Handbook of Research on Educational Design and Cloud Computing in Modern Classroom Settings* (pp. 1–21). Hershey, PA: IGI Global. doi:10.4018/978-1-5225-3053-4.ch001

Kovacevic, Z., Klimek, B., & Drower, I. S. (2018). Refugee Children and Parental Involvement in School Education: A Field Model. In K. Norris & S. Collier (Eds.), *Social Justice and Parent Partnerships in Multicultural Education Contexts* (pp. 139–161). Hershey, PA: IGI Global. doi:10.4018/978-1-5225-3943-8.ch008

Kratky, A. (2018). Personal Touch: A Viewing-Angle-Compensated Multi-Layer Touch Display. In F. Cipolla-Ficarra (Ed.), *Optimizing Human-Computer Interaction With Emerging Technologies* (pp. 232–247). Hershey, PA: IGI Global. doi:10.4018/978-1-5225-2616-2.ch009

Kuang, Y. (2018). Application of the "Teaching Innovation Practice Platform" in English Reading Instruction: A Case Study of a Public Middle School in Shanghai. In H. Spires (Ed.), *Digital Transformation and Innovation in Chinese Education* (pp. 249–271). Hershey, PA: IGI Global. doi:10.4018/978-1-5225-2924-8.ch014

Kubilay, S., & Yardibi, N. (2018). Refugee Parents' Preferential Values in Education. In Ş. Erçetin (Ed.), *Educational Development and Infrastructure for Immigrants and Refugees* (pp. 72–84). Hershey, PA: IGI Global. doi:10.4018/978-1-5225-3325-2.ch004

Kumar, T. P. (2018). Impact of Corporate Social Responsibility on Service Performance in Mediating Effect of Brand Equity With Reference To Banks in India. In Rajagopal, & R. Behl (Eds.), Start-Up Enterprises and Contemporary Innovation Strategies in the Global Marketplace (pp. 88-99). Hershey, PA: IGI Global. doi:10.4018/978-1-5225-4831-7.ch007

LaPlante, J. M. (2018). Unequal Opportunities and Inequitable Outcomes: Rethinking Education Finance Policy Design for a Global Society. In H. Levine & K. Moreno (Eds.), *Positioning Markets and Governments in Public Management* (pp. 209–239). Hershey, PA: IGI Global. doi:10.4018/978-1-5225-4177-6.ch016

Lau, B. T., & Win, K. M. (2018). Differentiated Animated Social Stories to Enhance Social Skills Acquisition of Children With Autism Spectrum Disorder. In V. Bryan, A. Musgrove, & J. Powers (Eds.), *Handbook of Research on Human Development in the Digital Age* (pp. 300–329). Hershey, PA: IGI Global. doi:10.4018/978-1-5225-2838-8.ch014

Lee, J. K., & Chirino-Klevans, I. (2018). Cosmopolitanism in a World of Teachers: American Student Teachers in a Chinese School. In H. Spires (Ed.), *Digital Transformation and Innovation in Chinese Education* (pp. 232–248). Hershey, PA: IGI Global. doi:10.4018/978-1-5225-2924-8.ch013

Lee, S. (2018). Expatriate Cantonese Learners in Hong Kong: Adult L2 Learning, Identity Negotiation, and Social Pressure. In D. Velliaris (Ed.), *Study Abroad Contexts for Enhanced Foreign Language Learning* (pp. 151–168). Hershey, PA: IGI Global. doi:10.4018/978-1-5225-3814-1.ch007

Lee, S. C. (2018). Mother America: Cold War Maternalism and the Origins of Korean Adoption. In F. Topor (Ed.), *Ethical Standards and Practice in International Relations* (pp. 157–186). Hershey, PA: IGI Global. doi:10.4018/978-1-5225-2650-6.ch007

Li, Y., & Wang, X. (2018). Seeking Health Information on Social Media: A Perspective of Trust, Self-Determination, and Social Support. *Journal of Organizational and End User Computing, 30*(1), 1–22. doi:10.4018/JOEUC.2018010101

Livers, S. D., & Lin, L. (2018). Elementary Teacher Candidates' Perspectives on the Teaching and Learning of English Learners. In U. Thomas (Ed.), *Advocacy in Academia and the Role of Teacher Preparation Programs* (pp. 23–41). Hershey, PA: IGI Global. doi:10.4018/978-1-5225-2906-4.ch002

López-Cózar-Navarro, C., & Priede-Bergamini, T. (2018). Nascent Social Entrepreneurship: Economic, Legal, and Financial Framework. In A. Carrizo Moreira, J. Guilherme Leitão Dantas, & F. Manuel Valente (Eds.), *Nascent Entrepreneurship and Successful New Venture Creation* (pp. 132–152). Hershey, PA: IGI Global. doi:10.4018/978-1-5225-2936-1.ch006

Lu, S. (2018). Financial Literacy Education Program Post Financial Housing Crisis: Community Based Financial Literacy Education Program. In S. Burton (Ed.), *Engaged Scholarship and Civic Responsibility in Higher Education* (pp. 49–66). Hershey, PA: IGI Global. doi:10.4018/978-1-5225-3649-9.ch003

Luyombya, D. (2018). Management of Records and Archives in Uganda's Public Sector. In P. Ngulube (Ed.), *Handbook of Research on Heritage Management and Preservation* (pp. 275–297). Hershey, PA: IGI Global. doi:10.4018/978-1-5225-3137-1.ch014

Luyombya, D., Kiyingi, G. W., & Naluwooza, M. (2018). The Nature and Utilisation of Archival Records Deposited in Makerere University Library, Uganda. In P. Ngulube (Ed.), *Handbook of Research on Heritage Management and Preservation* (pp. 96–113). Hershey, PA: IGI Global. doi:10.4018/978-1-5225-3137-1.ch005

Lytras, M. D., Papadopoulou, P., Marouli, C., & Misseyanni, A. (2018). Higher Education Out-of-the-Box: Technology-Driven Learning Innovation in Higher Education. In S. Burton (Ed.), *Engaged Scholarship and Civic Responsibility in Higher Education* (pp. 67–100). Hershey, PA: IGI Global. doi:10.4018/978-1-5225-3649-9.ch004

Mafumbate, R. (2018). Child Resilience, Survival, and Development: Voices of Orphans in Zimbabwe. In I. Tshabangu (Ed.), *Global Ideologies Surrounding Children's Rights and Social Justice* (pp. 239–252). Hershey, PA: IGI Global. doi:10.4018/978-1-5225-2578-3.ch015

Malmierca, M. J. (2018). Cloud Computing for Rural and Isolated Schools. In K. Koutsopoulos, K. Doukas, & Y. Kotsanis (Eds.), *Handbook of Research on Educational Design and Cloud Computing in Modern Classroom Settings* (pp. 376–394). Hershey, PA: IGI Global. doi:10.4018/978-1-5225-3053-4.ch018

Maroofi, F. (2018). Knowledge Management and Organizational Performance in Service Industry: Transformational Leadership Versus Transactional Leadership. In N. Baporikar (Ed.), *Global Practices in Knowledge Management for Societal and Organizational Development* (pp. 194–212). Hershey, PA: IGI Global. doi:10.4018/978-1-5225-3009-1.ch009

Mattson, T., & Aurigemma, S. (2018). Running with the Pack: The Impact of Middle-Status Conformity on the Post-Adoption Organizational Use of Twitter. *Journal of Organizational and End User Computing*, *30*(1), 23–43. doi:10.4018/JOEUC.2018010102

Medhekar, A., & Haq, F. (2018). Urbanization and New Jobs Creation in Healthcare Services in India: Challenges and Opportunities. In U. Benna & I. Benna (Eds.), *Urbanization and Its Impact on Socio-Economic Growth in Developing Regions* (pp. 198–218). Hershey, PA: IGI Global. doi:10.4018/978-1-5225-2659-9.ch010

Meletiou-Mavrotheris, M., & Koutsopoulos, K. (2018). Projecting the Future of Cloud Computing in Education: A Foresight Study Using the Delphi Method. In K. Koutsopoulos, K. Doukas, & Y. Kotsanis (Eds.), *Handbook of Research on Educational Design and Cloud Computing in Modern Classroom Settings* (pp. 262–290). Hershey, PA: IGI Global. doi:10.4018/978-1-5225-3053-4.ch012

Miller, J. (2018). Causes and Ramifications of Public Pension Fund Underfunding: A Case Study of the New Jersey Pension Funds. In H. Levine & K. Moreno (Eds.), *Positioning Markets and Governments in Public Management* (pp. 114–146). Hershey, PA: IGI Global. doi:10.4018/978-1-5225-4177-6.ch010

Milović, B. (2018). Developing Marketing Strategy on Social Networks. In S. Sarma (Ed.), *Global Observations of the Influence of Culture on Consumer Buying Behavior* (pp. 66–82). Hershey, PA: IGI Global. doi:10.4018/978-1-5225-2727-5.ch004

Mosweu, O., & Kenosi, L. S. (2018). Theories of Appraisal in Archives: From Hillary Jenkinson to Terry Cook's Times. In P. Ngulube (Ed.), *Handbook of Research on Heritage Management and Preservation* (pp. 24–46). Hershey, PA: IGI Global. doi:10.4018/978-1-5225-3137-1.ch002

Mukherjee, S., & Pradeep, K. (2018). Does Internationalization of Business-Group-Affiliated Firms Depend on Their Performance? In Rajagopal, & R. Behl (Eds.), Start-Up Enterprises and Contemporary Innovation Strategies in the Global Marketplace (pp. 153-165). Hershey, PA: IGI Global. https://doi.org/ doi:10.4018/978-1-5225-4831-7.ch011

Mutisya, P. M., & Conway, C. S. (2018). Quality Mentoring: A Prerequisite for Faculty at HBCUs. In C. Conway (Ed.), *Faculty Mentorship at Historically Black Colleges and Universities* (pp. 15–34). Hershey, PA: IGI Global. doi:10.4018/978-1-5225-4071-7.ch002

Nagabhushan, P. (2018). Mean Level Changes in College Students' Academic Motivation and Engagement. In *Engaging Adolescent Students in Contemporary Classrooms: Emerging Research and Opportunities* (pp. 142–174). Hershey, PA: IGI Global. doi:10.4018/978-1-5225-5155-3.ch006

Naranjo, J. (2018). Meeting the Need for Inclusive Educators Online: Teacher Education in Inclusive Special Education and Dual-Certification. In D. Polly, M. Putman, T. Petty, & A. Good (Eds.), *Innovative Practices in Teacher Preparation and Graduate-Level Teacher Education Programs* (pp. 106–122). Hershey, PA: IGI Global. doi:10.4018/978-1-5225-3068-8.ch007

Nirmala, T., & Aram, I. A. (2018). Newspaper Framing of Climate Change and Sustainability Issues in India. *International Journal of E-Politics, 9*(1), 15–28. doi:10.4018/IJEP.2018010102

Novak, J. I., & Loy, J. (2018). Digital Technologies and 4D Customized Design: Challenging Conventions With Responsive Design. In V. Bryan, A. Musgrove, & J. Powers (Eds.), *Handbook of Research on Human Development in the Digital Age* (pp. 403–426). Hershey, PA: IGI Global. doi:10.4018/978-1-5225-2838-8.ch018

Ögeyik, M. C. (2018). Measuring Phonological and Orthographic Similarity: The Case of Loanwords in Turkish and English. In D. Buğa & M. Coşgun Ögeyik (Eds.), *Psycholinguistics and Cognition in Language Processing* (pp. 49–67). Hershey, PA: IGI Global. doi:10.4018/978-1-5225-4009-0.ch003

Oling-Sisay, M. (2018). Don't Touch My Hair: Culturally Responsive Engagement in Service-Learning. In O. Delano-Oriaran, M. Penick-Parks, & S. Fondrie (Eds.), *Culturally Engaging Service-Learning With Diverse Communities* (pp. 43–55). Hershey, PA: IGI Global. doi:10.4018/978-1-5225-2900-2.ch003

Ololube, N. P., Ingiabuna, E. T., & Dudafa, U. J. (2018). Effective Decision Making for Knowledge Development in Higher Education: A Case Study of Nigeria. In N. Baporikar (Ed.), *Global Practices in Knowledge Management for Societal and Organizational Development* (pp. 382–399). Hershey, PA: IGI Global. doi:10.4018/978-1-5225-3009-1.ch018

Oritsejafor, E. O. (2018). Enhancing Competitiveness of Public Utilities in Nigeria: The Case of the Power Holding Company of Nigeria (PHCN). In H. Levine & K. Moreno (Eds.), *Positioning Markets and Governments in Public Management* (pp. 240–252). Hershey, PA: IGI Global. doi:10.4018/978-1-5225-4177-6.ch017

Otunla, A. O., & Olatunji, O. T. (2018). Clients' Perception, Extent of Adoption, and Level of Satisfaction With Multi-Platform Advertising Media Strategies (MuPAMS): Among Business Organisations in Ibadan, South-Western Nigeria. In K. Yang (Ed.), *Multi-Platform Advertising Strategies in the Global Marketplace* (pp. 54–80). Hershey, PA: IGI Global. doi:10.4018/978-1-5225-3114-2.ch003

Owuor, N. A. (2018). Oil and Gas Discoveries in Kenya: Important Global Exploration and Production Value Chain Lessons for the Society. In M. Risso & S. Testarmata (Eds.), *Value Sharing for Sustainable and Inclusive Development* (pp. 322–337). Hershey, PA: IGI Global. doi:10.4018/978-1-5225-3147-0.ch015

Özdemir, E., & Yılmaz, M. (2018). Omni-Channel Retailing: The Risks, Challenges, and Opportunities. In A. Kumar & S. Saurav (Eds.), *Supply Chain Management Strategies and Risk Assessment in Retail Environments* (pp. 97–118). Hershey, PA: IGI Global. doi:10.4018/978-1-5225-3056-5.ch006

Panko, T. R., & George, B. P. (2018). Animal Sexual Abuse and the Darkness of Touristic Immorality. In M. Korstanje & B. George (Eds.), *Virtual Traumascapes and Exploring the Roots of Dark Tourism* (pp. 175–189). Hershey, PA: IGI Global. doi:10.4018/978-1-5225-2750-3.ch009

Paraschiv, M. M. (2018). Elif Shafak's Works: A Means of Preventing Honor Based Violence. In M. Badea & M. Suditu (Eds.), *Violence Prevention and Safety Promotion in Higher Education Settings* (pp. 36–49). Hershey, PA: IGI Global. doi:10.4018/978-1-5225-2960-6.ch003

Paravastu, N., Simmers, C. A., & Anandarajan, M. (2018). Non-Compliant Mobile Device Usage and Information Systems Security: A Bystander Theory Perspective. *International Journal of Information Systems and Social Change*, *9*(1), 1–25. doi:10.4018/IJISSC.2018010101

Pathak, B. (2018). Process Documentation of Interfaith Peacebuilding Cycle: A Case Study From Nepal. In B. Cook (Ed.), *Handbook of Research on Examining Global Peacemaking in the Digital Age* (pp. 70–93). Hershey, PA: IGI Global. doi:10.4018/978-1-5225-3032-9.ch006

Pathak, S. J. (2018). Women Painters of Mithila: A Quest for Identity. In N. Mahtab, T. Haque, I. Khan, M. Islam, & I. Wahid (Eds.), *Handbook of Research on Women's Issues and Rights in the Developing World* (pp. 370–381). Hershey, PA: IGI Global. doi:10.4018/978-1-5225-3018-3.ch023

Patro, C. S., & Raghunath, K. M. (2018). Corporate Social Responsibility: A Conscientious Take. In M. Risso & S. Testarmata (Eds.), *Value Sharing for Sustainable and Inclusive Development* (pp. 75–99). Hershey, PA: IGI Global. doi:10.4018/978-1-5225-3147-0.ch004

Pérez-Uribe, R. I., Torres, D. A., Jurado, S. P., & Prada, D. M. (2018). Cloud Tools for the Development of Project Management in SMEs. In R. Perez-Uribe, C. Salcedo-Perez, & D. Ocampo-Guzman (Eds.), *Handbook of Research on Intrapreneurship and Organizational Sustainability in SMEs* (pp. 95–120). Hershey, PA: IGI Global. doi:10.4018/978-1-5225-3543-0.ch005

Perrotta, K. A., & Mattson, M. F. (2018). Using Counterstories and Reflective Writing Assignments to Promote Critical Race Consciousness in an Undergraduate Teacher Preparation Course. In U. Thomas (Ed.), *Advocacy in Academia and the Role of Teacher Preparation Programs* (pp. 42–64). Hershey, PA: IGI Global. doi:10.4018/978-1-5225-2906-4.ch003

Poli, A., Gambini, A., Pezzotti, A., Broglia, A., Mazzola, A., Muschiato, S., ... Costa, F. (2018). Digital Diorama: An Interactive Multimedia Resource for Learning the Life Sciences. In F. Cipolla-Ficarra (Ed.), *Optimizing Human-Computer Interaction With Emerging Technologies* (pp. 52–82). Hershey, PA: IGI Global. doi:10.4018/978-1-5225-2616-2.ch003

Presadă, D. (2018). Literature and Aesthetic Reading as Means of Promoting Nonviolence. In M. Badea & M. Suditu (Eds.), *Violence Prevention and Safety Promotion in Higher Education Settings* (pp. 94–109). Hershey, PA: IGI Global. doi:10.4018/978-1-5225-2960-6.ch006

Punetha, H., Kumar, S., Mudila, H., & Prakash, O. (2018). Brassica Meal as Source of Health Protecting Neuraceutical and Its Antioxidative Properties. In A. Verma, K. Srivastava, S. Singh, & H. Singh (Eds.), *Nutraceuticals and Innovative Food Products for Healthy Living and Preventive Care* (pp. 108–131). Hershey, PA: IGI Global. doi:10.4018/978-1-5225-2970-5.ch005

Puri, R., & Sengupta, P. (2018). Application of Statistics in Human Resource Management. In D. Bhattacharyya (Ed.), *Statistical Tools and Analysis in Human Resources Management* (pp. 15–37). Hershey, PA: IGI Global. doi:10.4018/978-1-5225-4947-5.ch002

Putnik, N., & Milošević, M. (2018). Trends in Peace Research: Can Cyber Détente Lead to Lasting Peace? In B. Cook (Ed.), *Handbook of Research on Examining Global Peacemaking in the Digital Age* (pp. 1–18). Hershey, PA: IGI Global. doi:10.4018/978-1-5225-3032-9.ch001

Rana, S., & Sharma, R. (2018). An Overview of Employer Branding With Special Reference to Indian Organizations. In N. Sharma, V. Singh, & S. Pathak (Eds.), *Management Techniques for a Diverse and Cross-Cultural Workforce* (pp. 116–131). Hershey, PA: IGI Global. doi:10.4018/978-1-5225-4933-8.ch007

Randa, I. O. (2018). Leveraging Knowledge Management for Value Creation in Service-Oriented Organisations of Namibia. In N. Baporikar (Ed.), *Global Practices in Knowledge Management for Societal and Organizational Development* (pp. 145–167). Hershey, PA: IGI Global. doi:10.4018/978-1-5225-3009-1.ch007

Rekun, M. S. (2018). A Swift Kick: Russian Diplomatic Practice in Bulgaria, 1879-1883. In F. Topor (Ed.), *Ethical Standards and Practice in International Relations* (pp. 49–72). Hershey, PA: IGI Global. doi:10.4018/978-1-5225-2650-6.ch003

Rodil, K., Nielsen, E. B., & Nielsen, J. B. (2018). Sharing Memories: Co-Designing Assistive Technology with Aphasic Adults and Support Staff. *International Journal of Sociotechnology and Knowledge Development, 10*(1), 21–36. doi:10.4018/IJSKD.2018010102

Samli, R. (2018). A Review of Internet Addiction on the Basis of Different Countries (2007–2017). In B. Bozoglan (Ed.), *Psychological, Social, and Cultural Aspects of Internet Addiction* (pp. 200–220). Hershey, PA: IGI Global. doi:10.4018/978-1-5225-3477-8.ch011

Sánchez-García, J. C., & Hernández-Sánchez, B. R. (2018). Nascent Entrepreneurs, Psychological Characteristics, and Sociocultural Background: Psycho-Sociocultural Background of Nascent Entrepreneurs. In A. Carrizo Moreira, J. Guilherme Leitão Dantas, & F. Manuel Valente (Eds.), *Nascent Entrepreneurship and Successful New Venture Creation* (pp. 111–131). Hershey, PA: IGI Global. doi:10.4018/978-1-5225-2936-1.ch005

Santana-Mansilla, P., Costaguta, R., & Schiaffino, S. (2018). A Multi-Agent Model for Personalizing Learning Material for Collaborative Groups. In F. Cipolla-Ficarra (Ed.), *Optimizing Human-Computer Interaction With Emerging Technologies* (pp. 343–375). Hershey, PA: IGI Global. doi:10.4018/978-1-5225-2616-2.ch015

Santos, C. E., Lima de Oliveira, D., & Freitas, M. D. (2018). The Role of Pibid in Graduation Courses: Discussing Teachers' Education. In Z. Djoub (Ed.), *Fostering Reflective Teaching Practice in Pre-Service Education* (pp. 218–234). Hershey, PA: IGI Global. doi:10.4018/978-1-5225-2963-7.ch012

Sarkar, J. (2018). Methodological Considerations for Research in Compensation Management. In D. Bhattacharyya (Ed.), *Statistical Tools and Analysis in Human Resources Management* (pp. 142–168). Hershey, PA: IGI Global. doi:10.4018/978-1-5225-4947-5.ch007

Sarofim, S., & Tolba, A. (2018). When Age, Religion, and Culture Matter: The Impact of Aging, Religiosity, and Cultural Differences on Consumers' Emotions and Behavior. In S. Sarma (Ed.), *Global Observations of the Influence of Culture on Consumer Buying Behavior* (pp. 261–278). Hershey, PA: IGI Global. doi:10.4018/978-1-5225-2727-5.ch015

Schroth, S. T., & Helfer, J. A. (2018). Differentiated Fieldwork and Practicum Experiences: Matching Teacher Candidate Assignments to Their Skills and Needs. In D. Polly, M. Putman, T. Petty, & A. Good (Eds.), *Innovative Practices in Teacher Preparation and Graduate-Level Teacher Education Programs* (pp. 306–326). Hershey, PA: IGI Global. doi:10.4018/978-1-5225-3068-8.ch017

Schwartz, H. M. (2018). States via Markets and Markets via States: Symbiosis and Change, Not Conflict. In H. Levine & K. Moreno (Eds.), *Positioning Markets and Governments in Public Management* (pp. 1–10). Hershey, PA: IGI Global. doi:10.4018/978-1-5225-4177-6.ch001

Semali, L. M. (2018). Indigenous Knowledge as Resource to Sustain Self-Employment in Rural Development. In S. Chhabra (Ed.), *Handbook of Research on Civic Engagement and Social Change in Contemporary Society* (pp. 142–158). Hershey, PA: IGI Global. doi:10.4018/978-1-5225-4197-4.ch008

Seraphin, H., & Gowreesunkar, V. (2018). On the Use of Qualitative Comparative Analysis to Identify the Bright Spots in Dark Tourism. In M. Korstanje & B. George (Eds.), *Virtual Traumascapes and Exploring the Roots of Dark Tourism* (pp. 67–83). Hershey, PA: IGI Global. doi:10.4018/978-1-5225-2750-3.ch004

Shahidi, N., Tossan, V., & Cacho-Elizondo, S. (2018). Assessment of A Mobile Educational Coaching App: Exploring Adoption Patterns and Barriers in France. *International Journal of Technology and Human Interaction, 14*(1), 22–43. doi:10.4018/IJTHI.2018010102

Sikira, A. N., Matekere, T., & Urassa, J. K. (2018). Engaging Men in Women's Economic Empowerment in Butiama District, Mara Region, Tanzania. In N. Mahtab, T. Haque, I. Khan, M. Islam, & I. Wahid (Eds.), *Handbook of Research on Women's Issues and Rights in the Developing World* (pp. 252–268). Hershey, PA: IGI Global. doi:10.4018/978-1-5225-3018-3.ch015

Silveira, D. G. (2018). Diffusion of Innovation and Role of Opinion Leaders. In S. Sarma (Ed.), *Global Observations of the Influence of Culture on Consumer Buying Behavior* (pp. 83–93). Hershey, PA: IGI Global. doi:10.4018/978-1-5225-2727-5.ch005

Simard, D. A., Martin, M., Mockry, J., Puliatte, A., & Squires, M. E. (2018). Introduction: Mental Health and Well-Being of College Students. In M. Martin, J. Mockry, A. Puliatte, D. Simard, & M. Squires (Eds.), *Raising Mental Health Awareness in Higher Education: Emerging Research and Opportunities* (pp. 1–20). Hershey, PA: IGI Global. doi:10.4018/978-1-5225-3793-9.ch001

Sosnin, P. (2018). Experimental Actions With Conceptual Objects. In *Experience-Based Human-Computer Interactions: Emerging Research and Opportunities* (pp. 47–97). Hershey, PA: IGI Global. doi:10.4018/978-1-5225-2987-3.ch003

Sosnin, P. (2018). Lack of Naturalness in Human-Computer Interactions. In *Experience-Based Human-Computer Interactions: Emerging Research and Opportunities* (pp. 9–46). Hershey, PA: IGI Global. doi:10.4018/978-1-5225-2987-3.ch002

Spaseski, N. (2018). Fractal and Wavelet Market Analysis in Pattern Recognition. In *Alternative Decision-Making Models for Financial Portfolio Management: Emerging Research and Opportunities* (pp. 254–309). Hershey, PA: IGI Global. doi:10.4018/978-1-5225-3259-0.ch007

Spaseski, N. (2018). Theory and Modelling. In *Alternative Decision-Making Models for Financial Portfolio Management: Emerging Research and Opportunities* (pp. 1–19). Hershey, PA: IGI Global. doi:10.4018/978-1-5225-3259-0.ch001

Spires, H. A., Green, K. E., & Liang, P. (2018). Chinese Parents' Perspectives on International Higher Education and Innovation. In H. Spires (Ed.), *Digital Transformation and Innovation in Chinese Education* (pp. 272–287). Hershey, PA: IGI Global. doi:10.4018/978-1-5225-2924-8.ch015

Spires, H. A., Himes, M., & Wang, L. (2018). Designing a State-of-the-Art High School in Suzhou, China: Connecting to the Future. In H. Spires (Ed.), *Digital Transformation and Innovation in Chinese Education* (pp. 191–210). Hershey, PA: IGI Global. doi:10.4018/978-1-5225-2924-8.ch011

Squires, M. E., Martin, M., Mockry, J., Puliatte, A., & Simard, D. A. (2018). Campus-Wide Initiatives. In M. Martin, J. Mockry, A. Puliatte, D. Simard, & M. Squires (Eds.), *Raising Mental Health Awareness in Higher Education: Emerging Research and Opportunities* (pp. 77–104). Hershey, PA: IGI Global. doi:10.4018/978-1-5225-3793-9.ch005

Standing, K., & Parker, S. L. (2018). Girls' and Women's Rights to Menstrual Health in Nepal. In N. Mahtab, T. Haque, I. Khan, M. Islam, & I. Wahid (Eds.), *Handbook of Research on Women's Issues and Rights in the Developing World* (pp. 156–168). Hershey, PA: IGI Global. doi:10.4018/978-1-5225-3018-3.ch010

Stępień, B., & Hinner, M. (2018). From Love to Rebuff: How Culture Shapes the Perception of Luxury Goods Among Consumers. In S. Sarma (Ed.), *Global Observations of the Influence of Culture on Consumer Buying Behavior* (pp. 24–47). Hershey, PA: IGI Global. doi:10.4018/978-1-5225-2727-5.ch002

Tantau, A. D., & Frăţilă, L. C. (2018). Trends and Conclusions for Business Development in the Renewable Energy Industry. In *Entrepreneurship and Business Development in the Renewable Energy Sector* (pp. 351–376). Hershey, PA: IGI Global. doi:10.4018/978-1-5225-3625-3.ch010

Terry, D. L., & Amudalat, E. A. (2018). Data Documentation and Informed Consent in Research. In C. Sibinga (Ed.), *Ensuring Research Integrity and the Ethical Management of Data* (pp. 127–154). Hershey, PA: IGI Global. doi:10.4018/978-1-5225-2730-5.ch008

Toma, S. I., Marinescu, P., & Grădinaru, C. (2018). Creating Shared Value in the 21st Century: The Case of Toyota Motor Company. In M. Risso & S. Testarmata (Eds.), *Value Sharing for Sustainable and Inclusive Development* (pp. 155–184). Hershey, PA: IGI Global. doi:10.4018/978-1-5225-3147-0.ch007

Travis, F. T. (2018). Long-Term Changes in Experienced Yoga Practitioners: Growth of Higher States of Consciousness. In S. Telles & N. Singh (Eds.), *Research-Based Perspectives on the Psychophysiology of Yoga* (pp. 35–51). Hershey, PA: IGI Global. doi:10.4018/978-1-5225-2788-6.ch003

Tripp, L. O., Love, A., Thomas, C. M., & Russell, J. (2018). Teacher Education Advocacy for Multiple Perspectives and Culturally Sensitive Teaching. In U. Thomas (Ed.), *Advocacy in Academia and the Role of Teacher Preparation Programs* (pp. 161–181). Hershey, PA: IGI Global. doi:10.4018/978-1-5225-2906-4.ch009

Tshabangu, I. (2018). Child Poverty and Social Inequalities in Africa: A Social Justice Perspective. In I. Tshabangu (Ed.), *Global Ideologies Surrounding Children's Rights and Social Justice* (pp. 74–87). Hershey, PA: IGI Global. doi:10.4018/978-1-5225-2578-3.ch005

Tugjamba, N., Yembuu, B., Gantumur, A., & Gezel, U. (2018). Research Study on Climate Change Education for Sustainable Development in Mongolia. In P. Ordóñez de Pablos (Ed.), *Management Strategies and Technology Fluidity in the Asian Business Sector* (pp. 192–214). Hershey, PA: IGI Global. doi:10.4018/978-1-5225-4056-4.ch012

Upadhye, B. D., & Bandopadhyay, N. (2018). The Taxonomy of Methodological Approaches in Marketing Research: Retrospect and Prospect. In Rajagopal, & R. Behl (Eds.), Start-Up Enterprises and Contemporary Innovation Strategies in the Global Marketplace (pp. 276-293). Hershey, PA: IGI Global. https://doi.org/doi:10.4018/978-1-5225-4831-7.ch021

Uvanesh, K., Nayak, S. K., Sagiri, S. S., Banerjee, I., Ray, S. S., & Pal, K. (2018). Effect of Non-Ionic Hydrophilic and Hydrophobic Surfactants on the Properties on the Stearate Oleogels: A Comparative Study. In A. Verma, K. Srivastava, S. Singh, & H. Singh (Eds.), *Nutraceuticals and Innovative Food Products for Healthy Living and Preventive Care* (pp. 260–279). Hershey, PA: IGI Global. doi:10.4018/978-1-5225-2970-5.ch012

Vallverdú, J., Nishida, T., Ohmoto, Y., Moran, S., & Lázare, S. (2018). Fake Empathy and Human-Robot Interaction (HRI): A Preliminary Study. *International Journal of Technology and Human Interaction, 14*(1), 44–59. doi:10.4018/IJTHI.2018010103

Van Deur, P. (2018). Assessing Self-Directed Learning at School Level. In *Managing Self-Directed Learning in Primary School Education: Emerging Research and Opportunities* (pp. 61–77). Hershey, PA: IGI Global. doi:10.4018/978-1-5225-2613-1.ch003

Van Deur, P. (2018). Case Study: The Relationship Between Curriculum Focus on Inquiry and Self-Directed Learning. In *Managing Self-Directed Learning in Primary School Education: Emerging Research and Opportunities* (pp. 95–111). Hershey, PA: IGI Global. doi:10.4018/978-1-5225-2613-1.ch005

Van Deur, P. (2018). Describing Self-Directed Learning in Primary Students. In *Managing Self-Directed Learning in Primary School Education: Emerging Research and Opportunities* (pp. 33–59). Hershey, PA: IGI Global. doi:10.4018/978-1-5225-2613-1.ch002

Vargas-Hernández, J. G., Almanza-Jiménez, R., Calderón, P. C., & Casas-Cardenaz, R. (2018). Organizational Learning and Performance Under the Approach of Organizational Theories. In N. Baporikar (Ed.), *Global Practices in Knowledge Management for Societal and Organizational Development* (pp. 106–125). Hershey, PA: IGI Global. doi:10.4018/978-1-5225-3009-1.ch005

Vega, J. A., Arquette, C. M., Lee, H., Crowe, H. A., Hunzicker, J. L., & Cushing, J. (2018). Ensuring Social Justice for English Language Learners: An Innovative English as a Second Language (ESL) Endorsement Program. In D. Polly, M. Putman, T. Petty, & A. Good (Eds.), *Innovative Practices in Teacher Preparation and Graduate-Level Teacher Education Programs* (pp. 48–66). Hershey, PA: IGI Global. doi:10.4018/978-1-5225-3068-8.ch004

Verma, A. K., Singh, A., & Negi, M. S. (2018). Nutriproteomics: An Advance Methodology of Nutrichemical Analysis. In A. Verma, K. Srivastava, S. Singh, & H. Singh (Eds.), *Nutraceuticals and Innovative Food Products for Healthy Living and Preventive Care* (pp. 1–23). Hershey, PA: IGI Global. doi:10.4018/978-1-5225-2970-5.ch001

Verma, J., & Verma, R. (2018). Innovation in the Provision of Medical Services in India. In Rajagopal, & R. Behl (Eds.), Start-Up Enterprises and Contemporary Innovation Strategies in the Global Marketplace (pp. 16-27). Hershey, PA: IGI Global. doi:10.4018/978-1-5225-4831-7.ch002

Verrini, A. (2018). Strategists From the Past, as Encrypted Cognitive Maps, Whose Access Code Is the Will of Learning Solutions. In L. dall'Acqua, & D. Lukose (Eds.), Improving Business Performance Through Effective Managerial Training Initiatives (pp. 196-209). Hershey, PA: IGI Global. https://doi.org/ doi:10.4018/978-1-5225-3906-3.ch009

Veselinova, E., & Samonikov, M. G. (2018). Driving Brand Equity With Radical Transparency. In *Building Brand Equity and Consumer Trust Through Radical Transparency Practices* (pp. 18–62). Hershey, PA: IGI Global. doi:10.4018/978-1-5225-2417-5.ch002

Veselinova, E., & Samonikov, M. G. (2018). Henkel: Radical Transparency and Sustainability. In *Building Brand Equity and Consumer Trust Through Radical Transparency Practices* (pp. 337–389). Hershey, PA: IGI Global. doi:10.4018/978-1-5225-2417-5.ch009

Veselinova, E., & Samonikov, M. G. (2018). The 3M Company: How to Use Radical Transparency to Generate Value for the Company. In *Building Brand Equity and Consumer Trust Through Radical Transparency Practices* (pp. 185–318). Hershey, PA: IGI Global. doi:10.4018/978-1-5225-2417-5.ch007

Vila, A. R. (2018). Latin American and Caribbean Literature Transposed Into Digital: Corpus, Ecosystem, Canon, and Cartonera Publishing. In F. García-Peñalvo (Ed.), *Global Implications of Emerging Technology Trends* (pp. 34–58). Hershey, PA: IGI Global. doi:10.4018/978-1-5225-4944-4.ch003

Vorkapic, C. F. (2018). Yoga for Children. In S. Telles & N. Singh (Eds.), *Research-Based Perspectives on the Psychophysiology of Yoga* (pp. 104–120). Hershey, PA: IGI Global. doi:10.4018/978-1-5225-2788-6.ch007

Vu, N. T. (2018). Pros and Cons of Integrating Non-Financial Services in Microfinance. In S. Hipsher (Ed.), *Examining the Private Sector's Role in Wealth Creation and Poverty Reduction* (pp. 171–199). Hershey, PA: IGI Global. doi:10.4018/978-1-5225-3117-3.ch008

Wani, K. A., Manzoor, J., Anjum, J., Bashir, M., & Mamta. (2018). Pesticides in Vegetables: Their Impact on Nutritional Quality and Human Health. In A. Verma, K. Srivastava, S. Singh, & H. Singh (Eds.), *Nutraceuticals and Innovative Food Products for Healthy Living and Preventive Care* (pp. 132-157). Hershey, PA: IGI Global. https://doi.org/ doi:10.4018/978-1-5225-2970-5.ch006

Weiss-Randall, D. (2018). DOI Theoretical Framework: Adopting Innovative Technologies. In *Utilizing Innovative Technologies to Address the Public Health Impact of Climate Change: Emerging Research and Opportunities* (pp. 144–166). Hershey, PA: IGI Global. doi:10.4018/978-1-5225-3414-3.ch005

Weiss-Randall, D. (2018). Sustainable Development. In *Utilizing Innovative Technologies to Address the Public Health Impact of Climate Change: Emerging Research and Opportunities* (pp. 167–203). Hershey, PA: IGI Global. doi:10.4018/978-1-5225-3414-3.ch006

Whitelaw, L., & Taddei, L. M. (2018). Using Reflection to Explore Cultural Responsiveness of Preservice Teachers. In Z. Djoub (Ed.), *Fostering Reflective Teaching Practice in Pre-Service Education* (pp. 166–188). Hershey, PA: IGI Global. doi:10.4018/978-1-5225-2963-7.ch009

Wongsurawat, W., & Shrestha, V. (2018). Information Technology, Globalization, and Local Conditions: Implications for Entrepreneurs in Southeast Asia. In P. Ordóñez de Pablos (Ed.), *Management Strategies and Technology Fluidity in the Asian Business Sector* (pp. 163–176). Hershey, PA: IGI Global. doi:10.4018/978-1-5225-4056-4.ch010

Woodman, K., & Kourtis-Kazoullis, V. (2018). Facebook, Tele-Collaboration, and International Access to Technology in the Classroom. In F. Cipolla-Ficarra (Ed.), *Optimizing Human-Computer Interaction With Emerging Technologies* (pp. 274–286). Hershey, PA: IGI Global. doi:10.4018/978-1-5225-2616-2.ch011

Woods, R. J., Johnson, S., & Pope, M. L. (2018). Teaching in an Anti-Deficit Pedagogical Mindset. In U. Thomas (Ed.), *Advocacy in Academia and the Role of Teacher Preparation Programs* (pp. 190–205). Hershey, PA: IGI Global. doi:10.4018/978-1-5225-2906-4.ch011

Wright, M. (2018). Cyberbullying: Description, Definition, Characteristics, and Outcomes. In F. Cipolla-Ficarra (Ed.), *Optimizing Human-Computer Interaction With Emerging Technologies* (pp. 161–182). Hershey, PA: IGI Global. doi:10.4018/978-1-5225-2616-2.ch006

Xu, D. (2018). Multimodal Semiotics in China. In H. Spires (Ed.), *Digital Transformation and Innovation in Chinese Education* (pp. 60–79). Hershey, PA: IGI Global. doi:10.4018/978-1-5225-2924-8.ch004

Yaokumah, W., & Kumah, P. (2018). Exploring the Impact of Security Policy on Compliance. In F. García-Peñalvo (Ed.), *Global Implications of Emerging Technology Trends* (pp. 256–274). Hershey, PA: IGI Global. doi:10.4018/978-1-5225-4944-4.ch014

Yaokumah, W., & Okai, E. S. (2018). Inter-Organizational Study of Access Control Security Measures. *International Journal of Technology and Human Interaction, 14*(1), 60–79. doi:10.4018/IJTHI.2018010104

Zheng, X., Liu, H., Lin, D., & Li, J. (2018). Achieving Rural Teachers' Development Through a WeChat Professional Learning Community: Two Cases From Guangdong Province. In H. Spires (Ed.), *Digital Transformation and Innovation in Chinese Education* (pp. 307–318). Hershey, PA: IGI Global. doi:10.4018/978-1-5225-2924-8.ch017

About the Author

Baimba Yilla, Ed.D., has over two decades of experience as a Foreign Service Officer with the US Department of State. In this role, he provides expertise in diplomacy, international relations, and national security to advance US foreign policy around the world, including in his previous postings in countries in Southeast Asia, the Middle East, Africa and at the United Nations in New York. Baimba is also an Adjunct Professor at Marymount University. He serves as a Lead Doctoral Faculty Mentor supporting doctoral candidates as they complete their Dissertation in Practice for the Doctor of Education degree in Educational Leadership and Organizational Innovation. Baimba is passionate about educational leadership and what it can do to help us address our socio-economic, political, and environmental challenges, as well as shape the lives of individuals and the course of a nation's history. This passion is what underpins Baimba's research interests. He has and continues to explore education and its impact on public policy for lasting social transformation through the lens of history, institutions, politics, human behavior, ethnicity and global leadership. Baimba is married with children.

Index

M

N

P

Q

R

S

V

www.ingramcontent.com/pod-product-compliance
Lightning Source LLC
LaVergne TN
LVHW061538290926
849162LV00004B/831